The Year of the Gerbil

The Year of the Gerbil

How the Yankees Won (and the Red Sox Lost)
the Greatest Pennant Race Ever

Con Chapman

Rutledge Books, Inc. Danbury, CT

Cover photo ©1978 Major League Baseball Productions.
Major League Baseball trademarks and copyrights used with
permission of Major League Baseball Properties, Inc.

Rutledge Books, Inc.
107 Mill Plain Road, Danbury, CT 06811
1-800-278-8533
www.rutledgebooks.com

Manufactured in the United States of America

Cataloging in Publication Data
Chapman, Cornelius J.
    The year of the gerbil

    ISBN: 1-58244-008-5

    1. Baseball -- United States -- History -- 20th century

796.357

To Laura and Whit and Reed,
for the Saturdays I missed writing this.

Introduction

In living memory, there are three events in the history of the Boston Red Sox that a fan of the team who has reached a certain age will inevitably recall along with an image of his or her whereabouts at the time. The first came in the twelfth inning of the sixth game of the 1975 World Series, when Red Sox catcher Carlton Fisk hit a home run to give his team a 7-6 victory over the Cincinnati Reds, tying the series at three games apiece. The most recent occurred in the tenth inning of the sixth game of the 1986 World Series, when Red Sox first baseman Bill Buckner allowed a ground ball hit by Mookie Wilson of the New York Mets to go between his legs, thereby enabling the Mets to win, 6-5, and tie that series at three all. The third is the moment on the afternoon of October 2, 1978, when, in the top half of the seventh inning of a one-game playoff to determine the champion of the American League's eastern division, Russell Earl "Bucky" Dent, a light-hitting shortstop who had hit only four home runs during the regular season, lofted a fly ball into the net above Fenway Park's left-field wall to score himself and two other New York Yankees and thereby give his team a 3-2 lead that led to a one-run victory.

The two events first named above occurred during American baseball's annual and final tournament, and even though the Red Sox lost both series, four games to three, the Boston team's players* could at least find consolation in the fact that they were playing on baseball's ultimate stage. After all, even the losers of the World Series receive commemorative rings that they can show to their grandchildren or hock to a pawnbroker, depending on their capacity for thrift. The game that turned with the last-described home run, however, was the culmination of a long decline, fall and revival that left the Red Sox short not only of the World Series but also without the American League pennant or even a division championship, prizes they were considered destined to win. The home run hit by Bucky Dent is remembered by Red Sox fans with more bitterness as a result.

In the annals of the New York Yankees, Bucky Dent's home run is a minor event; a 300-page history of the Yankees

---

* The author is of the view that an individual member of the Red Sox should be referred to as a "Red Sock," or, in light of the fact that socks are sold in sets of two, as a "pair of Red Socks," as in "Bill Lee was one of the most colorful pairs of Red Socks ever to grace the franchise's wardrobe." Sportswriters in New England instead adhere to a convention, which will be followed in this book, by which each player is referred to as a "Sox" pitcher, catcher, etc. (or in a more ungainly manner as simply a "Sox"), rather than a "Sock", contrary to the rules of sportswriting grammar applied to other teams. Thus, for example, Babe Ruth is referred to as the greatest "Yankee" of all time. This usage represents the converse of the rule whereby the plural versions of certain words—such as "deer" and "buffalo"—are formed without adding an "s".

published in 1981 devoted one sentence to it. In the saga of the Boston Red Sox, however, the event has come to summarize the work and symbolize its theme, in much the same way that Achilles' heel is invoked by those who have never read *The Iliad*. This difference in perspective is understandable: The New York Yankees during their prime were the most dominating team in the history of baseball, as dominant as any American professional sports franchise ever, with the possible exception of the Boston Celtics in basketball. During the period from 1949 through 1958 the Yankees won nine American League pennants, and would have won a tenth but for the fact that the Cleveland Indians set a league record in 1954 by winning 111 games, besting the Yankees' total of 103 wins, which normally would have been enough to take first place. During the period from 1926 through 1964 the Yankees had 39 consecutive winning seasons and finished first 26 times. The Yankees have won more pennants and World Series, and have more players in the Hall of Fame, than any other team. During their glory years the Yankees made a practice of beating everybody, not just the Red Sox, while the Sox have gone fourscore years without winning a World Series and have repeatedly been beaten in the later stages of pennant races, often by the Yankees. Thus, the difference between a Bostonian's view of Dent's home run and a New Yorker's impression of the same event can be compared to another uneven rivalry depicted in the literature of New England: to Ahab, the white whale was an obsession; to Moby Dick, the captain of the Pequod was an hors d'oeuvre.

This is the story of the season that ended for the Boston Red Sox on October 2, 1978, and of the hopeful expectations that led up to it and caused the team's failure on that day to seem all the more galling. This is also the story of New York and Boston and their conflicting roles in the American morality play that is neatly exemplified in the baseball rivalry between the New York Yankees and the Boston Red Sox. Finally, this is the story of the friction between an older, Depression-era generation of baseball management—Billy Martin of the Yankees and Don Zimmer of the Red Sox, and a younger, college-educated generation of baby boomer baseball players, represented most notably by Reggie Jackson of the Yankees and Bill Lee of the Red Sox—that made the heated atmosphere of the 1978 American League Eastern division race more combustible. In the Chinese celestial calendar, 1978 was the year of the horse, but for the Red Sox it was the year of the gerbil.

Hubris

The 1975 World Series is considered by some to be the best ever played, and the sixth game of that series is considered by many to be the greatest game in the history of American baseball's championship. A plurality (if not the majority) of those who currently subscribe to these views are followers of the Boston Red Sox, however. Looking at the matter from a more general perspective, there are games, both World Series and playoff, and home runs—both before and after the night that Carlton Fisk's blast sent the 1975 series to a seventh game—that are at least their equals, if not better. There have been, for example, two home runs that won a World Series on the last pitch thrown, the first by Bill Mazeroski of the Pittsburgh Pirates in 1960, the second by Joe Carter of the Toronto Blue Jays in 1993. By any objective standard these home runs were at least as dramatic as Fisk's in the famous sixth game of 1975. And there was the home run by Bobby Thompson in the bottom of the ninth inning of the

The Year of the Gerbil

third game of a three-game playoff that won the 1951 National League pennant for the New York Giants over the Brooklyn Dodgers after the Giants had mounted one of the greatest comebacks in American professional sports, winning 37 of their last 44 games.

As for other World Series, the 1991 matchup between the Atlanta Braves and the Minnesota Twins—dubbed the "worst-to-first" series because each team had finished in last place the year before—must surely be counted as more exciting than the 1975 series; five games were decided by one run and four were settled by the final swing of the bat, including the seventh game, which was decided in the tenth inning after being tied at the end of nine innings, the first such deadlock in the history of the World Series. The 1960 series between the Pirates and the Yankees must surely rank as the best of all time if the improbable triumph of an apparently over-whelmed underdog is the standard by which we should judge athletic contests (with Mazeroski's home run thrown in for good measure). In that series the Yankees set records for hits, runs and batting average, outscored the Pirates by 55-27 and won three games by scores of 16-3, 10-0 and 12-0. The Pirates won their victories by the paltry aggregate of seven runs, but they won four games, not three.

The 1975 series has its own claims to distinction, of course. Five of the seven games were decided by one run, two were decided in the ninth inning and two required extra innings. In all but the first game the team that won came from behind to do so—Boston led in all seven games, and had six runners thrown out at the plate in the first six games. The 1991 series has faded from the memories of many who

2

watched it, however, a phenomenon that some baseball purists attribute to the fact that neither Minneapolis nor Atlanta had much in the way of baseball history to sustain the images of those games played late into the night, the Twins being relatively recent arrivals from Washington, D.C., and the Braves being nomads twice-moved, once from Boston. The 1991 series is thus a seed that fell on barren ground, while the 1975 series had deep roots; it matched baseball's first avowedly professional team, Cincinnati, founded in 1869, against a team founded in 1901, neither of which had ever played anywhere but the city it then represented.

The 1960 series suffers from other disadvantages in any comparison with the 1975 series. It was filmed using the comparatively rudimentary techniques of the early days of televised sports, with fewer cameras to capture the action from different angles, and it thus lacks the superior production values that viewers have come to expect. Fisk's home run, for example, was supposedly captured on film in the form we have seen so many times because one of the many cameramen assigned to the game was distracted by one of Fenway Park's numerous Norway rats. The 1960 series was also witnessed by far fewer viewers than the 1975 matchup, as it was played in the days before major league baseball agreed to play World Series games at night in order to maximize broadcasters' advertising revenues. The 1975 series generated the largest television audience of any series up to that time, and the image of Fisk's home run, even though it fell into the left-field screen at 12:34 a.m., was thus seen by more eyes than Mazeroski's trot around Forbes Field's diamond at a more respectable hour of the day. The 1975 series would endure by dint of repetition of Fisk's shot alone, however, as no World Series marketing effort since the early hours of October 22nd in that year would be complete without a replay of his home run off Cincinnati Reds pitcher Pat Darcy. Thurman Munson, Fisk's opposite number on the Yankees and his opponent in a celebrated altercation in August of 1973 when Munson crashed into Fisk at the end of an aborted squeeze play, used to complain that Fisk got more attention for one home run in 1975 than Munson received for the entire 1976 season, when the New York catcher was named Most Valuable Player in the American League.

Thus, like all items of religious dogma, the 1975 World Series has achieved its status as an icon, and Fisk's home run has been certified as the relic of a Red Sox saint, on grounds that don't withstand a close examination. A loss in the World Series, like political corruption and prostitution, becomes more charming with the passage of time, but the Red Sox emerged from the 1975 World Series as the heroes of a grateful nation of neutral sports fans who will always root for the team that is behind in a championship series in the hopes of prolonging the amount of high-caliber televised sports available for viewing. Fisk's use of body English to keep the ball he hit from curving foul appears, to those who believe in such things, to be successful, thus satisfying the tendency among baseball fans to credit the supernatural as the cause of their teams' successes and failures, perhaps because men and women become baseball fans at an age when the strict dictates of reason are weaker than the irrational elements of their personalities. Among Red Sox fans this disposition is especially pronounced, and individuals who display its symptoms have named their torment "The Curse of the Bambino". They suffer from the delusion that a hex was placed on the team in 1920 as a result of the short-sighted decision by Harry Frazee, the Red Sox owner at the time, to sell Babe Ruth—affectionately known as the Bambino—to the New York Yankees. As evidence, they cite the incontrovertible fact that the team has not won a World Series since 1918, while the Yankees have won 34 league championships and have won the World Series 23 times since acquiring Ruth. To a skeptical observer, this equation confuses succession with causation. To Red Sox fans, it is a truth they hold to be self-evident.

Fisk's home run is the quintessential Red Sox triumph in that it came not in the last but in the sixth game of a World Series, a premature climax that gave the team a final chance to win or lose the series in the seventh game. Lose it they did, confirming the fatalistic view of life that New Englanders have either succumbed to or sought to overcome, depending on each individual's taste, since the time of the Puritans. Viewed in light of this tradition, the Red Sox are the team that New England deserves, but they were also chosen as the embodiment of American baseball tradition at a time when the nation was searching not for heroes, but antiheroes. Remember, in the year preceding the 1975 World Series an American president had resigned for the first time in history, and the memory of the nation's inglorious withdrawal from South Vietnam was still alive in the country's consciousness.

In truth, however, except for the periods of famine that followed the sale of Babe Ruth (28 years between World Series appearances), the Red Sox have not been that bad a team. They have played in the World Series nine times, winning five and losing four. They have been involved in postseason play five times in the past two decades: 1975, 1986, 1988, 1990 and 1995. What they haven't done is win the World Series since 1918, a period of frustration surpassed only by the two teams from Chicago, the White Sox (who last won a World Series in 1917) and the Cubs (who have gone without such a victory since 1908). Moreover, in the years since the end of World War II, the Red Sox have come within one game of winning the World Series on four occasions, losing in 1946 and 1967 to the St. Louis Cardinals, in 1975 to the Reds, and in 1986 to the New York Mets. The perennial chorus of complaint that issues from Fenway Park thus leads one to suspect that the New England Zeitgeist, chilled by hard winters and shaped by dour tradition, causes Red Sox fans to be happy only when they are unhappy, and to wear their knowledge of the team's failures—like the Red "B's" on their caps—as a modern-day version of the scarlet letter worn by Hester Prynne.

What followed the final out of the 1975 series, a pop-up by Carl Yastrzemski to Cesar Geronimo off relief pitcher Will McEnaney, has been described as a sea change for which Red Sox management was unprepared. In 1976 a decision by a federal court of appeals in the case of *Kansas City Royals Baseball Corporation v. Major League Baseball Players Association** upheld an arbitrator's decision that Andy Messersmith of the Los Angeles Dodgers and Dave McNally of the Montreal Expos had satisfied their obligations to their respective teams by playing out one-year "renewal" contracts after their previous agreements had expired. Prior to that case, players were

---

* 532 F.2d 615 (8th Cir. 1976). As Casey Stengel used to say, you could look it up.

bound to their teams by what was known in the legal jargon applicable to the game as the "reserve" clause, which had permitted owners (since 1879) to renew players' contracts from year to year by placing their names on a list that would put them beyond the reach of other teams under the terms of an agreement among the clubs' owners that evolved into Major League Rule 3(g), the "no-tampering" rule. In the Messersmith/McNally case the owners argued, with some justification, that the terms of the 1973 collective bargaining agreement between the teams and the players permitted the Dodgers and the Expos to renew Messersmith's and McNally's contracts under the existing system. The owners' view was that the terms of the 1973 agreement did not require them to arbitrate matters having to do with the reserve system. The federal court disagreed with the owners, noting that grievances regarding the reserve clause had been submitted to arbitration under prior collective bargaining agreements between the players and owners, and that the 1973 agreement had modified the reserve clause by expressly requiring arbitration of such disputes.

The Messersmith/McNally case did not affect the Red Sox alone, of course, and Red Sox general manager Dick O'Connell wasn't the only executive in major league baseball who had never had to deal with free agents before—none of them had. The contention that Red Sox management was incompetent or too inflexible to deal with the onset of free agency, or that its individual members were simply benighted, is equally disputable; after all, in 1976 the Sox attempted to acquire Hall of Fame relief pitcher Rollie Fingers and his teammate Joe Rudi from the Oakland Athletics for $1,000,000 each, but commissioner Bowie Kuhn voided the sales as not in the best interests of baseball. Kuhn would later display a similar distaste for the rigors of the marketplace as they affected him personally by escaping from the collapse of his New York law firm, Myerson & Kuhn, to the debtors' haven of Florida, where a man's home is not only his castle, it's surrounded by a legal moat that puts it beyond the reach of his creditors.

In 1976 the Red Sox fell to third place following their honorable defeat in 1975, but the principal cause of this decline in their fortunes was place injury, not bad management. On May 20th of 1976, in the first game of the season between the Sox and the Yankees, the Sox held a 1-0 lead in the bottom of the sixth inning at Yankee Stadium when Otto Velez, the New York designated hitter, singled off left-handed pitcher Bill Lee with Lou Piniella on second base and Graig Nettles on first. As Dwight Evans fielded the ball in right field, Piniella rounded third base and headed home. Piniella, whose explosive temper would later be captured on videotape when he was manager of the Cincinnati Reds, rammed into Red Sox catcher Carlton Fisk at the plate. As Lee later told the story, Fisk tagged Piniella with the ball and his fist, and not necessarily in that order. A Boston police report of Babe Ruth's era would have called what followed an "affray". Velez descended on the combatants and Lee, who had won 17 games for the Sox in 1975, attempted to tackle him. Mickey Rivers hit Lee in the back of the head with what is commonly known as a sucker punch. Nettles then advanced on Lee, picked him up and dropped him, intentionally.

The shoulder of Lee's pitching arm hit the ground first and absorbed the greater part of the gravitational force exerted on him. Nettles lay on Lee, claiming afterward that he did so to keep Lee out of the continuing brawl, while Lee would later analyze Nettle's crude chiropractic as an attempt to further injure the pitcher's already-damaged shoulder. After a relative sense of decorum was restored, Lee got up, took a swing at Nettles with his now-injured left arm, missed, and Nettles connected with a counterpunch that put Lee down for good. The injuries to Lee included torn cartilage and a torn capsule surrounding his left shoulder socket. His arm would remain in a sling for most of the season, and he would win only five games while losing seven. Despite his injury, Lee was critical of the Yankees' skill in the martial arts. They were fighting, he said, like "a bunch of hookers swinging their purses."

The Red Sox also suffered the loss of their owner during the 1976 season, as Tom Yawkey died of cancer on July 9th. While the suggestion that professional baseball players might be emotionally affected by the death of the man who signs their paychecks may seem hopelessly quaint to those who have endured the loss of a baseball season and a World Series to labor-management strife during 1994, Yawkey and the Red Sox had a relationship that bordered on co-dependency, to use a currently fashionable phrase from popular psychology. That is, Yawkey always treated his players like his children, lavishing sums of money on them based on his love and affection for them and not their market value, and the players generally repaid him as overindulged children will do, by failing to be productive for lack of incentive. Fellow owner Calvin Griffith, not known for his generosity towards his players, diagnosed the matter thusly: "People in my situation have always considered the Red Sox the team that screwed things up for everyone else the way they pay."

A possibly apocryphal story will illustrate the Sox' system of paternalistic largesse. Pitcher Gary Bell joined the Red Sox in 1967 from the Cleveland Indians. His record for the year was 13-13, 1-5 with Cleveland and 12-8 with the Sox. Bell prepared himself for contract talks with general manager Dick O'Connell for the 1968 season by deciding on a figure he could live with, then adding $15,000 in order to have room to negotiate downward to his acceptable minimum. When O'Connell heard Bell's opening proposal, he simply turned to his secretary and said, "Mary, type up another one."

Whatever the cause, the 1976 Sox ended up in third place, fifteen games behind the division-leading Yankees, who went on to win the pennant, beating the Kansas City Royals, 3 games to 2 in the league championship series, when Chris Chambliss hit a home run on the first pitch from Royals' reliever Mark Littell in the bottom of the ninth inning of the final game of the series to break a 6-6 tie caused by George Brett's three-run homer in the eighth. The Yankees then lost the World Series in four games to Cincinnati. Again, for those with a predilection for finding in coincidence the evidence of supernatural causes, the Sox failure to build on the success of the 1975 season mirrored similarly disappointing seasons following the team's World Series appearances in 1946 and 1967.

Manager Darrell Johnson survived the outbreak of what came to be known as Legionnaire's disease at the hotel where he stayed while in Philadelphia to manage the American League team in the 1976 All-Star Game, but he didn't survive the disappointing performance that his players put on that summer. Johnson was fired shortly after the All-Star break and replaced by Don Zimmer, the team's third base coach. Zimmer replaced Johnson's apparent indifference towards his players—Johnson passed up the team's celebration of its 1975 American League Championship win over the Oakland Athletics to drink beer in his office with the A's Joe Rudi—with a relationship that, while it would soon grow strained, at least connected him to them. Zimmer tinkered with the line-up, bringing Butch Hobson up from the minors to replace Rico Petrocelli at third base, and managed the team to fifteen wins in their last eighteen games, inspiring hope that the lost magic of 1975 could be regained.

The following season marked the first year in which baseball players freed by the Messersmith/McNally decision would take the field with teams that had signed them as free agents—free of the reserve clause, that is. The Red Sox acquired Bill Campbell from the Minnesota Twins in the free agent "re-entry" draft, while the Yankees picked up outfielder Reggie Jackson. The Sox had one of their most potent years offensively; their team batting average was .281 and their team slugging percentage (total bases divided by at bats) was .465. Four players drove in more than 100 runs—Jim Rice (114), Butch Hobson (112), Carl Yastrzemski and Carlton Fisk (102 each)—and George Scott, recently reacquired from the Milwaukee Brewers, had 95. The Sox led the major leagues with 213 home runs and set or tied eighteen major-league home run records. In one ten-game stretch the Sox hit 33 home runs; in a sweep of a three-game series with the Yankees they hit 16 home runs to New York's none. The 1977 season was proof of the truism that good pitching beats good hitting, however. The Yankees' pitching was the best in the American League East as the New Yorkers led the division with a 3.61 earned run average and 16 shutouts. The most valuable player on the Red Sox was undoubtedly the free agent reliever Campbell—his 31 saves led the major leagues—but his 13 wins also led the team, which meant that the Sox didn't have a dominating starter. The Sox ended up tied for second place with the Baltimore Orioles after losing two of three games to the Yankees in a mid-September series that gave New York a three and one-half game lead and allowed them to clinch the American League eastern division title.

The Red Sox' long history of fruitless struggle has caused a skeptical attitude to be a prerequisite to qualification as a true Red Sox fan, but this baseball variation on the flinty demeanor of the typical New Englander is generally nothing more than protective coloring. Beneath the brittle carapace of every hardened Boston fan lives an embittered soul who believed, at least once, that the Sox could go all the way. Nowhere is this phenomenon more apparent than among the Boston sportswriting corps, where a pessimistic point of view is as essential to admission to the Fenway Park pressbox as a press pass. The depth of each individual sportswriter's scorn for the Sox is proportionately matched by a corresponding capacity for belief in their ability to redeem themselves after so many years of failure. This duality has produced a regional strain of schizophrenia among New England reporters who cover the Sox: "Pennant Fever Grips Hub" is the imaginary headline that Boston sportswriters perennially invoke to mock the hopes of Red Sox fans when the team begins a season with a successful record, yet no one is quicker to pronounce a rookie a phenom, or to indulge in wild hopes for a recently-acquired veteran past his prime, than a supposedly cynical veteran of the Red Sox press contingent. With apologies to Yeats, too long a sacrifice can make a stone of the heart, but it can also make a mush of the head. Reggie Jackson was not the first to point out that this native negativism on the part of Sox fans and the press could affect the mood of the team and thus its performance, but his analysis of the phenomenon is as good as any Viennese psychoanalyst's:

> When you were with the Yankees, you just handled the Red Sox. You knew you were going to beat them. They just didn't play well against New York. The papers would get on them and the fans expected them to get beat. The Red Sox players didn't expect to play well.

It was this peculiar journalistic strain of manic-depression that led the Boston media, in the depths of the bitter winter of 1977, to read into the entrails of the 1977 season the portents of a dynasty only one year after most of the same paid plaudits were writing off the team as mismanaged, disoriented and hopelessly behind the times of free agency. How can the Red Sox miss winning the pennant in 1978, asked the Boston *Globe* in February, two weeks after a blizzard buried the Boston area in snowdrifts four feet high and caused fans to think of warmer times to come, alluding to the power that the team had displayed the year before. After all, the 1978 team would feature an important improvement over the 1977 squad, one whose significance can be explained in the Greek classical mode of Red Sox baseball analysis.

In the finest examples of tragedy, Aristotle tells us, the hero's misfortune results from some error on his part and not from his vice or depravity. The perennial error of the Red Sox, their tragic flaw, is to indulge in hubristic pride in their hitting while they fail to attend to their pitching. In the winter preceding the summer of 1978, however, the Sox tried to fix their problem like an Oedipus in shock therapy, acquiring Mike Torrez, winner of seventeen regular season and two World Series games for the Yankees the year before; Dick Drago, a former Sox pitcher with five saves and a 3.41 earned run average the previous season for the California Angels and the Baltimore Orioles; and Tom Burgmeier, another reliever acquired from the Minnesota Twins who had seven saves in 1977 and an 8-1 won-lost record the year before. The last two pitchers would be added to a bullpen whose mainstay, Bill Campbell, had been the best relief pitcher in the major leagues the two previous years. Mike Paxton, a sophomore right-hander, had won ten games against five losses in his rookie year while posting a 3.83 earned run average, and a rookie right-handed pitcher, Jim Wright, showed promise. The final piece of the pitching puzzle seemed to fall into place when the Sox traded Rick Wise, a pitcher whose best season had just ended, to the Cleveland Indians for Dennis Eckersley, a pitcher with three years' experience who would eventually win the Most Valuable Player award as a reliever for the Oakland A's. In the estimation of both Bill Lee and Carl Yastrzemski, the two players whose personalities marked the opposite ends of the team's emotional spectrum, the 1978 Sox had the best pitching they had seen since their respective careers with the team began.

The most telling of these transactions was the Torrez acquisition, because it seemed to reverse a long history of deals in addition to the sale of Babe Ruth in which the Yankees got the better of the Red Sox. A collection of New York Yankee records and statistics currently available divides players into three different categories: first, Yankees inducted into the Hall of Fame; second, Yankees obtained from the Red Sox; and third, Yankees obtained from the Red Sox who have been inducted into the Hall of Fame. During the period from 1921 through 1930 the Red Sox finished last every year but one, while the Yankees went to the World Series their first time and five more times, winning thrice. As one Red Sox fan was heard to mutter during those years, however, "Yankee dynasty, my ear. That was a Boston dynasty in pinstripes." It is almost as if Red Sox general managers lose their customary reserve when they get within sight of the Manhattan skyline, like Boston Brahmin ladies on a Fifth Avenue shopping spree. When Tom Yawkey bought pitcher Hank Johnson from the Yankees in 1933, the first year he owned the club, the Boston *Record*, reflecting on the oddity of the transaction in view of the fact that Harry Frazee had sold fifteen Red Sox to the Yankees in the previous five years, ran the story under the headline "Man Bites Dog".

The Sox have particularly specialized in trading away good pitching to the Yankees, which helps to explain Boston's perennial deficiency in this regard. In the most significant Yankee-Red Sox trade in the decade preceding the Torrez acquisition, the Yankees obtained Sparky Lyle from the Sox for Danny Cater and Mario Guerrero in 1972. On the Red Sox' side of the ledger for that deal, Cater lasted three years, playing in about half of the Sox' games each year and batting .262, while Mario Guerrero spent two years as a part-time shortstop with the Sox before being traded to the St. Louis Cardinals. Lyle, on the other hand, holds seven Yankee pitching records, including most relief appearances (420), most saves (141) and most wins plus saves (198), and his total number of relief strikeouts (454) is second only to Goose Gossage's 506.

The Yankees' other advantageous acquisitions of pitchers from the Sox include a trade for Carl Mays in exchange for two minor league players and $40,000 in 1919. Mays was the Yankees' leading relief pitcher during the period from 1920 to 1923, winning 26 games for New York in 1920 and then 27 more in 1921 to lead the league. In 1920, the Yankees obtained pitcher Waite Hoyt and three other players from the Red Sox for four second-string players; Hoyt is in the baseball Hall of Fame and his career winning percentage (.613) still ranks fourth highest among Yankee pitchers. The Yankees acquired Sox pitchers Bullet Joe Bush and Sad Sam Jones from the Red Sox before the 1922 season; Bush won 62 and lost 38 for New York in three seasons, while Jones was 21-8 for the Yankees in 1923 and 67 and 56 over five seasons. In 1923 the Yankees traded infielder Norm McMillan (a .260 lifetime hitter), outfielder Camp Skinner (.196 lifetime) and pitcher George Murray (career record, 20-26, 5.38 e.r.a.) for Sox pitcher Herb Pennock, who had two twenty-win seasons for the Yankees, achieved the third-best career winning percentage (.642) in Yankee history, and ended up in the Hall of Fame. In 1930 the

Hubris

Red Sox swapped Red Ruffing for Yankee outfielder Cedric Durst and $50,000; Durst played one season for the Sox, batting .245, while Ruffing holds the Yankee record for most complete games (262), and his 231 career wins are second in the Yankee record books only to Whitey Ford's 262. He is also in the Hall of Fame. Sixteen Red Sox pitchers over the years have won more than 200 games; five of them—Sad Sam Jones, Luis Tiant, Herb Pennock, Red Ruffing and Waite Hoyt—left to go to the Yankees. Hoyt, who won ten games in two years with the Red Sox before arriving in New York, was once asked to give the secret of pitching success. "Get a job with the Yankees," he said.

Pitching wasn't the only aspect of their game that the Red Sox improved as they headed into the 1978 season, however. They added defensive depth, signing utility infielders Jack Brohammer and Frank Duffy and outfielder Gary Hancock. They also traded for Jerry Remy, who would take over second base from Denny Doyle, an infielder at the end of his career who didn't have Remy's range or speed on the bases. Remy was a native of Massachusetts, having been born in Fall River and raised in Somerset, and the trade that sent reserve outfielder Rick Miller to the California Angels in exchange for the second baseman was accordingly popular with Red Sox fans. For once the Sox seemed, on paper at least, to have it all.

It is a perpetual conceit of New Englanders to admire their own industry to excess and suppose that the rest of the world is not working just as hard, however. Just as the textile mills moved south and the personal computer revolution bypassed Route 128, Boston's version of California's Silicon Valley, the Red Sox, their fans and the local press were more interested

17

that winter in their own trades and purchases than in the progress the Yankees made in the improvement of their prospects. The Yankees had a strong rookie right-handed pitcher in Jim Beattie. They acquired first baseman Jim Spencer in a trade with the White Sox. Like the Sox, they picked up free agent pitchers—Andy Messersmith, Rawley Eastwick and, most importantly, Rich Gossage, who would be on the mound when the last pitch of the last game of the Red Sox' 1978 season was thrown. As the embers of speculation and wishful thinking that fueled that winter's hot stove league died down, however, and Red Sox pitchers and catcher arrived in Winter Haven, Florida, to begin spring training, Sox fans were optimistic that their team could finally win it all.

The Straw that Stirred the Drink

On Thanksgiving Day, 1976, Reginald Martinez Jackson signed a four-paragraph note on stationery of Chicago's Hyatt Regency Hotel, agreeing to become a New York Yankee. "We are going on this adventure together," the note concluded. "I will not let you down." The delivery of that written promise to George Mitchell Steinbrenner, the Yankees' owner, concluded a process that began less than a month earlier when the Yankees, along with a group of twelve other clubs that did not include the Boston Red Sox, selected negotiating rights to Jackson as part of baseball's first free agent re-entry draft. The wooing of Reggie Jackson by the teams that first expressed interest in him on November 4, 1976, at New York's Plaza Hotel turned into a cross-country (and, with the Montreal Expos in the running, cross-border) pursuit of a kind that had never been seen before in American baseball. The courtship of Reggie Jackson demonstrated to fans, baseball executives and players alike that, for the first time in the history of American sports, the player—not the owner—was king.

That Reggie Jackson was around when labor relations in professional baseball took this particular turn was serendipity of the highest order; the ballplayer with perhaps the largest ego in the history of the game was available to play the leading role in a drama that demanded an actor with both a flair for the grand gesture and a mouth capable of projecting to the cheap seats. Reggie Jackson filled both these requirements. The outsize character of Jackson's personality was summed up best by his Oakland A's teammate Darold Knowles in baseball vernacular understandable even to those who didn't know a walk from a balk—"There isn't enough mustard in America to cover that hot dog."

Jackson derived a particular satisfaction from hitting home runs, with the attention of the whole stadium focussed on him as he stopped and watched the ball leave the stadium as a golfer watches a well-hit shot soar down the fairway (a gesture perfected, if not invented, by him), then jogged around the bases to applause meant only for him (if playing at home) or the stillness that meant he had silenced the crowd at a road game. Each home run had a gustatory appeal for Jackson, with every four-bagger being a "'tater" that gave him heartier nourishment than that provided by a skimpy single. George Scott, the powerful Red Sox first baseman whose love of the culinary arts was sometimes pursued to excess, is reported to have had the following conversation with Jackson:

The Straw that Stirred the Drink

Jackson: Where was that pitch you hit out last
  night?
Scott: It was right in my kitchen.
Jackson: Did you cook it?
Scott: I smoked it, Buck, I really smoked it.
Jackson: Me, I gotta go hunt for them.
Nobody throws Reggie one in his kitchen.

When asked to describe the home run he hit off Dodger pitcher Elias Sosa in the sixth game of the 1977 World Series,
Jackson joked that it was "room service. I could see the mustard on it coming to the plate."

Jackson's nature and the attention he demanded and
received throughout his career understandably produced
more than a little resentment on the part of his teammates.
On one occasion while a member of the Oakland A's, Jackson
was celebrating a game-winning home run in the A's clubhouse with a handful of Baby Ruth and O. Henry candy bars
on the incorrect assumption (or the pretext) that they were
named after legendary home run-hitters Babe Ruth and
Hank Aaron. "What kind of candy bar do you think they'll
name after me?" Jackson asked. "The shithead bar,"
answered teammate Sal Bando.* Jackson's exploits as a hitter
would later gain him sufficient renown for a concoction
known as the "Reggie Bar" to appear on dime-store shelves.
His fielding skills lagged far behind, however, causing his

---

* Jackson may have been the first major leaguer to have a candy bar named after
him since the Baby Ruth bar was actually named for the daughter of President
Grover Cleveland, and the O. Henry bar was named after the author, not Hank
Aaron. There is now a candy bar named after Albert Belle, the Chicago White Sox
slugger.

Yankee teammate Graig Nettles to ask, "What does he need another candy bar for? He's already got the Butterfingers."

Jackson's personality both attracted and repulsed the reporters who covered the team. Jackson was good copy, but he was also a man hungry for press coverage, and as a result his answers to reporters' questions and his frequent soliloquies to the assembled press were duly recorded but often reported with a tone of ironic wonder. "If bullshit were religion," a reporter observed after one particularly rococo Jacksonian improvisation, "he'd be the Pope." Since Jackson joined the Yankees on the strength of the highest bid in an auction that had been conducted before the national news media, the value of his services was broadcast to the wider world and the jealousy felt by his new teammates was compounded. When a large crowd of reporters and photographers gathered to cover Jackson's arrival at the Yankees' training camp in St. Petersburg in 1977, the players noticed. "You'd think we had just won the f___ing World Series or something," muttered team captain Thurman Munson. They hadn't the year before, but they would that year and the next with Jackson's help.

Jackson would attribute the cool reception he received when he joined the Yankees to racism, but there is reason to believe that his perception was impaired by a certain lack of self-awareness. He was capable of describing himself in epic terms —"I am like a storm when I hit," he once told a reporter, and then spun the simile out in a manner as confusing as a tornado:

First there's sleet—slow, sharp sleet out of dark skies. Then comes a mass of clouds and a howling wind. And thunder—very noisy, very frightening thunder. The wind now grows in intensity—leaves are blowing everywhere off trees of every description, limbs and boughs are snapping off and falling. There is a great noise. There is a heavy, heavy downpour all around. But you just wait—that's only the way it is now. Only once in a while, like rain. Someday, though, my hitting will be just like this (gesturing to the fair weather). Every day, as sure as that sun is up there, my hitting will be all there. All around. Everywhere you look.

A disaffected teammate hearing the foregoing self-analysis by Jackson might be forgiven for agreeing that he was indeed like the weather; if you didn't like him you could always stick around since he was bound to change.

While Jackson was adept at this sort of tall-tale telling, he seemed never to know or to care what effect his admiration for himself would have on his teammates. He particularly liked to make unfavorable comparisons of his teammates' intelligence to his own. On one occasion Jackson bragged to Carlos May that he had the highest I.Q. of anyone on the Yankees. "I don't give a damn what your I.Q. is," May responded. "What am I even talking to you for," Jackson said. "You can't even spell 'I.Q.'" In another case Jackson told Mickey Rivers, whom some teammates called "The Chancellor" because it was unlikely this distinction would ever be conferred on him by an institution of higher learning, that Jackson had an I.Q. of 160. Rivers came back with a response he figured would be devastating. "Out of what,

Buck, a thousand?" Jackson's high regard for himself so alienated other members of the Yankees that it was primarily
responsible for the continuation of the career of Fran Healy, a
journeyman catcher from Holyoke, Massachusetts, who was
valuable to the Yankees for a reason other than his skills as a
player; he was Jackson's only friend on the club. In the words
of Elston Howard, a Yankee coach at the time, Healy was "our
Henry Kissinger," referring to the former Secretary of State
who was known for his globetrotting diplomacy between
enemy nations.

Jackson's penchant for self-dramatization, and his view of
his role on the Yankees, were perhaps best exemplified by a
comment he made in spring training of 1977 to freelance
writer Robert Ward, who was working on an article for *Sport
Magazine.* "You know," Ward quoted Jackson as saying before
he had ever played an inning of baseball for the Yankees,

> this team, it all flows from me. I've got to keep it
> all going. I'm the straw that stirs the drink. It all
> comes back to me. Maybe I should say me and
> [catcher and team captain Thurman] Munson.
> But really he doesn't enter into it. He's being so
> damned insecure about the whole thing. I've
> overheard him talking about me.

Munson had indeed been talking about Jackson, express-
ing indirectly through sarcasm his resentment of the money
Jackson was making and the attention he was getting as the
Yankees' new hero. When he was made captain of the
Yankees, Munson had elicited a promise from owner George

Steinbrenner that he would be the highest-paid member of the team. Steinbrenner agreed to pay Jackson more, but absolved himself of the obligation to increase Munson's salary by the rationalization that while Jackson would make $400,000 more than Munson, the difference represented bonus money rather than regular salary, a distinction that Munson recognized as one born of self-interest. Scripture tells us there is more rejoicing over one lost lamb than all the sheep in the fold. To bring that truism into the age of free agency, there is more rejoicing over one free agent than all the regulars on the roster.

Jackson recognized Munson's value to the team, but at the same time he offered a deprecating view of the captain's contribution to the marketing of the Yankees: "Munson's tough too," Jackson admitted to Ward.

> He's a winner but there is just nobody who can put meat in the seats [meaning fans in the stands] the way I can. That's just the way it is. Munson thinks he can be the straw that stirs the drink, but he can only stir it bad.

Before Jackson's comments appeared in the article titled "Reggie Jackson in No-Man's Land", advance copies of the magazine had circulated among the Yankees and Jackson and Munson had made some tentative attempts at a rapprochement. When the story became public, however, Jackson's metaphor for himself was broadcast to the world of baseball fans and echoed back by the press, who upset with every question to his teammates whatever measure of repose had been achieved since the Yankees' new slugger had first conjured up the image of himself at the center of a miniature whirlpool. He had succeeded in placing himself squarely in the position he had imagined.

For manager Billy Martin, Jackson would not, could not, be the team's leader regardless of how much the free agent desired or deserved to play that role. In the *Sport Magazine* article, Ward asked Martin whether the team would have leadership problems now that Jackson had joined them. "We already have a team leader," said Martin. "Thurman Munson." Munson was Martin's ideal as a player—a man who took the game so seriously he seemed to confuse it with life itself, as opposed to Jackson, who while he worked at his game did so only for the glory and the comfort it could bring him. That Jackson could even imagine himself as the leader of the Yankees at that point in his tenure with the team gives one an indication of his capacity for self-delusion. The Yankees' hatred of Jackson as an opposing player had been so deep that as recently as 1976, the year before he signed with New York, Yankee players had rewarded pitcher Dock Ellis with a pile of $20 bills dropped in his locker, Salvation Army-style, after he hit Jackson in the face with a pitch in a game against the Orioles. Eine Kleine Chinmusik, in the Yankees' view, was just what Jackson needed.

When Jackson joined the Yankees the team was experiencing what for them was a virtual drought in terms of a world championship. They had lost to the Cincinnati Reds, four games to none, in 1976, the year before he joined the team. That World Series appearance had been their first in twelve years, and they had lost their two previous appearances in the autumn tournament as well, as the St. Louis

The Straw that Stirred the Drink

Cardinals beat them four games to three in the 1964 series, and the Los Angeles Dodgers swept them in 1963. Their last series victory had been in 1962, when they beat the San Francisco Giants, four games to three. For a franchise that had at different times won seven and eight world championships in a row, the team's dry spell in the sixties and seventies had been like the Israelites' forty-year stroll in the desert. Still, at the end of the 1976 season, the Yankees' record in World Series play was twenty wins and ten losses, so the current version of the team was regarded with the sort of optimism that college football boosters tend to accord a highly-regarded but untried junior varsity squad at a university used to New Year's Day bowl games.

With Jackson in the lineup in 1977, the Yankees won the eastern division of the American League, the American League Championship, 3 games to 2 over the Kansas City Royals, and the World Series, 4 games to 2 over the Los Angeles Dodgers. Jackson played in 146 games that year, had 150 hits (including 32 home runs, 2 triples and 39 doubles), drove in 110 runs and batted .286. The season did not go smoothly, however. After the initial furor over Jackson's self-regarding trope had died down, he remained isolated from his teammates and alienated from Martin, who resented Jackson's comfortable relationship with Steinbrenner. As for Steinbrenner, he seemed to find in Jackson the object of a desire that often finds expression in an older, successful man's craving for a younger, attractive woman; the need to conquer by money that which he might have won by other wiles in his youth, and the need to display his prize. In Tom Wolfe's famous phrase, Jackson was the free-agent equivalent of

Steinbrenner's trophy wife, the thing of baseball beauty that the Yankee owner possessed because he could outbid his fellow owners, who were stuck with their earnest rookies and dowdy veterans. Jackson, responding to a reporter's question, confirmed the parallel. "He wanted me more than the others," Jackson explained. "It's like chasing a broad."

Jackson's affinity with Steinbrenner sprang from another source as well. Jackson, like Steinbrenner, was a businessman, or at least the sort of opportunistic vehicle that other businessmen and women use to lend credibility to dubious or fledgling ventures—the person with the face or name recognized by the public who stamps a likable image on an otherwise mundane enterprise. Jackson owned car dealerships, the ultimate personality-driven business next to restaurants, but his interest in this area of commerce seemed to be driven more by his love of cars than by a desire to make a buck. When Jackson first joined the Yankees, he overheard utility infielder Fred Stanley mention that his parents, who lived in Arizona, were looking to buy a new car but were leery of spending $11,000 on it. "You wanna car for your folks?" Jackson asked. Stanley said he did, and Jackson sold him the model his parents wanted for $4,000 less. By such means Jackson may have won some friends on the Yankees, but he most surely did not develop a successful automobile dealership. Jackson was also in the business of selling raw land in Arizona, a fact which may explain why he returned to baseball after his retirement as a player to coach for the Yankees.

Billy Martin, by comparison, was a career baseball man, the hired help who minded the operation that did more to nurture Steinbrenner's ego than it did to fill his wallet.

The Straw that Stirred the Drink

"Before I came to New York as the Yankees owner," Steinbrenner noted, "I always wanted to go to a place like '21' and I could never get in. I bought the Yankees and we held our first press conference there. Suddenly I had a whole room at '21'. That's what it means to own the Yankees." In that sense, Martin was the stable hand for Steinbrenner's highly-paid thoroughbreds, and Jackson was the horse the owner currycombed himself. In the words of Elston Howard, "Billy was jealous of him, hated the attention Reggie got, couldn't control him." Martin had been opposed to Steinbrenner's decision to pursue Jackson; Steinbrenner chose to ignore him.

It is difficult to imagine a greater divergence between the paths of two players who both reached the major leagues than that which separated Billy Martin's experience in baseball from Reggie Jackson's. Billy Martin never attended college, although he was offered a partial scholarship by Santa Clara University. Instead, in the spring of his senior year at Berkeley High School in his hometown in California, Martin traveled to a Brooklyn Dodgers tryout for high school graduates who were at least nineteen years old. He hitched a ride to San Mateo, California with three other players and spent the night in jail after a policeman found the four of them sleeping on top of a dugout. He lied about his age and educational accomplishments and got four hits in a practice game the next day; the Dodgers said they would call, but they didn't, or if they tried to, Martin didn't find out about it because his family didn't have a phone. In a typical expression of Martin's truculent temperament, he never forgave the Dodgers for the slight, and he would repay them by beating them in the World Series three times as a player and twice as a manager.

The Year of the Gerbil

Martin graduated from high school and joined the Oakland Junior Oaks, where he was spotted by a scout named Jimmy Hull, who recommended him to a scout for the Oakland Oaks of the Pacific Coast League. He was signed for $200 a month; Martin later said he would have paid for the privilege of playing professional baseball (assuming he had the money), so strong was his desire to be a ballplayer. Hull told him to report to the Idaho Falls club, then playing a series in Phoenix. The following conversation, recounted to New York *Post* sportswriter Maury Allen, then ensued:

> **Hull:** You got any clothes, kid?
> **Martin:** Just what I'm wearing.
> **Hull:** Where's your high school graduation suit?
> **Martin:** My uncle died and they buried him in it.
> **Hull:** You got a suitcase, kid?
> **Martin:** Nope. Never went anywhere.
> **Hull:** Here's three hundred dollars. Go buy yourself a new suit, some shirts, some ties and a suitcase. You can keep the rest. Then have your dad drive you to the train station.
> **Martin:** I can't. He's working on the trucks.
> **Hull:** How about your mother?
> **Martin:** Can't. She don't drive. Besides, we don't have a car.

Hull drove Billy to the train station after the Martin family held a going-away party. "That was some exciting day," Martin recalled. "I was off to play ball. I was a professional. I had dreamed about this day ever since I was a little kid. . . Everybody came to the house to congratulate me, all my uncles and aunts and cousins, my brother Tudo, my uncle Ratcy, my uncle Sluice, my cousin Killer, they were all there." It was, Martin said later, "a great family night." Martin's mother was pregnant with him when she threw his father out of the house for sleeping with students from the University of California at Berkeley, and thus his notion of a family night may deviate slightly from the generally-accepted norm.

Jackson also came from a broken home; his mother had left his father when Reggie was very young for reasons similar to those that caused the breakup of Martin's parents, and Jackson grew up with his father and two older brothers. Jackson, however, had been the prime prospect developed by a recognized college baseball power—Arizona State University—whose 1966 team produced seven players, including Jackson, who signed major league contracts. Jackson was selected by the Oakland A's as the second pick in the second free agent draft ever, and he was signed by A's owner Charlie Finley for $85,000 after Jackson doubled Finley's opening offer of $50,000. His signing was the subject of a press conference at a time when he had played fewer than 100 organized baseball games. For Reggie Jackson, the way to the major leagues was made straight by his talent and circumstances. For Martin, who once declined to read a book in high school because, as he told his teacher, "I'm going to be a baseball player and baseball players don't have to read books," the equanimity bordering on indifference with which Reggie Jackson approached the game of baseball was tantamount to sacrilege. To an urban sophisticate like Jackson, the intensity that Martin brought to every pitch, every play, and every game, was déclassé, a form of religious fanaticism.

Martin's resentment of Jackson grew as the 1977 season progressed, with intermittent outbursts the visible evidence of the pressure that built up unseen. On June 18th the Yankees were in Boston for a Saturday game that would be telecast nationally. In the sixth inning, with Jackson in right field, Sox leftfielder Jim Rice hit a pop-up that fell in front of Jackson as he loped in from his position deep in Fenway's power alley. Jackson, the sort of fielder who on a good day made easy catches look hard, saw no reason to exert himself unnecessarily on a play he couldn't make, and he lobbed the ball back to the infield since Rice was no threat to stretch the single into a double. Martin, enraged by Jackson's apparent lack of hustle, sent in Paul Blair in mid-inning to substitute for Jackson, a tactic he had used before with other, less sensitive players to shame them. As Jackson reached the dugout, Martin exploded at him. "You show me up, I'll show you up," the manager screamed. "What did I do?" Jackson shouted back at him, more in bewilderment than anger, like a husband who's forgotten the flowers on Valentine's Day. "You didn't hustle. Nobody quits on me." More words were exchanged, and the two moved toward each other as Elston Howard and Yogi Berra moved between them. Mike Torrez told Jackson to go cool down in the clubhouse, and order was restored.

After this confrontation it seemed inevitable that Martin would be fired. Jackson was in the first year of a $3 million contract, and managers were to Steinbrenner what spouses were to a past generation of Hollywood stars—the position must be filled on a continual basis by a qualified individual who is nonetheless subject to removal at any time for any reason. Steinbrenner, while not close to Martin, nonetheless admired his aggressive style. He talked to both player and manager, and Jackson, in a gesture of some magnanimity given his leverage, told Steinbrenner that he didn't want to be the cause of Martin's leaving. "Don't fire him," Jackson said. Steinbrenner didn't, but after a brief respite, tensions continued to build.

Later that year when the Yankees reached the American League Championship Series, they were tied with the Kansas City Royals at two games apiece when Paul Splittorff was announced as the starting pitcher for the Royals in the fifth and deciding game. Martin chose not to start Jackson, ostensibly because Jackson did not hit well against Splittorff. "The record shows Reggie doesn't hit him," Martin explained to a reporter who asked whether Jackson would start and, when told that he wouldn't, why not. When Jackson was asked for his reaction, he said, with some bitterness, "I know what I can do—if he did we'd be better off."

Reporters in this situation play the role of go-betweens trying to drum up newsworthy controversy in much the same way that schoolyard promoters try to incite fistfights between potential adversaries. Jackson's comment was relayed to Martin, who pointed out the obvious —"I'm the manager of this club—I make out the lineup card." And, the manager added, "if he doesn't like it he can kiss my Dago ass." The contemptuous shorthand phrase for "Diego", referring generally to any dark-skinned male of Latin descent but used primarily to refer to Italians, was worn as a badge of pride by the Yankee manager. Paul Blair started in right field.

The Year of the Gerbil

The Royals got two runs in the first and held a 3-1 lead as the Yankees came to bat in the top of the eighth. Splittorff had tired, and Doug Bird, the Royals' best relief pitcher, was pitching. Willie Randolph singled, Thurman Munson struck out and Lou Piniella singled. With two on and two out, Martin sent Jackson up, proving the truth of his claim that he'd play Adolf Hitler if it would help him win. Jackson came through, fighting off a high fastball before singling to center on a two-strike pitch to close the lead to 3-2. The Yankees scored three more runs in the ninth and won 5-3. Jackson did not join in the team's celebration. Martin sneaked up on George Steinbrenner with a bottle of champagne and dumped it on the Yankee owner. "That's for trying to fire me," he said.

The antipathy between Martin and Jackson hung over the Yankees as they prepared for the World Series like the introit to a requiem mass. The Yankees won the first game in extra innings when Willie Randolph doubled and Paul Blair singled him home in the bottom of the twelfth. In the second game manager Martin started Jim Hunter, who was never known as "Catfish" until Kansas City A's owner Charlie Finley decided he needed a nickname. Hunter gave up home runs to Ron Cey, Steve Yeager and Reggie Smith in the first three innings, and Jackson, Hunter's teammate dating back to their days together with the Oakland A's, blamed Martin. "How could the son of a bitch pitch the man, how could he embarrass him like that?" Jackson asked in the open field at Dodger Stadium the next day. "The man [Hunter] should have never been in there." "Let him worry about playing right field and I'll do the managing," Martin responded to the tattling reporters. "Where the hell does he come off saying a thing like that?" Jackson had apparently overlooked Martin's capacity for cunning, learned on the Yankee bench next to his mentor Casey Stengel. By gambling on an improbable performance by Hunter, Martin was saving his best starters—Torrez, Gullett and Guidry—for the stretch, since no World Series was ever won in the second game.

The Dodgers had eclipsed the Yankees' sluggers in the first three games, hitting five home runs to New York's one, but Jackson homered in the fourth game, which the Yankees won, and the fifth game, which they lost, to make the score in games three for the Yankees, two for the Dodgers. Jackson's three home runs in the sixth game on three consecutive pitches from Burt Hooton, Elias Sosa and Charlie Hough won the sixth game for the Yankees to decide the series. Those home runs are the accomplishment that earned Jackson the nickname that has stuck with him—Mr. October—for coming through under the pressure of the ultimate test in American professional baseball. This time, unlike the celebration that followed the American League Championship Series, Jackson was the center of attention as the warmth of the occasion burned off the chill that had persisted between the newcomer by free agency and his teammates. Jackson started the victory speech that seemed called for by the occasion —"After all we've gone through here"—and then walked off, an open champagne bottle in his hand, to the manager's office. Martin stood up and greeted him, and Jackson went to shake his hand. In an instant the two were hugging. The only thing the manager said was, "You did a helluva job, big guy."

The Loyal Order of
the Buffalo Heads

*W*ebster's *Dictionary* defines "fraternal order" as "a society, often secret, of members banded together for mutual benefit or for work toward a common goal." Such groups often adopt animal totems—Lions, Elks, Moose. And, both in folklore and in truth, their stated charitable functions are sometimes a mask for mere fellowship enhanced by the consumption of alcohol. They offer a refuge from the pressures of work and the monotony of daily routine under the guise of some higher social purpose.

The Loyal Order of the Buffalo Heads was formed in 1977 by regular members Ferguson Jenkins, Rick Wise, Jim Willoughby and Bill Lee, and adjunct member Bernie Carbo. Just as the Masons have different degrees to distinguish varying levels of esoteric achievement, the Buffalo Heads had both the aforementioned hierophants as well as neophytes Dick Pole, Rick Jones, Tom House and Tom Murphy, pitchers all. The order's choice of its mascot was based on research by Jenkins. "My Indian friends consider the buffalo the ugliest, dumbest animal in captivity," he told a reporter. Regardless of the particular quality Jenkins had in mind when he selected the group's symbol, the intended reference was manager Don Zimmer, whom Jenkins had dubbed "Buffalo Head" in much the same way that a tribe of Indians would refer to one of their members by the name of an animal whose qualities they thought he exemplified.

The organization's primary purpose was the protection and preservation of, and prevention of cruelty to, pitchers, since its founders shared the perception that they worked in a clubhouse atmosphere that was hostile to their kind. Ferguson Jenkins, president-by-acclamation, succinctly described the philosophy of manager Don Zimmer they were organized to fight: "The man knows nothing about pitching or pitchers. He's a lifetime .230 hitter who's been beaned three times. He hates pitchers. We will never see eye-to-eye." Lee seconded the motion: "Don dislikes all pitchers as a basic prejudice. If you've been beaned and nearly killed twice, you're going to want to make pitchers live in fear." Unlike the mystical themes that form the basis for organizations such as the Masons and the Knights of Columbus, this statement of organic beliefs was at least partly based on fact. In his twelve years in the major leagues Zimmer had been a mediocre player, playing for five different teams and never batting higher than .262 in a full season, and he had been severely injured by two pitches that struck him in the head during the early years of his career.

The Loyal Order of the Buffalo Heads

The formation of the Loyal Order of the Buffalo Heads coincided with a period during which Zimmer may indeed have mistreated some of his pitchers, and not just by the subjective standards that pitchers invoke to justify their failures. During 1977 the Sox had no starting pitching to speak of and, after Bill Campbell, not much relief pitching. Luis Tiant began the season with a contractual holdout and as a result was out of shape and unable to finish games that he could have completed in other springs. His humdrum record of 12-8 was the best of any starter, and he was the only pitcher in the rotation who didn't end up in the bull pen at least twice, but his earned run average of 4.53 was the worst of his career. Rick Wise and Reggie Cleveland floated in the same doldrums of mediocrity, each winning eleven games with earned run averages of 4.78 and 4.26, respectively. Ferguson Jenkins won ten and lost ten, but he won only three games in the second half of the season and none of them against a team capable of the middle-class respectability that a .500 won-lost record confers. Lee complained openly, and Zimmer came close to engineering the left-hander's release in late July before John Claiborne, assistant general manager, intervened. While Bill Campbell was the outstanding relief pitcher in the major leagues that year, he was so overworked, and so overburdened by the strain of his screwball, that by season's end he was receiving cortisone shots on a weekly basis.

Tiant, Wise, Jenkins, Cleveland and Lee all complained as they struggled individually, each taking a verse from the pitcher's litany of suffering, which reads thusly: "I'm not getting enough work (Lord, we need a four-man rotation). I'm getting too much work (Lord, get somebody warming up).

I'm getting the wrong kind of work (Lord, I'm not a long reliever)." One would expect, given this hagiography of pitching martyrs, that the Sox as a team would have been sacrificed at an early point in the 1977 season, but Zimmer still managed to keep them alive long enough to finish within two and a half games of the Yankees. In retrospect, to paraphrase A.J. Leibling, the 1977 Sox pitching staff may have been the biggest collection of adolescent neurotics since the Children's Crusades, with Bill Lee playing the role of Stephen the Shepherd Boy.

In addition to its charitable purpose, the Loyal Order of the Buffalo Heads provided its members with the opportunity to indulge in the conviviality fueled by spirits that is characteristic of American fraternal orders. Several of the Buffalo Heads used drugs, including Lee, who had first tried marijuana while a student at the University of Southern California, and who continued to use it throughout his career, once drawing a fine in 1979 for saying, in answer to a reporter's question whether the Red Sox had a problem with marijuana, "Hell no, how could they? I've been using that stuff since 1968 and I've never had a problem with it." Willoughby indulged as well, once smoking hashish with Lee before a game in Seattle in which Lee ended up pitching in relief of Rick Wise. Lee attributed his superior performance that day—five and two-thirds innings, two runs allowed—to the calming effects that the drug had on him. "It was quite an experience," Lee recounted. "I could see every play in my mind moments before it actually occurred. . .My concentration was so intense that there were no fans present and no hitters at the plate. It was just me, my catcher, and his signs." Or so the pitcher within him thought. Lee, by his own admission, also used cocaine, mescaline, mushrooms and peyote, but avoided amphetamines. "They made you feel stronger than you really were, making you believe you could blow the ball past people," Lee explained. His strength lay in his control and the diverse speeds of his pitches, which helped compensate for his lack of an overpowering fastball. Among the other lodge members, at least Jenkins was a probable user; he was arrested on drug charges after he retired from baseball.

The drug of choice among the Buffalo Heads, however, was clearly alcohol. Lee himself viewed drinking as an occupational hazard of major league baseball that, for some players, turned into an occupation. "The games present [ballplayers] with excuses to drink," he said. "If we have a good game, we want to celebrate. If we were horseshit, we want to forget. Young players drink to fit in, to take part in the camaraderie and relieve the boredom. When a player sees his career coming to an end, it's a more dangerous time. He tends to drink a lot more than he used to, knowing that his days in the sun are almost at an end and there's nothing he can do about it."

The travel required by major league baseball affords players with ample opportunities to imbibe. "The partying," Lee would recall after his playing days were over, "begins at the airport," where players kill time in the terminal lounge. If the flight doesn't take off as scheduled, the alcohol intake on the groundside of the airport increases. "When we finally do board our plane," Lee said, "the first thing they do is start pounding drinks into you. There are usually open bars on board and we had our methods of getting a little bit more than our normal allotment of liquid refreshments. I was often designated to distract the stewardess while the guys went in and grabbed all the two-ouncers of Scotch they could carry. While I set up a screen with the stewardess, another scouting party would be sent to keep management occupied. If you're ever on a plane with ballplayers and you see a bunch of them involved with their coaches in an intense discussion about the subtleties of the slider, you know the alcohol supplies are being raided. By the time the plane touches down most of them will be severely hammered."

Lee claimed, however, that there was no correlation between his level of alcohol consumption and his level of performance, unless it was an inverse one; the worse his hangover, the better his pitching. "There were days," he noted, "when I would get my nine hours of z's, get up with the dawn, do some calisthenics, have a great breakfast, and get to the ballpark early. I wouldn't make it past the first inning. On the other hand, there was many a time when I got to the stadium with my head on fire, still smelling of last night, and I'd go out and twist the opposition into pretzels."

The other Buffalo Heads shared Lee's fondness for alcohol. Willoughby, according to Lee, was a complex person who would be "serene and earth-oriented before a game," but "would pound six beers into himself and become a different guy, hellbent for leather," shortly thereafter. The Buffalo Heads as a group once succeeded in drinking enough beer in one sitting to create a mountain of beer cans reaching to a hotel room ceiling, finishing their feat at two o'clock in the morning. There was no official scorer present, however, and the accomplishment accordingly does not have the status of a major league record for a single drinking session.

The Loyal Order of the Buffalo Heads

Like many of his generation, Lee came to view the critical decision in the choice of stimulants as one between hallucinogens such as marijuana on the one hand, and alcohol in its various forms on the other, with the former representing the healthier, preferable option. "The difference between alcohol and marijuana is that alcohol is an aggressive drug that hampers the raising of consciousness. . .A guy who guzzles a bottle of VO in an evening is much worse off than a guy who does a few joints." This dichotomy ignores a spectrum of extremes other than that represented by the portraits at the opposite ends of the rogues' gallery of Yankee inebriants, namely, pitcher Steve Howe with his cocaine habit and Mickey Mantle and his transplanted liver. The category of choices ignored by Lee is that calculated by degrees of self-restraint, with total abstinence at one extreme, chronic intoxication at the other and a self-regulating continence somewhere in between.

That this dimension of assessment should not have occurred to a member of the Buffalo Heads is perhaps typical of professional athletes generally, who bear many of the marks of a leisure class (as described by Thorstein Veblen) that engages in conspicuous consumption as evidence of its wealth. Baseball players, who engage in what is a slow-paced pastoral game by comparison to most other sports, occupy the higher strata of this leisure class, and pitchers, who are rarely asked to work more than once every five days, are located at perhaps the furthest remove from daily toil of all professional athletes with the possible exception of placekick holders in football. Professional baseball players abstain from drudgery to such an extent that they retain young boys to carry and hand them their bats, which rarely weigh more than a businessman's briefcase, much as affluent golfers hire caddies to tote their clubs. They indulge in sport, an unproductive pastime that exemplifies the predatory impulse, the point of each game and the season itself being victory over opponents. And they often indulge in drink and drugs to excess, demonstrating that they have the excess wealth needed to purchase intoxicants and the leisure time to indulge in them. As Veblen put it,

> The ceremonial differentiation of the dietary is best seen in the use of intoxicating beverages and narcotics. If these articles of consumption are costly, they are felt to be noble and honorific. . . Drunkenness and the other pathological consequences of the free use of stimulants therefore tend in their turn to become honorific, as being a mark, at the second remove, of the superior status of those who are able to afford the indulgence. Infirmities induced by over-indulgence are among some peoples freely recognised as manly attributes.*

Sober or drunk, the Buffalo Heads' were at a disadvantage in their battle against their manager since Zimmer could consign a starting pitcher to a relief-pitching role or simply

---

* Thorstein Veblen, *The Theory of the Leisure Class*, Book-of-the-Month Club Edition, 1981, pp. 70-71. Not to put too fine a point on it, the Buffalo Heads' choice of their totem and the preference that professional sports teams in general display for fierce animals (or supposedly-fierce humans, as in the case of the Indians and the Braves) as mascots echoes another observation by Veblen, namely, that the predatory aspect of leisure-class activity is reflected in the "predilection shown in heraldic devices for the more rapacious beasts and birds of prey." *Id.*, p. 18.

decide not to use a particular pitcher at all, whether as starter or reliever. Thus, Lee, Wise and Jenkins all ended up in the bull pen, and Zimmer overlooked reliever Willoughby (31 appearances in 1977) while he overworked Bill Campbell (69 appearances that year). Campbell was 30-14 with 51 saves and an earned run average just slightly above or below three runs per nine innings during 1976 and 1977; during 1978, when the Sox were desperate for pitching down the stretch, Campbell appeared in only 29 games, had only 4 saves, a 7 and 5 record, and a 3.91 earned run average. His best years were behind him at that point, and he left the Sox for the Chicago Cubs in 1982 and retired in 1983.

Lee in particular felt the brunt of Zimmer's policy of intentional disuse. "Zimmer was intent on breaking up the Loyal Order," Lee concluded later. In 1977 Zimmer sent Lee to the bull pen, telling him it was for his own good. "Don claimed that pitching in relief would give me a chance to build my arm back up [after his injury at the hands of Graig Nettles]. Then he did his best to make sure I couldn't get into a ballgame." When Lee finally did make it into a game in relief, it was by a sort of southpaw highjacking. Zimmer had called for left-hander Ramon Hernandez to warm up, but Hernandez couldn't get loose. Zimmer came to the mound and signaled for the left-hander, but Lee, who hadn't been asked to warm up and who had thrown only two pitches, started the walk to the pitcher's mound. "I didn't call for you," Zimmer yelled at Lee. "Relax," Lee said, as ever the model of studious insouciance. "I'm just coming out to help Ramon. He can't make it today. You need a left-hander, and I'm going to prove to you that my arm is sound." "I want it to be known that I did not want you out here," Zimmer replied. "If you hurt yourself, it's not my fault." Lee, who was a candidate for release at that point in the season, struck out the batter and by the spring of 1978 had worked his way back into the starting rotation.

Men "go mad in herds, while they recover their senses slowly, and one by one," we are told by Charles Mackay in *Extraordinary Popular Delusions and the Madness of Crowds*. The Buffalo Heads were enough of a herd to incite each other to acts that, for men paid large sums of money to do what they apparently loved to do best, surely qualified as lunacy. On the night of September 17, 1977 and into the morning of the next day, the order indulged in a revel that concluded, by Lee's account, with Lee and Jenkins finishing off a last bottle of wine at five in the morning. Lee, trained as a Catholic in his childhood but an apostate thereafter, seemed to have retained the Roman Church's doctrine that the body is a temple of the Holy Ghost; he concluded that night's defilement of his senses with a manic cleanup designed to restore the sanctity of his corporeal cathedral, jogging five miles around a lake near Baltimore's Memorial Stadium shortly after arriving at the park. When he returned to the visitors' clubhouse after his run he found Bernie Carbo asleep behind an ultrasound machine, Rick Wise and Jim Willoughby recuperating in the trainer's room, and Ferguson Jenkins nowhere at all.

It was "Thanks, Brooks Day," in Baltimore, a celebration of the notable career of Brooks Robinson, the long-time Orioles third baseman. After the game began, Lee reported, he found Jenkins in the bull pen, asleep in the golf-cart-like vehicle that carries relief pitchers to the mound. By the second inning Mike Paxton, the Sox starter, was weakening, and Zimmer had pitching coach Alvin Jackson call down to Walt Hriniak in the Sox bull pen for Jenkins to begin warming up. At first Hriniak couldn't find Jenkins. When he did, he found him (according to Zimmer's account) sleeping in the truck from which the game was being broadcast for television. Hriniak tried to cover for Jenkins, preferring the wrath of Zimmer to the task of waking Jenkins, who at six feet five inches and 205 pounds, would have required an extraordinary degree of leverage for the five-foot eleven-inch Hriniak. (Jenkins would later claim that Hriniak knew he had gone into the TV truck to watch a football game.) Hriniak eventually revealed the location of the corpse, pronounced him dead and Bob Stanley was brought in instead. Jenkins was revived, fined and reprimanded.

Zimmer's displeasure with Jenkins extended to the rest of the Buffalo Heads, and was expressed in gestures both large and small. At the end of the 1977 season Zimmer invited the players into his office one by one to give them his personal thanks for their efforts—all but the Buffalo Heads. On the same day the five senior members of the order—Lee, Jenkins, Willoughby, Wise and Carbo—posed for a group picture they knew would be their last together in Red Sox uniforms. Zimmer had given the word to the front office that he wanted the Buffalo Heads to roam somewhere else and, by the beginning of the 1978 season, the senior members of the lodge had been scattered in a diaspora that was both the product of Zimmer's wrath and its principal balm. Rick Wise was gone to Cleveland in the trade for Eckersley. Jim Willoughby was sold outright to the Chicago White Sox in a transaction that offended his somewhat prickly sense of amour-propre and Lee's generally accepted principle of baseball accounting, namely, that a dollar bill never struck out anybody. Lee lit a candle and placed it on Don Zimmer's desk as a sort of votive offering for the soul of his departed lodgemate. Ferguson Jenkins was sent to the Texas Rangers for John Poloni, a left-handed pitcher who had won one major league game in September of 1977. Unfortunately for the Red Sox, he never won another and was released after winning one minor league game and losing seven. Jenkins went 18 and 8 for the Rangers in 1978, his best season ever in terms of winning percentage, and won 53 more games before he retired in 1984 after 19 years in the major leagues. Pledges Rick Jones, Dick Pole, Tom House and Tom Murphy had been disposed of in 1977, with Murphy going to Toronto and the rest to Seattle. Lee and Carbo were the only ones left. As they jogged together in the outfield before the second game of the 1978 season against the Texas Rangers, in which the Sox would face Jenkins, Lee said to Carbo, "Now there's only two of us. We're the last remnants, a couple of bookends."

April

The 1978 season started inauspiciously for both the Yankees and the Red Sox, as each team dropped two out of its first three games, the Sox losing their first series to Chicago while the Yankees did the same against Texas. There were small portents of trouble for the Sox. Yaz dropped a fly ball in the second game of the season, thereby losing a $100 bet with shortstop Rick Burleson that he could repeat his feat of 1977, when he played the entire season without committing an error, the only regular outfielder in the American League to do so. New Sox pitchers Torrez and Eckersley didn't prevail in their first starts, as Torrez lost two leads in his opening-game defeat by the White Sox, and Eckersley was pulled after four innings in his first outing because, in Don Zimmer's estimation, he had "run out of gas" and the manager didn't want him to develop arm problems from throwing too many pitches in the chill of the early season. As a coach of the 1974 Sox,

Zimmer had seen Rick Wise suffer just such an injury when he pitched a four-hitter in the cold spring of that season. Wise won only two games the rest of the year.

In Greek mythology, Lachesis is the Fate who determines the length of the thread of one's life. With the extermination of the Buffalo Heads, the Sox' acquisition of a great deal of pitching talent in the winter following the 1977 season, and Bill Lee narrowly avoiding release during the summer of that year, it was fortuitous that she should have chosen to extend his career in the spring of 1978. Lee stopped the early run in the weave of the Sox with a 5-0 shutout of the White Sox in the third game of the season, thus beginning his tenth year under contract with the Red Sox with his first shutout since August 19, 1975, when he beat Wilbur Wood of the White Sox. Even in victory Lee could be an irritant to management, however. He was quoted on the day of the game in the Chicago *Sun-Times* as saying, "I can't possibly communicate with him," referring to Zimmer. General manager Haywood Sullivan answered Lee publicly by saying, "I don't mind a player self-destructing, but I don't like him trying to take someone down with him."

By the end of the first week of the season, both the Yankees and the Sox were looking decidedly mediocre, each with 1-3 records. The Sox then reeled off eight straight wins, including their first seven home games, beating the Indians twice and sweeping consecutive series with Texas and Milwaukee. In typical Sox fashion, Boston's surge owed more to hitting than pitching; both Jim Rice and Jerry Remy hit safely in the first seven games, Butch Hobson had RBIs in ten straight games, the fifteenth player in American baseball history to do so, and Remy added a new dimension to the tradi-tionally-plodding Sox offense with four steals in the first five games. The streak was ended by the Indians and exiled Buffalo Head Rick Wise as the Sox lost 13-4 in what was the first victory by any of the pitchers involved in the March trade that brought Eckersley to the Sox. "There was no vengeance involved," Wise responded when a reporter asked him how it felt to beat his former nemesis Zimmer, but Wise's words were belied by his actions; the day before he had sent out his copy of the group picture of the Buffalo Heads taken at the end of the 1977 season to be enlarged and framed. When asked what he thought of Wise's pitching, Zimmer replied, obliquely but not at all cryptically, "I thought Bob Stanley pitched well."

During this early-season era of good feelings even Lee seemed to be willing to subordinate his personality to the greater good of the team, and Zimmer diplomatically chose to ignore Lee's comments in Chicago. "He's a helluva competi-tor and pitcher," Zimmer told reporters after Lee struck out White Sox designated hitter Junior Moore in the ninth inning of the team's first win of the season. Lee matched Zimmer with an apparent willingness to deny, or at least annotate, his prior remarks about the manager: "What I was quoted as say-ing wasn't what I meant," he told reporters, in typically ellip-tical fashion. Seeming weary of his role as class clown, coun-tercultural spokesman and cosmic put-on artist, he cut off reporters' questions by saying, "I'd just as soon bury the whole Spaceman thing (referring to his nickname) and get on with pitching." Lee seemed to be at peace with himself and his pitching showed it. He won his first five decisions in April, an accomplishment that put him in a distinguished company with only Paul Splittorf, the Kansas City Royals' ace, and Frank Tanana of the California Angels, whose career record at that point was 70-49. Together, Lee and Dick Drago won or saved 7 of the Sox' first 11 wins. Since Eckersley had yet to win a game, Torrez had won only once and Tiant was on the disabled list, it was fair to say that Lee was carrying the pitching staff.

The Yankees' ledger book also showed a deficit in the pitching account. Goose Gossage, the relief pitcher who was supposed to give the Yankees the best bull pen in baseball, lost the first game of the season to Texas on a home run on an 0-2 count to Richie Zisk of the White Sox. After two fastballs, Gossage threw Zisk a slider trying to waste a pitch, but it stayed high and Zisk hit it into the left-field stands. The same thing happened four days later when he faced Larry Hisle of the Milwaukee Brewers—two quick strikes on fastballs and a slider for a home run. He gave up another home run in his next appearance and his record was 0-3. Catfish Hunter lost his first two starts, 9-6 to Texas and 6-1 to Baltimore. Hunter had been the most dominating pitcher in baseball during the first half of the seventies, with records starting in 1970 of 18-14, 21-11, 21-7, 21-5 and 25-12. He moved from the Oakland A's to the Yankees in 1975 and won 23 while losing 14, then went 17-15 the next year. In 1977 he was a health insurer's nightmare as he developed a urinary disorder, was hit on the toe by a line drive and developed arm trouble, the latter ailment being the result, thought some, of an adjustment to his motion to compensate for a hernia. His record fell to 9-9, his earned run average increased to 4.72, and he gave up 29 home runs in 143 innings, making him the most accommodating pitcher in baseball in that regard. Yankee fans and management looked to him for a comeback in the spring of 1978, but it was not yet in the offing. Ron Guidry pitched well in his opening day start but didn't finish and his team didn't win. Ed Figueroa, with two complete games and a 3-1 record, and Sparky Lyle, with two wins and one save, were the only New York pitchers whose arms were performing as required.

For Yankee fans Reggie Jackson was the principal cause for hope. He went 4 for 5 with 2 doubles in the Yankees' first win over the Texas Rangers. In the team's home opener against the White Sox, Jackson hit a three-run homer in his first at bat, producing all the runs New York would need to win, 4-2. It was his fifth consecutive home run in five (official) at bats in Yankee Stadium starting with the fifth game of the prior year's World Series and continuing through his one-walk, three home-run performance in the sixth game of the series; it was also his fourth home run on four consecutive swings in Yankee Stadium. His feat was honored by a shower of Reggie Bars from the stands, as the recognition that Jackson had predicted he would receive if he were to play in New York—that a candy bar would be named after him—had come to pass after only one season. The candy bars had been distributed to spectators at the game by the company that made them, and, as Jackson rounded the bases, two fans decided to wing their gifts towards home plate. The spontaneity of the act and the anonymity of the setting convinced most of the other people in the stands to throw their bars as well, and the game was delayed while the grounds crew, assisted by some of the hungrier and more enterprising kids in the stands, picked up the mess.

The reactions of the two ball clubs to the outburst varied. Here's Jackson's: "It was a nice gesture." Piniella, the batter on deck who had to wait through the cleanup: "It was a very thrilling moment—for Reggie." Billy Martin: "I felt like opening up a candy store." And White Sox manager Bob Lemon: "I think it was horse manure." Lemon took a sarcastic view of the product's quality: "It must be a great tasting candy bar if they throw it instead of eat it. They should advertise it as 'The candy bar made to throw.'" The Reggie Bar never developed the popularity of the Baby Ruth, the confection that Jackson wrongly thought he should be measured against, but not for lack of promotion. As his longtime teammate Catfish Hunter aptly put it, "When you unwrap a Reggie Bar, it tells you how good it is." The Reggie Bar remains available in the town where the author lives two decades after it was first introduced, despite the fact that its freshness date, like Jackson's hold on the attention of America's baseball fans, has long since passed.

On April 14th the Yankees held a Welcome Home luncheon at the Americana Hotel. It was an open day for the Yankees, who had been working in their fields of play since the team came north following spring training, and it would be their only day off for two weeks. Five players—Graig Nettles, Mickey Rivers, Thurman Munson, Roy White and Sparky Lyle—chose not to attend, or in White's case, to leave early. Two days later, Yankee owner George Steinbrenner decided the five should be fined $500 each for violating paragraph 3(b) of the standard major league contract, which required them to "cooperate in any and all reasonable promotional activities of the club." Yankee players' representative

April

Ken Holtzman told Marvin Miller, the president of the Major League Players Association, and the players' union returned the Yankees' fire with a volley an American Civil Liberties Union lawyer would have admired, filing a grievance claiming the luncheon was not strictly promotional because it benefitted a sectarian cause, namely, the instructional television activities of the Archdiocese of New York. Nettles sought personal dispensation on the grounds that his pregnant wife had a doctor's appointment and someone had to watch their three children; his plea was denied. Roy White, on the other hand, was excused by management from payment of his fine for answering to a higher call; he had an appointment with his tax lawyer.

In an earlier time, the fines would have been paid or ignored, depending upon the talent of the player involved and his value to the team, and the matter would have been done with. In an era governed by rules that reflected collective bargaining and the mistrust that had developed between the players and the owners, a minor spat turned into an official dispute that would not be resolved, by relief pitcher Sparky Lyle's estimation, "until Christmas." The incident left a particularly bitter taste in the mouths of the accused. "If they want someone to play third base," Nettles said, "they have me. If they want someone to go to luncheons, they should hire Georgie Jessel," the professional bon vivant known in his time as the Toastmaster General. Mickey Rivers was full of gall and wormwood. "It was our first free day here since spring training," he complained. "The Yankees aren't doing anything except for certain guys." A reporter asked him to be more specific—which guys? "There's a lot of certain guys around here," he muttered. Rivers's pique was not something to trifle with; earlier in the month he had pushed traveling secretary Gerry Murphy to the ground and tried to choke him when Murphy refused to accommodate Rivers's demand that his luggage be carried through customs in Toronto by a Yankee bag-wallah.

For Albert Walter "Sparky" Lyle, the former Red Sox who came to New York in the ill-fated trade for Danny Cater, l'affaire de luncheon was an occasion to annoy George Steinbrenner. Lyle's relationship with Steinbrenner had turned sour for reasons first laid out in the biblical parable of the workers in the vineyard (Matthew 20:1-16). The previous season Lyle had won the final two American League Championship games against Kansas City after the Yankees had fallen behind in the series, 2 games to 1, and had then won the first game of the World Series against the Dodgers. He had been rewarded by Steinbrenner with a spontaneous one-year extension of his existing three-year contract at his previous salary of $135,000 per year, with a $35,000 bonus thrown in as a lagniappe. To this offer, Lyle responded with a small-town boy's naivete: "Whatever you say is fine with me." As he was driving through New Mexico on vacation after the season ended, however, he heard that the Yankees had signed short-reliever Rich Gossage, a free agent who had played for the Pittsburgh Pirates the year before, to a $2,750,000, six-year contract. The last was now first, and Lyle, the primary reliever in the Yankee bull pen for the past six years, was—at least in his own mind—last.

But Steinbrenner didn't stop with Gossage. He paid the Atlanta Braves $100,000 for Andy Messersmith's contract, which meant he was paying (in Lyle's view) the sum of $366,666 per year (the $100,000 purchase price plus a third of Messersmith's three-year, $1,000,000 contract) to find out if the cofounder of free agency could pitch again after missing half of the last two seasons. Then the Yankees picked up Rawley Eastwick, another pitcher whose days of excellence were behind him, to a five-year, $1,100,000 contract. When Lyle continued his former practice of showing up late for spring training, Steinbrenner issued a press release saying that if Lyle didn't recognize his moral and contractual obligation to report on time, the Yankees wouldn't waste their time trying to find him. This pronouncement was exemplary of a pattern of disinformation that Steinbrenner has followed over the years, saying one thing publicly that he knows to be half-true privately; Cedric Tallis of the Yankees knew where Lyle was, as he had spoken to him the morning the press release was issued. Since Lyle had already agreed to his contract for 1978, he did not have the leverage he had in prior years when he would come to camp late because he was unsigned. Now, he arrived at camp earlier than usual in recognition of his contractual status, and Steinbrenner paid a Fort Lauderdale high school band to greet Lyle at the airport with a banner that said: "WELCOME TO FORT LAUDERDALE SPARKY—FINALLY." A little more than a week later, Lyle told Steinbrenner he wanted to be traded.

The Yankees refused to trade Lyle, instead embarking on a program of brainwashing that was as intense as any practiced during the Korean War. They told him they had tried to trade him (to the Texas Rangers) but couldn't. Lyle knew better, namely, that the Yankees had turned down the trade, not the Rangers. Then they told him that they couldn't trade him because he had won the Cy Young Award the previous year. Lyle—a former teammate and drinking buddy of Bill Lee who, like Lee, seemed to live solely in the present—said he didn't care; the glory of the award was over for him the day he received it, he claimed, even though on that day he felt so excited and proud he could have "farted in public." So he told them that if they wouldn't trade him (instead of couldn't) he was entitled to more money. Finally, the Yankees said they would pay him $250,000 for an added year to his contract, meaning three years hence. Lyle turned it down. Steinbrenner was reportedly ready to pay him an extra $50,000 per year for the life of his contract if he would pitch an inning in a spring training game against the Reds. Lyle complied, got out of the inning on eight pitches, and refused to pitch any more. The team and its principal reliever faced an irretrievable breakdown.

On April 16th Lyle retired seven of eight batters to save the final game of a three-game sweep of the White Sox. On April 18th he went to Steinbrenner to tell him he was quitting. Steinbrenner, in a rare moment freed from the burden of his blustering public persona, agreed that Lyle had a legitimate beef. He promised to take care of Lyle once things quieted down. He knew that Lyle couldn't survive without his salary, and he got the pitcher to admit as much. What Steinbrenner wanted was for Lyle and the others who skipped his luncheon to drop their grievance, and this was communicated to the pitcher by manager Billy Martin as a go-between for Al Rosen, president of the Yankees. If they did, Steinbrenner would come up with more money for Lyle. Lyle said no.

Jackson, meanwhile, continued to confirm his value by deeds that matched his frequent and incendiary words; he hit a lead-off home run in the bottom of the ninth inning against the Orioles on April 18th to give the Yankees the win and a .500 record for the first time that season at 5-5. He stole two bases April 22nd in a 4-3 win over Milwaukee; those steals marked Jackson's passage from petit to grand larcenist as he crossed the 200-stolen base threshold for his career when he dusted himself off after the first one. In the ninth inning of a game against the Twins on the last day of April he got an infield hit, went to second on a wild throw and scored the winning run on a single by Chris Chambliss.

The Sox stumbled at the end of the month, ending April with a 2-1 loss to the Texas Rangers and Ferguson Jenkins. That defeat represented the team's third loss in eight days to pitchers whom they had traded away over the winter, the other two being the loss to the Indians and Rick Wise on April 22nd and a 5-4 loss to Texas and Reggie Cleveland on April 28th. Jenkins was bitter about his treatment by Zimmer in 1977 and was willing to talk about it. "I told Bill Lee two days ago that the pitchers Zimmer got rid of will win 80 games between them," Jenkins told reporters after beating the Sox and Lee on April 30th. "You can't give away pitching, veteran pitching. Why did he? I can't answer except to say personality. It was with me. Nobody knew when he was going to pitch last year, and when I spoke out I was dumped. It was a cruel, monstrous thing that happened to a pretty good pitching staff," he groused in an overwrought dramatization reminiscent of Vivian Leigh's Scarlett O'Hara. For the record, the actual performance of the five principal pitchers from the 1977

Red Sox who were not with the club for the full 1978 season was exactly one-half as good as Jenkins predicted; Jenkins (18), Cleveland (6), Wise (9), Willoughby (1) and Tom Murphy (6) won a total of 40 games in 1978.

Jenkins would continue his campaign of complaint throughout the season from other outposts of the American League. "I got shoved into the bull pen by a fat, ugly bald man who doesn't know anything about pitching," he would later complain to a Minneapolis writer. Dodger scout Charlie Metro brought the quote to the attention of Zimmer, who told a reporter, "I'm going to write him a letter and tell him he's right on three counts. I'm fat, ugly and bald. He may be right on the other count too, but if he were still here I wouldn't be. I'd have been fired."

The first month of major league baseball in 1978 ended with the Yankees in third place in the American League East with a 10-9 record, the Red Sox in second place at 11-9, and the Detroit Tigers in first place at 13-5.

New York and Boston

I f baseball had a Bible, the story of the rivalry between
Boston and New York would appear in the Book of
Genesis. Before the current version of baseball developed on the Elysian Fields of Hoboken, New Jersey, a
picnic ground across the Hudson River from New
York, there was "Boston Ball", also known as the
"Massachusetts Game" or "town ball". That earlier variation
of the game differed from the New York style of play in that
runners were retired from the base paths by hitting them with
a soft ball thrown at them, instead of touching them with the
ball or placing it "in the hands of an adversary on the base."
It is thus both literally and metaphorically true that as baseball moved southward from Boston to New York it was transformed from softball to hardball.

If baseball were drama, the Red Sox would be a little
theater production of a classical tragedy that comes off as
farce, while the Yankees would be a long-running Broadway

hit that, while periodically staged by lesser casts, regularly repays its angels with box-office success. There is, of course, a Broadway play—*Damn Yankees*—about a Faustian bargain to beat the perennially-triumphant New Yorkers, based on the novel *The Year the Yankees Lost the Pennant* by Douglass Wallop. There is no *Damn Red Sox*, nor is one likely to be produced in the lifetime of any Boston fan living today. Being a fan of the Yankees has rarely involved the sort of sacrifice that other baseball fans must make from time to time, or for years on end, as in the case of the Red Sox. As a result, rooting for the Yankees has been compared by different sportswriters in different times to rooting for U.S. Steel or General Motors (when those corporations were the envy of the industrial world) or for the Nazis. The rest of America expects a certain minimal portion of abrasiveness and arrogance from every New Yorker, the way it expects cordiality from Southerners and shallow mysticism from Californians, but the Yankee fan is an enhanced version of this regional stereotype as a result of the team's history of success. In the 1938 MGM movie *Boys Town*, Mickey Rooney plays a cocky orphan from New York who boasts that he roots for the Yankees. Another orphan sums him up with two words: "You would."

This duality in America's national pastime replicates in the realm of sports a larger contrast between the two regions: New York is the Empire State and New York City is the Big Apple, the place where, as the song goes, if you can make it there you can make it anywhere. New York's Wall Street is the capitalist capital of America, while Boston's stock exchange is at best a regional affair. Will Rogers came up with a homely metaphor for New York's precedence in this regard: America's cow grazes

all over the pasture, he said, but it gets milked in only one corner—New York. Boston, on the other hand, is a place where
wealth has long been viewed as a consideration secondary to
breeding, an attitude summed up by the Boston Brahmin in the
John P. Marquand novel who, when asked how he made his
money, replies "We don't make our money, we have it." While
proper Bostonians once pretended to disdain newly-accumu-
lated wealth, their contempt (to the extent that it persists to this
day) is decidedly Pecksniffian. For example, an article in the
Boston *Globe* in 1978, the year under consideration here,
described the comparatively greater salaries an individual
could expect to receive in various trades if he or she were to ply
them in New York City rather than Boston. The idea of a New
York newspaper reporting the cuts in pay a person would suffer by moving to Boston is improbable, since in this respect
Boston is no worse to a New Yorker than anyplace else.

The typical New Englander is thus skeptical of wealth at
the same time that he or she is envious of it. The skepticism
springs from the knowledge that financial rewards entail
financial risk, and the envy is the result of forces too obvious
to require explanation. New England's aversion to financial
risk is perhaps best exemplified by its distinction as the birth-
place of the spendthrift trust, the instrument by which the
region's mill owners and China traders kept their descendants from dissipating inherited fortunes in riotous living.
Through these arrangements, the capital of New England
was held by trustees who were loath to put the funds at risk
for fear of violating the grave obligation imposed upon them
as fiduciaries. As Elmer Davis put it in a 1928 article in
Harper's, the trustees of New England "cannot take a chance.

. . .And without taking a chance no region in a slump is likely to get itself out." *Fortune* magazine expressed the same view in an article on the business climate in New England five years later, noting that "A society may be embalmed in a can of trusts as a cod may find eternal youth in brine."

This indigenous fear of risk has been handed down through the generations in Massachusetts in the same way that low-number license plates make their way to cars currently on the road from old Yankee ancestors who could afford automobiles before their neighbors. In 1980, when Apple Computer first issued stock to the public, residents of Massachusetts were prohibited from participating because the state's regulators decreed that the company's offering was too risky. The shares were sold on the New York Stock Exchange in one of the most successful public offerings ever to investors everywhere but Massachusetts, and purchasers of the stock profited handsomely.

The different seeds from which these regional strains have grown are exemplary of the later flowering they produced. New York was populated early on by Dutch settlers, descendants of a great trading nation capable, in moments of collective commercial frenzy, of such speculative excesses as the Tulipomania of the 1600s, in which the value of lovely but useless articles—tulip bulbs—was bid up to levels far exceeding their intrinsic worth by a population universally attuned

---

* The term "Yankee" has Dutch origins, although they are somewhat cloudy. It is derived from "Jan Kees", which means "John Cheese" in Dutch, and was probably first used by non-Dutch as a disparaging nickname for Hollanders. It was later applied by the colonial Dutch in New York to English settlers in Connecticut, and has since come to refer generally to a native of any northeastern state or, in the South, to any northerner.

to the prospect of selling them again at a profit. The Netherlands, a nation without natural resources, grew wealthy by hard work and by trading what little they had—mainly herring—for things of greater value. The fable handed down to us about the interaction between these people and the Indians who inhabited the land that became New York is that the Dutch were sharp enough to acquire Manhattan island for $24 worth of trinkets. The tale that we tell about the Pilgrims of the Massachusetts Bay Colony implies that, without the help of the agricultural skills of Squanto, a native of the Plymouth region, their community, with a socialist form of government they later abandoned, wouldn't have been around for the first Thanksgiving.

The Puritans preferred "honest gaine" through labor over the speculative pursuit of riches that caused the colonists in Virginia to succumb to gold fever and nearly perish as a result of their neglect of essential tasks, and they frowned upon excessive acquisitiveness. They fined Robert Keayne, the city's first import merchant, for price gouging, and compelled him to make a public confession of his "covetous and corrupt heart." Cotton Mather's "rules for trading" prohibited merchants from taking unfair advantage of their customers by selling above the "current price," meaning the price that a buyer who knows the value of a commodity would give for it. A seller who lived by this rule might find himself unprepared for the sharper attitudes of another clime when he went to buy something, which may explain why the Red Sox paid $400,000 in 1980 for Claude Edward "Skip" Lockwood, most recently of the New York Mets, a free agent relief pitcher in the fifteenth year of his career who produced only two saves and a 5.32 earned run average for the Sox before retiring.

Money is power, said a Boston preacher in the nineteenth century without a nod to Thomas Hobbes. He might have pilfered more profitably from Adam Smith, who pointed out that money's power is not intrinsic, but is unleashed only when one buys things. The regional contrast between Boston and New York in terms of financial acumen may be gleaned from the fact that when the Yankees bought Babe Ruth from the Red Sox in 1920, part of the consideration given by the Yankees was a loan, not an outright payment, and it was secured by a mortgage on Fenway Park. Thus, the Yankees not only obtained the best player in the game at the time and possibly ever, they got him in part with money they would get back later. They also could have foreclosed on the Red Sox' ball field itself if owner Harry Frazee had failed to make punctual payments on his promissory note.

The pinchpenny philosophy of the New Englander is so pervasive that tinctures of it can be found even in recent transplants from New York. Red Sox general manager Lou Gorman, formerly of the New York Mets, was asked why, in the thick of the 1990 pennant race with the Oakland A's, he passed up outfielder Willie McGee after the former star of the Cardinals' World Series teams of the 1980s became available for the waiver price. In response, Gorman asked a rhetorical question that has become a part of the Red Sox catechism of frustration: "What would we do with Willie McGee?" McGee, a former Most Valuable Player, two-time batting champion and three-time Golden Glove winner, went on to win the National League batting title that year. McGee was acquired by the Red Sox five years later during the pennant race of 1995 at a time when his skills had understandably declined; it was as if a WASP from Boston's North Shore had come home from a tag sale gloating to his wife about a great deal on a pair of used galoshes. The New Englander clasps his coin purse with both hands and turns away from potentially improvident expenditure while muttering the region's familiar homily: "Use it up, wear it out, make it do, do without."

New York is thus the place in America that serves as the hometown, usually adopted, of those who believe that money is life's report card. Boston, on the other hand, is often referred to as the Athens of America due to the large number of colleges and universities located there; it is, as a result, inhabited by more than a few people who believe that one's report card is, or ought to be, as good as money. Massachusetts in general and Boston in particular are thus known to the rest of the world as places where the life of the mind can be preferred over an existence of superficial acquisitiveness without attracting critical attention; the *Dictionary of American Slang's* definition of "Boston coffee" (tea) includes the explanation that the use of the term reflects the fact that "Boston is associated in the popular mind with an effete way of life."

The contemplative life and the attitudes associated with it are, of course, easier to maintain when one already has the cash that others so crassly strive for, and Massachusetts is also a state that might adopt as its motto "Don't touch the principal" on account of the inherited wealth that, meted out by trustees, sustains many of its inhabitants. This regional trait towards the intellectual is revealed by the tendency among those who write about the Sox to indulge in scholarly digression. A recent collection of essays about the Red Sox included fourteen footnotes; a similar collection of essays about the Yankees by the same publisher and of approximately the same length contained none. Robert Burton observed in his 1621 work, *The Anatomy of Melancholy*, that melancholy is a "common maul" of students, and results from "too vehement study." In choosing to cultivate his or her mind, a proper Bostonian who is also a Red Sox fan may accordingly have chosen a fertile field for the seeds of misery.

The "Athens of America" label has given rise to an analogy in which New York becomes baseball's Sparta, but the apparent parallelism disappears upon closer examination. The term "New York intellectual" is as much a part of the American vernacular as "New York deli." Athens was more populous and more densely populated than Sparta, as New York is by comparison to Boston. The Spartans are remembered for their austerity; New York is the American city that ranks second only to Hollywood, in popular imagination if not in truth, as a place where a life of unrestrained self-indulgence can be pursued. The golden age of Athens is remembered as a time of culture, sophistication and joyful living; Massachusetts is the puritanical state where sumptuary laws prohibited the working classes from wearing gold, silver, silk or hatbands for the better part of the seventeenth century. Sparta was a conservative oligarchy, New York is a liberal democracy, with five registered Democrats for every confessed Republican.

The only valid basis for the comparison would thus appear

to be that the soldiers of Sparta were supposed to be invincible, as were the Yankees in their time. That, and the fact that Sparta won the Peloponnesian Wars, which is why there are today teams named the "Spartans," but none called the "Athenians." John Cheever compared the 1978 Red Sox to the Trojans and the Yankees to the Greeks, but this comparison is inapt as well. The incident that started the Trojan War was the theft of Helen by Paris, the son of the Trojan king; the Red Sox, as anyone who has been a fan of the team for very long knows, rarely steal anything. And it is the Red Sox who, like the Greek warrior Achilles, are always felled by the improbable blow to a weak spot—their pitching arms—in otherwise-sturdy bodies.

There are several reasons for the prevalence of impertinent classical allusions in writings by Bostonians on the Red Sox. The first is that the progress of a Red Sox season often follows the form of a tragedy, moving from early-season happiness to October misery. The team is thus likely to be examined in light of things Greek, although the resemblances that are detected by some observers are often no closer than Greek salad is to Boston baked beans. The second is that, since Boston must depend on its reputation as an academic center in a way that New York need not, pride in the intellect becomes a form of local boosterism among Bostonians, in much the same way that small towns across America celebrate local foodstuffs such as lima beans or pork ribs as the means by which they distinguish themselves. A Boston sportswriter's allusions to Greek history, literature or mythology in describing the Red Sox are thus likely to be as affected as the smile that the mayor of such a provincial community displays when he swallows the local delicacy at the annual harvest festival, and should be taken no more seriously.*

After the obligatory Athens-Sparta analogy, the invocation of Oscar Wilde's Dorian Gray to describe an aging veteran, a comparison that links a pitcher banished to the bull pen with Charlie on the MTA (the man in The Kingston Trio song who never returned from a ride on Boston's subway), and the opening lines of *A Tale of Two Cities*, the average sportswriter covering the Sox will usually have exhausted his store of literary allusions. While this deficiency should benefit those who read Boston's sports pages to find out what actually happened in the previous day's game, its potentially salutary effect is usually nullified by an overabundance of quotations from obscure rock 'n' roll songs (the most common being "Lawyers, Guns and Money" by Warren Zevon) popular with the current baby-boom crowd of Boston sportswriters. As this generation of journalists ages, and their favorite groups end up in the cut-out bins at local record stores, these allusions have become slightly less accessible to the average Red Sox fan than quotations from Shakespeare.

The dichotomy between Boston and New York, while exaggerated in general and subject to numerous exceptions in particular, is nonetheless real. Nineteenth-century Boston was, in the cartography of Dr. Oliver Wendell Holmes (the

---

* Michael Gee of the *Boston Herald* seems to be the exception. In a recent column repeating the theme of Red Sox history as tragedy he referred to the "pity and terror" that Sox fans should feel when considering the possibility of meeting the Yankees, just as Aristotle would have. And in another, he noted that a particular loss by the New York Jets to the New England Patriots included all the elements of a tragedy except for a chorus and the fact that the Jets' coach didn't tear out his eyeballs at the end.

elder), the hub of the solar system. This boast was subsequently expanded by a sort of big bang of the communal ego so that Boston became a place so solipsistic (or provincial) that it was referred to, often by its inhabitants and frequently without irony, as the Hub of the Universe. "Hub Man Dies in NY A-Blast" proclaimed a parody of the Boston *Globe* several years back, putting into a headline's shorthand both the parochialism of which Bostonians are capable and their affected indifference to New York and all that it represents. More than a few news vendors had to refund money to patrons who hadn't heard the news, didn't realize it was fictional and saw nothing peculiar in the paper's angle on it. New York's view of itself in relation to the rest of America has perhaps been best expressed by the foreshortened maps of America produced by a number of artists showing Manhattan's streets looming larger in size and significance than the rest of the country from the Hudson westward.* Bostonians regard those who depart for New York with a mixture of contempt and affected puzzlement; the Boston Brahmin protagonist of John P. Marquand's *The Late George Apley* writes to his son, "Above all, I cannot imagine what you see in New York." In short, the New Yorker rolls his eyes northward towards Boston with condescension, and the Bostonian looks southward upon New York with disdain. The Yankee fan and the Red Sox fan do the same, in their smaller sphere of contest.

---

* The earliest was probably produced by industrial designer Daniel Wallingford, who moved from New York to Boston in 1935. The most widely-known of recent versions is undoubtedly that drawn by Saul Steinberg, which appeared as a cover of *The New Yorker* magazine.

The Year of the Gerbil

Boston may be the last stop on the road taken by shows bound for Broadway, but in terms of the arts, it might as well be the first since, to turn the chorus of "New York, New York" on its head, if you don't make it there, you don't make it anywhere. The distance between Boston's theater district and the popular stages of New York can't be measured in miles since the name "Broadway" is known around the world. By contrast, Boston's theater district has no popular name at all other than "Piano Row"—the now-unused nickname for the block of Boylston Street where the Colonial Theater is located, so-called because of the music stores that line its sidewalks—or the "Combat Zone," for the specially-zoned pornography area that surrounds it and which, at times when conscription has been in effect, appeared to have been invaded by servicemen. A discussion between two New York ladies in Henry James' *The Bostonians* is instructive on this point:

> **First lady:** Well, you must be pretty desperate, when you have got to go to Boston for your entertainment.
> **Second lady:** Well, there's a similar society there, and I never heard of their sending to New York.
> **First lady:** Of course not, they think they have got everything. But doesn't it make your life a burden, thinking what you can possibly have.

And later, discussing a New York club that decides to give a lecture series, one of James's characters says, "It is New York trying to be like Boston."

Boston's reputation as a cultural stepsister to New York's child star originated with the asceticism of the Puritans, the congregation haunted by the fear, in the words of H.L. Mencken, "that someone, somewhere, was happy." In 1673, a citizen of Springfield, Massachusetts, named Samuel Terry and eight others were fined by magistrate John Pynchon for putting on an "uncivill" play that was determined to be "Immodest and beastly." In 1876, the Puritanical school of literary criticism was institutionalized as the New England Watch and Ward Society, which was founded to stamp out books and plays considered to be offensive or dangerous to the public morals. Mencken had reason to know of the Puritanical morals that guided the Watch and Ward Society's aesthetic principles; he was arrested on the Boston Common and tried for selling pornography—an edition of his *American Mercury* magazine that contained an article on a small-town prostitute—in a case that tested the Society's system of informal censorship. In a contemporary world in which looser morals have triumphed, Bostonians bear the stigma of their history of civic righteousness like a transvaluation of Hester Prynne's scarlet letter; and like her, they wear their badge with a mixture of guilt and pride.

The Puritanical element of the New England temperament may help to explain why the Sox would trade a pitcher like Sparky Lyle to the Yankees when he was at the peak of his career. Lyle was a good reliever who averaged almost 14 saves a year in his five seasons with the Sox, but he began to produce at a quantum level higher immediately upon being traded to New York. In 1972, his first year with the Yankees, he saved 35 games, as many as he had in his last two years in

Boston and more than any pitcher in the league. He saved 27 the next year and led the league again in 1976 with 23 saves. In 1977 he became the first relief pitcher to win the American League Cy Young Award, the award given annually since 1956 to the best pitcher in each league.

Notwithstanding his gaudy statistics, in his days with the Red Sox Lyle had represented the initial manifestation of a proletarian style of the radical will that reached its apotheosis several years later in Bill Lee's rebellions, and as a result he was viewed with a Puritanical disapproval by some members of management and Clif Keane, a local talk-show host who would later come to dislike Lee for the same reasons. Lyle rode a motorcycle and stayed out so late that he was the roommate of choice for players who wanted to take advantage of the amorous opportunities that fall so readily in the path of major league baseball players. He violated the principle of Puritan thrift by initiating a practice of sitting on birthday cakes given to teammates by Red Sox fans, starting with one given to Rico Petrocelli. Petrocelli, a shortstop and third baseman with the Sox when Lyle broke in with the team in 1967, had received a cake from his fan club that he tried to hide from his teammates. Lyle, sensing the bourgeois individualism at work in the mind of Petrocelli, removed the cake from the locker where it had been hidden while the rest of the team was taking batting practice. When Petrocelli returned to the clubhouse after taking his swings, he saw Lyle standing naked with his back to a bench where the cake was sitting. "Look out for my cake," he yelled, but Lyle, feigning a deaf ear to his teammate's warning, squatted down. "Sorry about that," he said to the disheartened infielder. "Want a piece?"

Lyle's taste for night life violated the old Boston Brahmin's dictum (usually attributed to Rodman Weld, a forebear of William Weld, a governor of Massachusetts) that a Boston gentleman "never takes a drink before 3 o'clock or east of Park Street"—namely, before the stock market had closed or downtown among the unwashed and the madding crowd of business hustlers. After a night of drinking with Bill Lee in New York, Lyle is reported to have hailed a cab. When one stopped, Lyle asked the driver to take him to the Biltmore Hotel. The cabbie looked at Lyle and said simply, "You're leaning on it."

May

The Red Sox' play in the month of May was the best evidence of the team's potential that a doubtful fan could have asked for. The second month of the 1978 season was the most successful in the history of the franchise, with the team winning 23 and losing only 7. When the Red Sox won they won by power, primarily from Jim Rice, who hit 13 home runs that month, just one short of the club record set by Jackie Jensen in June of 1958. On May 28th Rice hit his 17th home run of the year, an event that caused statistic mavens to check the comparative pace of Babe Ruth and Roger Maris, the Yankee greats who share the record for home runs in a season. (They hold the record in joint custody, their two houses separated by an asterisk indicating that Maris's 61 home runs were hit in 162 games, while Ruth's 60 were hit in 154 games.) In their respective record-setting seasons, Ruth hit his 17th home run in the 47th game of the season while Maris hit his in the 48th game; Rice hit his in the Sox' 45th game of

1978. A right-handed hitter, Rice was honored for his prowess by one of the more flattering strategies in baseball history, a four-outfielder shift. In a game against Kansas City on May 9th, Royals manager Whitey Herzog moved third baseman Jerry Terrel to left field, second baseman Frank White to third base, and leftfielder Tom Poquette to left center. Rice went 2 for 4 anyway.

On May 11th, the Sox won their twentieth game of the season, a 5-4 victory over Baltimore, the earliest in the season they had won twenty games since 1946, the year in which they won the pennant but lost the World Series in the seventh game to the St. Louis Cardinals when Enos Slaughter scored all the way from first base on a shallow base hit by Harry Walker. Halfway through the month, on May 13th, the Sox took first place for the first time that season, with a 4-2 win over Minnesota.

The Sox' success was achieved despite one glaring weakness; namely, a lack of relief pitching. Bill Campbell, the mainstay that held up the mast of the team's pitching staff in 1977, was 1-3 with a 12.79 earned run average after losing two games to the Texas Rangers at the end of April, one on an 11th-inning home run to Richie Zisk and another two days later in the ninth inning. The pitcher he replaced in the second loss was Bill Lee, from whom Zimmer took the ball with a runner at second and one out. "I've got Campbell ready," Zimmer told Lee. "I'm going with him." "Fine," said Lee at the time, a little sharply. Later, in answer to a reporter's question, Lee was more congenial, saying "He (Zimmer) did the right thing," even though Campbell proceeded to give up a bloop double to Zisk and then a pinch-hit single to John Lowenstein to bring in the game-winning run. Campbell's slow start was worrisome inasmuch as Dick Drago also had developed soreness in his elbow and would be out for the better part of the month.

The answer to the team's relief pitching needs in the first part of the 1978 season, as improbable as it may seem now to most Red Sox fans, came in the person of Bob Stanley, the man who has Bill Buckner to thank for the fact that he is not now remembered as the goat of the Sox' loss of the 1986 World Series to the New York Mets. Stanley's record in 1978 was an incredible 15-2 with a 2.60 earned run average. In the early goings his arm would be all the Sox had in the bull pen. After his relief appearance on May 1st in a 9-6 victory against the Orioles, Stanley had appeared in three games in which seven men were on base when he took the mound; none scored.

The shortage of strong arms in the Sox bull pen could be overlooked for a reason in addition to the power that their lineup of sluggers was producing. They simply didn't need much relief pitching in the first part of the season since at the end of May their four principal starters were a combined 22-5, with Lee at 7-2, Tiant at 3-0, Eckersley at 5-1 and Torrez at 7-2. At one point in May, Bill Lee, Bob Stanley, Jim Wright and Mike Torrez put together 23 consecutive scoreless innings, with Torrez's performance on May 7th being the strongest of all as he threw just 90 pitches in beating the White Sox 5-0, his first shutout of the year. Torrez's early success was an unexpected dividend for Sox fans, since he had historically been a better pitcher in the second half of the season, when the weather was hotter, than in the cooler days before the break for the All-Star Game in July.

Still, there were signs of weakness in the Sox' infrastructure. Carl Yastrzemski had only 3 extra-base hits in his twenty games, the result, it was thought, of pain from a bone bruise on his right hand that had cysts underneath it. Fisk and Scott had bad backs and Drago, Campbell and Hobson had hurting elbows, with Hobson's pain causing him to make throwing errors; on May 9th nine Sox were suffering from some sort of ailment or injury. When the Sox lost 3-2 to Baltimore that day as the result of a home-run ball Tom Burgmeier threw to Eddie Murray, it was the sixth time the team had lost in the ninth inning of a game, the sign of a club that lacks the discipline or the finesse to win when victory is within its grasp. Bob Bailey, a player acquired on Don Zimmer's recommendation based on their time together with the Montreal Expos, was batting .067. Zimmer responded to criticism that Bailey was his pet by predicting that "he'll win four or five games for us." Rick Burleson went 0 for 20 at one point, and his batting average sank to .183.

The Sox could at least take comfort in the fact that the team's business affairs were in order following the death of owner Tom Yawkey after the American League approved the sale of the club in the middle of the month for $15 million to a limited partnership headed by former catcher Haywood Sullivan and former trainer Buddy Leroux as general partners. Leroux and Sullivan would each hold a 10 percent interest, their limited partners would own 60 percent of the team and former owner Jean Yawkey would retain a 20 percent stake. The league had previously turned down a proposal that called for the Leroux-Sullivan group to finance their purchase with borrowed money, and the reconfigured arrangement satisfied the other owners' concern that the new owners would wind up overextended if they were permitted to pay for their membership in the exclusive club of major league baseball franchises with other people's money. Thus Sullivan, a man whom Tom Yawkey, with his preternatural shyness, kept as an employee in part because the former catcher made him laugh, and Leroux, the man who repaired the moving parts that made the Red Sox machine run, ascended to the owner's box. The approval of the sale was important to the players as well. The previously proposed arrangement involved a bank loan heavily weighted with restrictions on the team's off-field activities, including one that placed a ceiling on raises that the club could give its players. Fisk for one was concerned about this covenant, and he was relieved that the players would be allowed to feast on the milk and honey of the Promised Land of free agency, to which Tom Yawkey, like Moses, had led them but could not enter.

The Sox came to the end of the month with an eight-game winning streak and the best record in baseball, but Bill Lee's failure to survive the first inning of a game on the last day of May against the Toronto Blue Jays seems, in retrospect, the watershed that divided his climb to the top of the American League's pitching statistics in the first part of the season from the decline that followed. When he beat the Orioles, 5-4 on May 11th, aided by a Dick Drago save on a day when Lee admitted he didn't have "good stuff," Lee tied Babe Ruth's record of 89 wins as a left-handed pitcher with the Red Sox. His teammates would commit enough errors in his next two starts to give Sox opponents eleven unearned runs, and his record would fall in one month from 6-0 to 7-4 on June 12th. While he would win three of his next five starts, the best string of pitching in his career was over as the shoulder he had injured in the 1976 brawl at Yankee Stadium began to hurt. "My shoulder's just tired," he said after being chased in the first inning of the game against Toronto. "I've tried to do too much. I pitched a lot in spring training, but then I haven't been knocked out of any games either. I guess it's my Catholic ethic, but I don't like to miss a start, and along the way I probably should have." He began to take an anti-inflammatory drug in the hope of easing the pain.

Good stuff or bad, Lee's record wasn't good enough to make Billy Martin pick him for the American League's All-Star team. As manager of the prior year's American League champions, Martin had the right to pick the league's pitchers for the All-Star Game, but he had developed an enduring enmity towards the left-hander after Lee insulted Martin at a news conference following his shoulder injury at the hands of Graig Nettles in 1976. Martin didn't pick Lee for the team, an omission that was viewed by more than a few observers as the product of spite.

At about the same time that Lee began to falter, Luis Tiant, a 37-year-old right-hander whose career to that point had been a series of hills and valleys (21-9 one season for Cleveland, he went 9-20 the next), began to regain the form of his better years. Three times a 20-game winner for the Red Sox, Tiant had slipped to 12-8 with a 6.53 earned run average in 1977, and he started the year slowly after dislocating a finger on a line drive by Detroit's Steve Kemp in spring training. He was on the disabled list at the start of the season and did not appear in a game until April was half over, pitching in relief of Dennis Eckersley against Milwaukee. On the same day Reggie Cleveland was sold outright to the Texas Rangers, and Tiant was forced back into the starting rotation. He pitched five perfect innings on April 29th against the Texas Rangers and then won seven consecutive games, a streak that ended June 30th when he lost a 3-2 decision to the Orioles after limiting Baltimore to five hits over eleven innings.

As with the Red Sox, the Yankees' starters had also begun to produce. Catfish Hunter got his first victory of the season on May 2nd, a 4-2 victory over Kansas City, a win that moved the Yankees into second place ahead of the Sox and behind the Detroit Tigers. A week later Hunter beat the Twins 3-1, with the help of Sparky Lyle's fifth save. It was Hunter's best effort, according to observers, in three years. Ed Figueroa's record improved to 4-1 on May 3rd when he beat Kansas City 6-5, and on May 5th, Ron Guidry won his third straight start, beating Texas 5-2, as the Yankees won their fifth game in a row. Sparky Lyle would, in his own words, single-handedly end the team's run of luck the next day when he failed to get either of two Texas runners out on a tap back to the mound, allowing the Rangers to take the lead and pad it later when Bump Wills followed what should have been the last out of the inning with a double that drove in two runs.

The Yankees' May wakening from their slumbers of April was not without a fair amount of early-morning grumbling, however. On a May 15th flight from Kansas City to Chicago, Yankee catcher Thurman Munson was needling Billy Martin about his seat in first class, a distinction without much of a difference because of the players' right, under their collective bargaining agreement with the major leagues, to an empty seat between every two players, paid for by their ball clubs. "What's your argument," Martin yelled at Munson. "I don't have an argument with you," he continued. "If you have an argument with me you can meet me in my room." As was the case throughout his career, Martin's native truculence and paranoia had been fueled by alcohol. Elston Howard, who as the American League's most valuable player in 1963 was the team's most visible link (besides Martin) to one of the Yankees' more recent dynasties, and (unlike Martin) an exemplar of the dignified demeanor of the model Yankee, could only shake his head as he watched the disturbance. "This is it," he said. "This is my last year. I can't take it any more."

The sense of bedlam that pervaded the Yankees' clubhouse was in large part attributable to the imperious temperament of the club's owner, George Steinbrenner. As John McMullen, one of Steinbrenner's co-owners once put it, "There's nothing so limited as being a limited partner of George." Edward Bennett Williams, perhaps the best known lawyer for a man who liked to say he was "knee deep in lawyers," succinctly described what was perhaps Steinbrenner's most debilitating flaw. "If something is wrong," Williams noted, "it has to be someone else's fault." Steinbrenner was thus known as a boss who would fire his employees on a whim, then call them back and reward them with benefits out of all proportion to the injury he had inflicted on them—a cruise to a tropical clime or college tuition for their children, for example. Early in the month Steinbrenner issued an edict forbidding any of his players from talking to former Yankee great Tony Kubek, now a television sportscaster, after Kubek was quoted as saying that

Steinbrenner was a man with "one of the most expensive toys in the world," but that he was manipulative and tried to rule his players by fear. The ban was imposed despite the fact that the most contentious debating society in the country would have had trouble finding someone to assert the negative of those propositions.

More than anything else, Steinbrenner's capacity for caprice caused his players to look constantly over their shoulders in fear of being released or traded. One day Sparky Lyle noticed clubhouse man Pete Sheehy handling some new nameplates used to identify the player's lockers. He picked one up and saw that it was for Jerry Narron, a catcher at the Yankees' minor league club in Tacoma, Washington. "What the hell does this mean?" asked Lyle. Sheehy said he liked to make up nameplates just in case a player was called up and that in Narron's case he was only guessing. The next day Fran Healy, the team's third-string catcher and Reggie Jackson's only friend and confidant on the club, was released. When he heard the news, Lyle told Sheehy, "Let me know when they're taking my nameplate down."

The Yankees seemed to thrive despite the turmoil that constantly afflicted their clubhouse like a low-grade infection; perhaps they needed it for the same reason that a New Yorker transplanted to Keokuk, Iowa, might miss traffic jams and incivility—their daily routine under the ownership of George Steinbrenner had caused them to become used to it. They put together a second five-game winning streak at the end of the month and at one point had won 20 out of 26 games. By May 28th the Tigers had lost 7 of their last 8 games and would not be in contention for the rest of the year. At the end of May, the

Sox had a 34-16 record—the best in baseball—but they were only three games ahead of the Yankees, whose quickened pace of 19 wins and 8 losses for the month put them at 29-17.

The Gerbil

While the Loyal Order of the Buffalo Heads represented a pleasant diversion for those fans who wanted more from their investment of time and attention in baseball than simple box scores, they would have seemed merely tiresome and immature without a proper foil. For the Buffalo Heads, Donald William Zimmer was a natural predator. As his nemesis Bill Lee put it,

> Zimmer thought we were a danger to his ball club. He was of the old school, and we were part of the counterculture. He and the front office thought that we were going to corrupt the morals of the rest of the team.

Zimmer walked away from the game in 1995 while a

coach for the Colorado Rockies after suffering from a loss of blood flow to his brain, only to walk back again the next year to serve as a bench coach for the Yankees who, as it turned out, won their first championship since 1978, beating the Atlanta Braves. During his career he managed three minor league and four major league teams, the three in the big leagues besides the Red Sox being the San Diego Padres, the Texas Rangers and the Chicago Cubs. His first managing job, for Knoxville in 1967, introduced him to a young player, then not yet twenty years old, who would make 72 errors in two seasons playing third base for the Cincinnati affiliate. When Zimmer had to activate himself to play first base after injuries depleted his roster, the first two batters up hit balls to third base, and wild throws sent Zimmer diving towards the home side of the bag, directly into oncoming base runners. "I turned to the rightfielder and made him come play first," Zimmer later recounted. "I told him if someone was going to get killed, it wasn't going to be me." While Zimmer might have avoided various physical injuries by ending his short stint as a born-again infielder, his young third baseman—one Bernardo Carbo—would return to torment him mentally if not physically as a member of the Buffalo Heads in their years together with the Red Sox.

From Knoxville, Zimmer moved up to the Reds' Triple-A club in Buffalo despite a 26-46 record in his first assignment. After two seasons there, Zimmer left to join the San Diego Padres organization, where he would be reunited with Buzzy Bavasi, his front office boss during his years with the Dodgers. Zimmer would manage the Padres' Key West, Florida, affiliate for $8,000 a year plus $4 a day in meal money. On the long drives back from road games (Key West being four hours from the nearest city and nearly ten hours from league opponent Cocoa), Zimmer would ask the driver to make a stop at a 7-11 store in Homestead, south of Miami, before the final stretch south. From the front seat, Zimmer would pass back bologna sandwiches, spread with the players' choice of mayonnaise or mustard, stretching the meal money to the point where it provided sustenance, if not delectation.

Zimmer coached in the big leagues with the Montreal Expos in 1971 and the San Diego Padres in 1972 before getting his first major league managing job when San Diego manager Preston Gomez was fired in April of 1972. Zimmer lasted two seasons, finishing last both times before being dismissed. At the time he was the lowest-paid manager in the big leagues, making less than his own coaches. He was unemployed for only six weeks after the date of his discharge by the Padres, however, joining the Red Sox whom he coached from 1974 through 1976 before taking over as manager from Darrell Johnson in 1976. He would hold that position for nearly five seasons, the longest tenure of any Red Sox manager since Pinky Higgins managed the team for eight straight years in the late 1950s and early 1960s.

Zimmer had been, as Ferguson Jenkins liked to recall, a mediocre player. He was the lifetime .230 hitter that Jenkins accused him of being; his career batting average was .235, although he had one commendable year at the plate, 1958, when he hit .262 in 127 games and had 17 home runs and 14 stolen bases. When George Scott broke out of an 0 for 36 slump in mid-September of 1978, a writer with a thirst for historical echoes of the occasion determined that Zimmer held the New

York Mets record for the longest batting slump, 0 for 34. Zimmer's career with the Dodgers was limited in time because he happened to fill the brief gap between the careers of two great Dodger shortstops, Pee Wee Reese and Maury Wills. He went to the All-Star Game once, in 1961. Personal statistics aside, Zimmer played on two Dodger teams that won the World Series, the first in 1955 when the franchise played in Brooklyn, the second in 1959 after they had moved to Los Angeles. That put Zimmer two world championships ahead of all the Buffalo Heads combined. (Carbo played on the Cincinnati Reds team that lost to the Baltimore Orioles in 1970, and Wise, Willoughby, Lee and Pole were members, along with Carbo, of the 1975 Red Sox team that lost to the Reds.)

Zimmer's only significant contribution to World Series history is noteworthy for the fact that he was absent from the field of play when it occurred, however. In the top of the sixth inning of the seventh game of the 1955 World Series, with the Dodgers leading the Yankees 2-0, Dodger manager Walter Alston sent in a pinch hitter for Zimmer, who had been playing second base in a right-handed platooning measure against Tommy Byrne, the Yankees left-handed starter. Jim Gilliam, a right-hander who had been playing left field, was brought in to play second, and Sandy Amoros, a fleet Cuban who threw left-handed, was moved into left. In the home half of the sixth, Billy Martin opened with a walk and Gil McDougald followed with a bunt single to bring up left-handed Yogi Berra, now remembered primarily as a cuddly illogician who is quoted nearly as often as Lewis Carroll, but then one of baseball's most potent hitters. With two men on and no one out, the outfield shifted around to right to prepare for Berra, who was expected to pull the ball. Instead, Berra lofted a fly ball down the left-field line that appeared certain to fall in for extra bases. Martin held up, but McDougald was already past second base when Amoros, who had been positioned in center field, caught the ball in his right hand as it was about to fall to the ground near the left-field foul line, a catch the right-handed Gilliam probably could not have made. Amoros turned and threw the ball to Pee Wee Reese behind third base, who threw it on to Gil Hodges at first to complete a double play.

When asked later whether he thought he had a chance to catch Berra's drive, Amoros answered as all athletes should when confronted with the witless cross-examination of the postgame interview—"I dunno, I just ran like hell." Dodger pitcher Johnny Podres settled down and the Dodgers had their first World Series in eight tries, while the Yankees had lost their first World Series after seven straight victories, a sequence that had begun twelve years earlier. Alston's decision to pinch-hit for Zimmer was, in the words of Dodger historian Peter Golenbock, "the most important strategic decision any Brooklyn manager ever made."

Despite his conflicts with the Buffalo Heads over off-field behavior, Zimmer in his time as a player had been no ascetic. He was known to be a racetrack companion of Duke Snider and Johnny Podres in his days with the Dodgers. He was a bowler, along with fellow Dodgers Carl Erskine, Pee Wee Reese and Clem Labine, in the days before bowling became a subject of study for sociologists and an object of condescension by comedians and was merely an occasion for drinking while ostensibly exercising. His temperament didn't mellow with age, either; in the year at issue here, he was still the holder of the league record for managerial rejections in two of the minor leagues in which he managed.

Zimmer's elevation to the position of manager came at a time when the heroes of 1975 were looking decidedly unheroic, but in circumstances that made him seem an accident. The 1976 season, the first in the era of free agency, gave the Red Sox the first holdouts in the history of the franchise—Carlton Fisk, Fred Lynn and Rick Burleson. All would end up signing new contracts with the team shortly before the new basic agreement between the owners and the players association became effective in early August, but the friction that their declaration of independence caused was palpable in the first half of the season. The team did not reach .500 until July 5th after they had failed on eight previous occasions when they were within one victory of doing so. Owner Tom Yawkey, who had always said he would own the Red Sox until he died and then decide what to do with them, expired four days later. At the All-Star break the team was 40-40, and their starting line-up was hitting a utility infielder's .250. They were nine and a half games behind the Yankees.

Darrell Johnson managed the American League team that lost in the 1976 All-Star Game, and the Sox opened the second half of the season by losing three of four to Kansas City and then two more to the Texas Rangers. General manager Dick O'Connell had been moving towards a decision to fire Johnson, but had temporized in light of the pennant Johnson had won the year before. After the 1-5 start to the season's second half, however, he felt he had to dismiss Johnson. Having delayed his decision too long, he had to move quickly, and there were no name-brand commodities on the market. "I liked Zimmer," O'Connell told a reporter some years later. And, O'Connell said, "he was the only person available."

Zimmer ended up with a .574 winning percentage in his five years as manager of the Red Sox, better than Dick Williams, Ralph Houk and Darrell Johnson, among other favorites of Sox fans and the Boston press. He also finished with a .508 percentage for his entire 14 years as a manager, which included stretches with some fairly awful teams, including the 1972-73 Padres (114-190) and the 1982 Texas Rangers (a .396 winning percentage in 96 games). He won one division championship, the National League East in 1989 as manager of the Cubs, for which he was named Manager of the Year. The Buffalo Heads' animadversions to the contrary, he must have known something about winning baseball games.

In fact, a case can be made that, next to Joe McCarthy, the former Yankee manager who guided that team to eight pennants in eleven years and later managed the Red Sox, Zimmer was the best manager over two full seasons or more that the team had in the sixty-year period from 1920, Babe Ruth's first season with the Yankees, through 1980, Zimmer's last year with the Red Sox. The roster of Red Sox managers during that period, and their records, are as follows:

Steve O'Neill (246 games, 1950-1951)	.606
Joe McCarthy (1948-1950)	.604
Zimmer (1976-1980)	.574
Eddie Popowski (14 games, 1969)	.556
Dick Williams (1967-1969)	.545
Eddie Kasko (1970-1973)	.540

Joe Cronin (1935-1947)	.539
Darrell Johnson (1974-1976)	.539
Ralph Houk (1981-1983)	.523
Ed Barrow (1918-1920)	.512
Pinky Higgins (1955-1962)	.501
Bucky Harris (1934)	.500
Pete Runnels (24 games, 1966)	.500
Lou Boudreau (1952-1954)	.497
Bill Carrigan (1913-16, 1927-29)	.494
Bill Jurges (1959-1960)	.484
Johnny Pesky (1963-1964, 1980)	.452
Hugh Duffy (1921-1922)	.442
Billy Herman (1964-1966)	.413
Frank Chance (1923)	.401
Marty McManus (1932-1933)	.386
Shano Collins (1931-1932)	.349
Lee Fohl (1924-1926)	.349
Heinie Wagner (1930)	.338
Rudy York (1 game, 1959)	.000

Zimmer can be faulted for not winning a World Series, a pennant or a division championship during his tenure, but no Red Sox manager during this period won a World Series, only three won pennants (Joe Cronin, 1946; Dick Williams, 1967; and Darrell Johnson, 1975), and only one won a division championship (Johnson, 1975) after the two leagues were split in 1969. The fact that Zimmer is now remembered in Boston mainly as a failure, the man who was at the helm of the ship of the Red Sox state in 1978, thus says more about the town and its peculiar personality than the man or his skills as a manager.

Bostonians make a great show of detesting snobbery, and they ought to, because they have so much of it around. There is social snobbery, based on lineage, and therefore limited to those who can claim a distinguished pedigree. There is moral snobbery, an inheritance from the censorious Puritans that is now broken out not for its original purpose, namely, the scorn of those who succumb to the temptations of the flesh, but rather for more mundane failings like voting Republican or failing to recycle plastic containers. There is financial snobbery, based on wealth, and therefore limited to those who possess, for the moment at least, money and the things that it buys. And there is intellectual snobbery, in some respects limited to those who possess demonstrable mental superiority or the apparently objective confirmation of a degree granted by a reputable institution of higher learning, but in fact available to every man and woman who can find someone, anyone, whom they consider to be their inferior in this regard. Once conventional wisdom in Boston has determined that a particular individual is intellectually defective, the culture of the city permits even those with comparatively meager allotments of gray matter to laugh at the supposed boob as part of a larger crowd that enjoys a feeling of collective superiority over the butt of a common joke. The task is made simpler if, as in Zimmer's case, the object of derision is capable of self-deprecation. "Bill Lee is a college graduate," Zimmer said to a sportswriter by way of comparison one day. "He's above me, and I don't try to understand him or those words he uses. I can't spell most of them anyway."

Whether Zimmer lacked the cognitive skills needed to be a successful major league manager is, as the figures above should

The Year of the Gerbil

demonstrate, highly doubtful. Of course, some question whether big-league managing requires *any* intellectual skills, while no one hesitates to laud particular managers who develop a reputation for being analytical or cerebral (St. Louis's Tony La Russa comes to mind). The former proposition is perhaps best summed up by the saying that, in order to be a good football coach you have to be smart enough to understand the game and dumb enough to think that it matters. The contrary point of view has been postulated by former Houston Oilers' coach Bum Phillips; a good coach, said Phillips in his Texas dialect, can take your'n and beat his'n or take his'n and beat your'n.

Zimmer put together three consecutive ninety-win seasons in the American League East during a three-year period in which the A.L. East division winner won the World Series in two seasons (the Yankees in 1977 and 1978) and won the American League pennant in the other (the Orioles in 1979). It accordingly seems safe to say that he must be fairly accomplished in the mental aspects of the game of baseball since it is difficult to prevail in any competitive endeavor on luck alone for such an extended period of time. Zimmer's answers to reporters' questions were grammatical even though they generally occupied a stratum of the atmosphere lower than the ozone that Bill Lee's thoughts traversed. At the start of the 1978 season, when rookie pitcher Jim Wright was showing promise, Zimmer was asked how he would make room for Tiant and eventually Bill Campbell when those pitchers were ready to pitch again: "Whom are we going to cut?" Zimmer asked rhetorically and hyper-grammatically.

Zimmer's sometimes contrarian approach to the game

96

caused the Boston *Globe*'s Peter Gammons to call him a genius after an 8-6 win over the Texas Rangers early in 1978 when Zimmer took off the bunt sign three times in a single game, producing singles by Dwight Evans and Butch Hobson and a double by Jerry Remy. Zimmer was a local hero in Chicago— although he managed the Cubs to three fourth-place finishes in his four years there—and he was a popular coach with the Colorado Rockies. Since he was more successful in Boston than either of those places, Zimmer's lack of favor with Boston fans and the press may thus have more to do with prejudice than objectivity.

There was an item in Zimmer's personal medical history that gave Red Sox fans and the press an occasion to belittle his intellect, however, if not an excuse for doing so. As a member of the Dodgers' St. Paul farm team in 1953 Zimmer was batting .300 and leading the American Association with 63 runs batted in and 23 home runs when he ducked into a high, inside curveball thrown by Jim Kirk, a right-handed pitcher for Columbus, Ohio. He didn't regain consciousness for thirteen days, having undergone two brain operations in the meantime. A year later, after Zimmer had recovered sufficiently to have collected 53 RBIs and 17 home runs, the Dodgers brought him up for good. In 1956 he took another pitch in the left cheekbone from Hal Jeffcoat of the Chicago Cubs and didn't see out of his left eye until Christmas morning of that year. As a result, Zimmer ended up with a metal plate in his head that was the basis for a goodly number of jokes, however unjustified, about his remaining brainpower.

Many Sox fans considered Zimmer déclassé for another reason. Boston is a college town where, as a local professor once put it, a man gets older every day while each year's crop of new students never ages. In an environment where one must thus confront the inevitable fall from a youthful state of grace on a daily basis, the urge to find a basis, however slight, on which to claim that one remains current with the fashions of the times is compelling. In 1978, the prevailing opinion in Boston was that Zimmer was, by comparison to the players he clashed with, decidedly uncool. Born in 1931 in Cincinnati, Ohio, Zimmer was everything that the Buffalo Heads were not. Zimmer chewed tobacco; the Buffalo Heads smoked leaves rather than chewing them, and then only to get high. Zimmer frequented Boston's dog tracks; when he was fined $250 in May of 1978 for bumping an umpire over a bad strike call in the ninth inning of a 2-1 loss to Toronto, Bill Lee's first defeat of the season, he told the press: "There goes my Saturday night at Wonderland," the greyhound track north of Boston. The Buffalo Heads would have journeyed to Revere or Raynham, the blue-collar towns where Boston's greyhounds run, only as a goof, a lark—as low camp. Zimmer came up through baseball's farm system; the Heads were of a generation for whom college baseball was a pleasant alternative to all-night bus rides back from minor league games and a place where one acquired a gloss of intellectual superiority that could serve as conversational fodder for the sort of ironic put-on that Bill Lee perfected. Zimmer's personal pharmacopoeia included nothing that couldn't be found at your local drugstore, and while he was known to imbibe in alcohol, he was a teetotaler by comparison with Darrell Johnson, his immediate predecessor.

Boston *Globe* sportswriter Ray Fitzgerald summed up

The Gerbil

Zimmer's dilemma after the Sox put together their seven-game winning streak in early April:

> Since the first game of the season when the Red
> Sox lost to the White Sox in the ninth inning, Don
> Zimmer has been under fire from the fans. The
> Red Sox manager, working on a one-year con-
> tract, has been blamed for everything from
> rained-out games to traffic jams around Fenway.
> Talk show addicts don't like the way he walks,
> talks or chews tobacco. They don't like his crew
> cut or the way he's built. They think he plays
> favorites and feel his way of life went out with
> saddle shoes and bobby sox.

Zimmer was viewed as a throwback in an era that wor-
shipped youth, and a drudge in a time that honored the cava-
lier. When the Yankees came to town for the first series of 1978
an out-of-town sportswriter told him he had missed the first
game of the series because of a daughter's graduation. "I'm 0
for 2," Zimmer replied, alluding to the travel he had endured
as a player, coach and manager and the sacrifices he had
made, missing his children's graduations. "Remember an
infielder in the Giants' organization, Bobby Etheridge?"
Zimmer asked.

> I was managing Salt Lake City and I got a call
> from the big club to say they were sending
> Etheridge to me from San Diego. I said "Fine, will
> he be here for tomorrow night's game?" They
> said, "We don't know." It's only about an hour

and a half by air, but it took him three days to get there. Then he told me "I'll play tonight but tomorrow I want to fly to San Diego and drive my wife back here. I'll miss the games Tuesday, Wednesday and Thursday." I said "How many kids do you have?" He said none. I asked if his wife could drive—"Oh sure," he said. "Look," I said, "how about you playing ball and letting her drive up here alone?" I could imagine when I was playing ball telling Charley Dressen I wanted time off to go home and drive my wife to Brooklyn. "Fine," he'd say, "but go to Mobile instead and have a good year there."

The obloquy heaped on Zimmer in the spring of 1978 was so persistent that a trip to the mound on May 2nd to replace Allen Ripley, a second generation Red Sox pitcher (son of Walt Ripley, 0-0, 1935) whose promise went unfulfilled, was notable only for the fact that Zimmer wasn't booed. At the time there were three fights in progress behind the visitors dugout; as a result, Zimmer observed, the fans didn't notice him until he had almost completed his return to the bench. At the time the Sox were 11-9 and three games behind the first-place Detroit Tigers. Six weeks later the Sox were in first place with the best record (42-19) in baseball, and team captain Carl Yastrzemski still felt compelled to give a statement to the press defending Zimmer. "We've got a manager," Yastrzemski said,

who stands by the bat rack every game. And when every guy comes to bat for every bat he has something encouraging to say. Let me say this—

The Gerbil

> I've been in the game for 18 years with a lot of dif-
> ferent managers, and I like it. It means something
> to me, and the rest of the guys.

After this testimonial, which sounded like a rough draft of an elegy for a departed manager, Yastrzemski lapsed into bathos: "Guys on this team care about one another. No one gets down on the other guy. We all go out and do our own thing in different ways but we care about each other."

In short, Zimmer was a square in a town that strives mightily to be hip. The origin of Boston's communal fear of being thought unsophisticated lies in its historical reputation as a cultural stepchild of New York and a Puritanical backwater where the erotic, the suggestive and the merely titillating were lumped together and—in the famous phrase—banned in Boston. New York has many problems, but, unlike Boston, the need to convince the world that it is a center of sophistication is not among them. Would Zimmer have been better loved as a manager in New York than in Boston? The example of Billy Martin is instructive. Martin was, in many ways, Zimmer's New York double—fiercely competitive, old-fashioned, a man who lived the game as if it were life itself and had no tolerance for those who, like Reggie Jackson and Bill Lee, displayed their contempt for career baseball men by frequent and blasé criticisms of the proposition that baseball was a serious endeavor rather than just a game.

Bill Lee and Reggie Jackson liked to give the impression that baseball was just one of a number of ways in which they could earn a living, with Lee suggesting that he would have been just as happy as a forest ranger (he majored in forestry at the University of Southern California) and Jackson pointing to his car dealerships and real estate investments as an indication of his business skills. While Lee may indeed have been like the lilies of the field, who neither toil nor spin but somehow survive, no one has seen him in a ranger's tower since he left the major leagues, although he now owns a farm in Vermont. As for Jackson, it is doubtful whether the investment opportunities that came his way would have found him if he had never advanced beyond the Class A Lewis-Clark Broncs of Lewiston, Idaho, and he certainly wouldn't have accumulated the capital needed to take advantage of them if that were the case.

For people like Martin and Zimmer, baseball wasn't a game, it was a job, the only job they ever had and the best one they could imagine. But New York loved Martin as strongly as the more vocal Red Sox fans and the majority of the Boston media despised Zimmer, even though Martin seemed to represent everything that a fan of Jackson's would detest, just as Zimmer personified the principles that a fan of Bill Lee's would scorn. Martin had a reservoir of good will among New York fans to draw on, filled with memories of his exploits with the great Yankee teams of the 1950s. Zimmer never played for the Red Sox and there was thus no comparable tide of favor to buoy him through difficult times. When the Sox traveled to New York for a two-game series in late June at a time when Martin's job hung in the balance while Zimmer's team was ahead of the Yankees by eight and a-half games, Martin was greeted with a standing ovation as he brought the lineup card to home plate before the first game. "Ain't it a shame that you've got to hear everyday that you might get fired?"

Zimmer asked Martin the first day. Martin, taking it all in, said simply, "This is worth all of it." When the crowd repeated its salute the next day, Zimmer wondered at the irony of their treatment at the hands of their respective fans. "How do you do it?" he asked Martin. "As far ahead as we are, I've never had an ovation like this." In the end, both Martin and Zimmer were winners, but Martin was a winner in the Yankee tradition, with (at the time) one World Series victory and two American League pennants to his credit, while Zimmer was a winner in the Red Sox tradition who would end up with a collection of near-misses—one fourth place, two third place, and two second place finishes—beside his name in the record book. And Zimmer had the misfortune to manage in Boston, where strategies for self-defeat are an integral part of the playbook.

The principal difference between Zimmer and Martin— the former a man at peace with himself, the latter fighting a constant battle with the world—became clear when Zimmer coached for Martin and the Yankees in 1983. At one point during the season Martin came upon an unfamiliar female reporter in the Yankee clubhouse and asked her what she was doing. She said she was a reporter for the *New York Times* taking a survey of the Yankees on the All-Star voting. Martin told her to get her ass out of the clubhouse and called her a hussy and a slut. The *Times* filed a formal complaint with the Yankees and the American League, and George Steinbrenner promised a full investigation of the incident. Martin testified that the reporter was wearing a low-cut dress with slits "up to here," as if he had a female dress code to enforce or (more preposterously) the inclination to do so. Zimmer was called as a witness along with trainer Mark Letendre and pitcher George Frazier. Letendre and Frazier said that Martin hadn't used those words. Zimmer said he hadn't heard Martin use the offending language but couldn't bring himself to give Martin the benefit of full-fledged corroboration—he claimed he hadn't been within earshot at the time. A.L. President Lee MacPhail acquitted Martin on the grounds of mistake (it was the reporter's first assignment in the clubhouse as she had not previously been a member of the *Times'* sports department) as well as temporary insanity, since Martin worked for Steinbrenner and was thus the subject of the constant rumors of firing that were as much a part of managing the Yankees as filling out the lineup card.

After testifying Zimmer said, "I can't wait for this year to be over. When it is, I'll be out of here so fast you won't even know I'm gone." On the final day of the season he dressed within three minutes and raced out the door to the parking lot where his wife was waiting with the car running.

June

The month of June is a time of tension for baseball's young and marginal players, since it is the month in which teams that have put off personnel decisions are forced to make deals by the onset of the trading deadline. A player is not exempt from the perils of baseball's bazaar until he has been in the majors for ten years, with five years playing for the same team. In the case of the Red Sox, the players who did not qualify under this standard, and who thus were watching the calendar with more trepidation than their seniors, included Bill Lee and Bernie Carbo, the Last of the Buffalo Heads.

Carbo occupied a secure place in the hall of Red Sox heroes from the then-recent past by virtue of his exploits in the 1975 World Series. Carbo hit a pinch-hit home run in the third game of the series, which the Cincinnati Reds won in the tenth inning when Carlton Fisk and Cincinnati pinchhitter Ed Armbrister became entangled after Armbrister hit a high-bouncing sacrifice bunt and failed to get out of Fisk's way. Fisk, perhaps angered or distracted by Armbrister's apparent interference, threw wildly to second base, allowing Cesar Geronimo to take third and to score when Joe Morgan singled to center over a drawn-in outfield three batters later. Three games later, the Reds were ahead in the series by three games to two, with a 6-3 lead in the eighth inning. Lynn led off with a single and Rico Petrocelli walked. Sparky Anderson brought in Rawley Eastwick, who struck out Dwight Evans and got Rick Burleson to fly out. Carbo was brought in to pinch-hit again, but Eastwick, who would win two games of Cincinnati's four, seemed overpowering. He got two quick strikes on Carbo, and almost struck him out on a pitch Carbo was barely able to foul off with a swing that Carlton Fisk called the worst in the history of baseball and *New Yorker* writer Roger Angell likened to "someone fighting off a wasp with a croquet mallet." On the next pitch, Carbo drove a high fastball into the center-field bleachers, thereby making possible the home run by Fisk that is more widely remembered today.

Carbo was a player of unrealized potential, with sufficient talent to have hit .310 with 21 home runs in his rookie season with Cincinnati; he never reached .300 in hitting or 20 home runs again. As a result, he is now remembered primarily for his home run in the fabled sixth game of the 1975 series and for the unself-conscious eccentricity that earned him a place as the only non-pitcher in the Loyal Order of the Buffalo Heads. Carbo's antics caused him to be viewed by the respectable burghers of organized baseball as possessing the trustworthiness of a carnival roustabout, and they accordingly turned him into one of the game's most mobile transients—he was hustled in and out of eight major league franchises in his ten-year career, two of them (St. Louis and Boston) twice. In St. Louis he kept a stuffed gorilla (which he took with him on road trips) named Mighty Joe Young after the primate of the cinema who never achieved King Kong's fame. In Knoxville, with Zimmer as his manager, he was on third base one day after hitting a triple in the bottom of the ninth inning. "Tag up on a fly ball," Zimmer, coaching third, told him. Hal McRae hit a long fly ball to center, and Zimmer turned to watch Carbo run home after it was caught. What he saw was Carbo with his foot on the bag, looking back at him. "What are you waiting for?" Zimmer screamed. "For you to tell me to go," Carbo replied with an impassive air. In the summer of '75 Carbo crashed into the bull pen at Fenway Park to make a catch that saved a home run in a game against the Yankees. The plug of tobacco he had been chewing popped out with the impact, and he spent ten minutes looking for it on the warning track; when he found it, he put it in his mouth again and play resumed.

Carbo infuriated more managers than Zimmer. He irritated Sparky Anderson in Cincinnati, Red Schoendienst in St. Louis, Del Crandall in Milwaukee and Darrell Johnson in Boston. He nearly came to blows with Jeff Torborg in Cleveland, and he refused to take fielding practice with the Sox in the summer of 1978. At the end of the 1976 season, when Boston and Milwaukee were negotiating the trade that would send Cecil Cooper to the Brewers and George Scott back to Boston, the Brewers had one final demand. "We don't make the deal," Brewer general manager Jim Baumer told the Red Sox negotiators, "unless you take Carbo back." A fellow member of the Red Sox, asked by Carbo if he wanted to join the Buffalo Heads for an evening of carousing, summed up management's view of Carbo with this blunt assessment: "I'd rather be caught with a girl in my hotel room than be seen coming in with you."

Where Lee acted the part of the class clown, showing off when it would both irritate those in charge and amuse his fellows, Carbo seemed, on the surface at least, to be a genuine naif or wise fool, the village idiot of Fenway Park, the New England town green of the Red Sox. In his book *Beyond the Sixth Game*, Boston *Globe* writer Peter Gammons recounted a story that captured this aspect of Carbo's personality:

> In 1974, losing 5-0 in Detroit, Darrell Johnson couldn't figure out why Carbo tried to steal second and was thrown out. So he called him over to the dugout. "I got the steal sign," Carbo told him.
>
> "What is the steal sign?" Johnson asked him, figuring Bernardo had forgotten.
>
> "Any combination adding up to five," answered Carbo, referring to Johnson's system of adding the value of two signs together to get a number that signified the specific sign.
>
> "What was the value of the first sign?" asked Johnson.
>
> "Two."

"What about the second?"

"Two."

While his skills had declined over the years, Carbo remained the fulfillment of fantasy as a possible pinch hitter. He is not among the top ten pinch hitters by average in Red Sox history, but his career home run percentage of 4.6, or nearly one home run for every twenty at bats, places him ahead of Dwight Evans, Carlton Fisk, Butch Hobson and Jackie Jensen, and just slightly behind Jim Rice, Tony Conigliaro, Jimmie Foxx and Ted Williams among other Boston sluggers. He led the Sox in on-base percentage in 1976 and 1977 and in the latter season he was 4-for-14 in pinch-hitting appearances. His 15 home runs that year carried out to a fearsome 6.6 home run percentage, or nearly one home run every fifteen times at bat. This was equal to Jimmie Foxx's career average, and trailed Jim Rice's 6.8 average of 1978, the best slugging season in Rice's career, by a margin not detectable without the aid of a calculator.

So why, on June 15th, the day of the trading deadline, was Carbo sold? As Zimmer put it, either diplomatically or mendaciously, it was "nothing personal." The move came at a time when Carbo was playing out his option season while seeking a five-year contract at the age of 30. He hadn't played since May 21st, when he jammed his right ankle sliding into second base in Detroit. However potent his skills as a hitter, he could not play center field at a major league level and thus forced realignments in the Sox outfield when one of the starters was hurt. "When I put a lineup out there for defense," Zimmer explained to reporters, "I'd much rather have Rice, Yastrzemski and Evans than an outfield of Rice, Evans and Carbo. Now you've upset two positions. Besides, I want Evans right where he is." On a team loaded with hitters, the fourth-best hitting outfielder with inadequate fielding skills was not indispensable. In any event, as the French proverb goes, the graveyards are full of indispensable people.

On the other hand, a paranoid mind could find in the deportation of Carbo a sign that Zimmer and general manager Haywood Sullivan had achieved their intention of remodeling the Sox' pad by throwing out the psychedelic colors and replacing them with more muted tones. And since the intoxicated mind is more likely to infer malicious intent from innocent acts, it should not have surprised Red Sox management that Bill Lee viewed the sale of Carbo as evidence of a conspiracy against the Buffalo Heads and a bad omen for the Red Sox' fortunes. Both Lee and Carbo expected to be traded on June 15th, and when they had heard nothing by the end of the day they celebrated in their typical fashion by going drinking.

When Lee read the papers the next morning, he learned that Carbo had been sold to the Cleveland Indians for $15,000, "pocket change" in Lee's estimation. Lee went to Fenway Park, tore his nameplate off his locker and cleaned it out, and walked out of the clubhouse and off the team. He then went to the Jordan Marsh department store, where he honored an engagement to cook a spinach lasagna before a crowd of primarily female shoppers who probably didn't know him from Dick Radatz. One baseball Annie kissed him as he got on the elevator to go, and a janitor put to him the question that no one in the crowd of gastronomes had thought to ask. "Pretty lousy about Carbo, huh?" "Today," Lee replied, "just cost us the pennant, friend."

The Boston *Herald*'s front page the next morning bore the banner headline: "Angry Bill Lee Quits Sox." The Boston *Globe* was more discreet, averting its gaze from the drama of Lee's departure the way relatives might look away when a dispute breaks out between husband and wife at a family reunion out of a desire to preserve an otherwise successful marriage by ignoring an isolated incident of discord. The *Globe* focussed instead, as is its wont, on the human interest element of the story, quoting Lee's wife, Mary Lou Lee, on the subject of her husband's overwrought state. "Bill's been really mad all day," she said. "I just dropped him off. I hope he calms down." Clif Keane, a radio talk-show host with a low opinion of Lee, asked general manager Haywood Sullivan "Did Bill Lee get a cortisone shot in the shoulder or the head?" at the team's press conference the next day. George "Boomer" Scott, the Sox' big daddy of a first baseman, summed up the situation in three words: "Spaceman take off."

Lee had torn his telephone off the wall and owner Haywood Sullivan had to telegram him to summon him to a meeting. Lee's father and his wife persuaded him to attend. When he met with Sullivan and co-owner Buddy LeRoux, he challenged Sullivan to a fight, a challenge that Sullivan accepted but which LeRoux broke up. "I'd have killed the son of a bitch," Lee said afterwards, words not normally associated with the pacific state of mind that he claimed to pursue. Lee calmed down eventually, but he was unrepentant. When Sullivan told him he'd have to dock him a day's pay for being absent without leave, Lee asked him how much that would be. Five hundred and thirty-three dollars, Sullivan told him. "Great," said Lee. "Make it $1,500 and I'll take the whole weekend." After the price had thus been negotiated, Sullivan sent Lee down to the clubhouse to face Zimmer, where Lee made a fateful prediction: "You're going to rue the day you got rid of Carbo," he said. "The day will come when you're going to need him. There will be a crucial spot in a crucial game when only his bat can save us. Only he won't be here." Again, George Scott divined the essence of the situation: "Spaceman splash down."

Lee's decision to take a stand on this issue was particularly ill-timed. His shoulder was hurting and he was entering a slump from which he wouldn't recover. Still, with Mike Torrez tied with Frank Tanana as the winningest pitcher in the American League with 8 victories, Tiant at 4-0 and Eckersley at 5-1, the Sox' pitching seemed sufficiently strong for Haywood Sullivan to turn down a chance to pick up Oakland A's pitcher Rick Langford for $400,000 the week of the trading deadline. "What would we do with him?" Sullivan sneered at an inquiring reporter in the Seattle press box. "We've got enough pitching," a reply that foreshadowed Lou Gorman's imprudent decision to pass on Willie McGee twelve years later. And he was right, at least at the time; his four starters were a combined 27-7 and on June 12th, the Sox had achieved their widest margin over a second place team since September of 1975, six games, as the Yankees lost 9-6 to the Angels and the Sox beat Seattle, 5-2.

At the same time that the Red Sox' pitching appeared to have achieved a Cy Young-like level of superiority not seen in

Red Sox uniforms since Cy Young wore one (1901-1908), the Yankees' staff began to show signs of wear. Manager Billy Martin began the month of June by stigmatizing Rawley Eastwick and Andy Messersmith as "George's boys," an accurate reflection of the fact that they had been signed by owner George Steinbrenner without consulting Martin and a recurrent theme in the threnody that accompanied Martin's managerial career from Detroit to Minnesota to Texas and now to New York, namely, that he couldn't win with other people's players. Both Eastwick and Messersmith were due to come off the disabled list, and Ken Holtzman, the former Oakland Athletic, was put on the disabled list to make room for one of them, reportedly because he had a bad back. He did have stiffness in his back, and he wore a back brace, but he thought he was capable of pitching and he objected to his consignment to inactive status.

Don Gullett pitched his first start of the season for the Yankees on June 4th against the Oakland A's, giving up three hits, one walk, two runs and getting only one batter out. It was Gullett who Sparky Anderson had predicted would end up in the Hall of Fame sometime after he started the seventh game of the 1975 World Series, to which Bill Lee had responded, when told by a reporter of Anderson's comment, "I don't care where Gullett's going, because after this game I'm going to the Eliot Lounge," a bar that formerly stood at the corner of Commonwealth and Massachusetts avenues in Boston where runners make the turn for the final sprint to the finish line of the Boston Marathon. Anderson's prediction didn't seem unlikely at the time; Gullett had a 91-44 career record with the Reds when the Yankees picked him up as a free agent after the

1976 World Series. He had pitched the opening game of that World Series for the Reds, and, after a 14-4 season with the Yankees in 1977, he would start the opening game of the 1977 World Series for them, becoming the first pitcher to pitch opening games of consecutive World Series for different teams, a statistic now useful primarily for winning bets in bars. While Lee may have made it to the Eliot Lounge, Gullett didn't make it to the Hall of Fame, and after his initial outing of the '78 season it appeared unlikely that he would ever return to his former stature among major league pitchers.

At one point things were going so badly for the Yankees that, at the tail end of a seven-game losing streak that began in May, coach Gene Michaels was ejected from a game in a time warp that began a day after the event complained of and concluded before the next game started. Lou Piniella had been called out at first by umpire Larry McCoy in a June 5th game against Seattle. Piniella protested, with some justification in the eyes of more than a few observers, and McCoy ejected him. The next night when Michaels brought the lineup card to the plate he mentioned the call that went against Piniella to umpire Steve Palermo and Palermo summarily ejected him before the "Star-Spangled Banner" had been played. Adding the ejection of Billy Martin the night before to the subtotal of Michaels and Piniella, the Yankees had scored a bad conduct trifecta.

It was during this stretch that rumors of Martin's imminent dismissal began to reach a critical mass, like a floor vote building to the nomination of a candidate at an old-time political convention. On June 9th Maury Allen, a New York *Post* columnist and author of several books about the Yankees,

brought a clipping from a column by fellow *Post* sportswriter
Dick Young into the team's clubhouse that predicted Martin
would soon be fired. The strain of serving under George
Steinbrenner would try the patience of managers before and
after Martin, but for the former World Series hero and running
buddy of such Yankee icons as Joe DiMaggio and Mickey
Mantle, the suffering brought on by Steinbrenner's meddling
was multiplied by three further elements: First, Martin was
thin-skinned by nature and would resent interference from
the front office and ball club owners at every stop in his
career; second, Steinbrenner affected an intimacy with Reggie
Jackson, who Martin loathed more than any player he had
ever managed; and third, Martin had, in the perceptive analysis of Sparky Lyle, wanted only two things in his life—to play
for the Yankees and to manage them—and now Steinbrenner
stood in the way of the latter. If Martin wanted to remain the
manager of the Yankees, he would have to harken to
Steinbrenner's caprices, whatever they may have been on a
given day. This troubled Martin: "I hate," he observed to Lyle,
"to eat shit."

Martin's tendency to melodrama wore on his players, but
more than was normally the case because Martin was in the
third year of his tenure with the Yankees, a fairly extensive
term for him. His longest prior stint of employment was the
period just short of three years that he had spent with the
Detroit Tigers, whom he managed from October 2, 1970, until
September 2, 1973. Martin had been hired as manager of the
Yankees on August 2, 1975, and thus had already progressed
through the stages of initial elation and subsequent disap-
pointment that historically characterized his relations with his

players, and had passed into a period of cynicism. In the later, darker periods of his managing engagements, he tended to lash out at his players in his frustration at their lack of perfection, and his confrontation with Thurman Munson on the flight from Kansas City to Chicago on May 15th served as a sort of dog-eared page in the book that Yankee players kept on Billy Martin; this was a passage worth remembering, since it marked the point at which Martin exploded at the most dedicated student and manager's pet in the Yankees' current class. The players were tired of the tension caused by Martin's tenuous position, but they were at the same time fearful of and peeved at him.

On June 10th Thurman Munson was hit in the throat by a foul tip and Bucky Dent suffered a severe hamstring pull when he dove for a ball hit up the middle in a game against the Angels. Two of the four most important positions in the Yankees' defense would be occupied by understudies for a while, in Dent's case for more than a month, while the team's pitching staff was undergoing renovations that caused temporary disruptions in service. Ken Holtzman, who had threatened to sue the Yankees at the beginning of the month for the indignity of his demotion to the disabled list, was traded to the Chicago Cubs for a minor league pitcher whose earned run average was bigger than his hat size. Dick Tidrow's thumb was injured, as was Don Gullett's shoulder. Rawley Eastwick, another retread from the 1975 Reds team that beat the Red Sox in the World Series, was traded to Philadelphia. Catfish Hunter and Andy Messersmith had yet to recover from their arm injuries. Jim Beattie complained that he wasn't being used correctly. And Sparky Lyle, the prior year's Cy

Young Award winner whose envy of other players' salaries caused him to retreat into a posture psychologists refer to as "passive aggression," became so depressed by talk of the Yankees' anticipated signing of Rod Carew for somewhere around $4,000,000 that he decided to take an unapproved leave of absence on June 13th. Before he left, he told Billy Martin that he wouldn't go AWOL if Martin thought it would cause Steinbrenner to fire the manager. Martin, still scatologically obsessed in his depression, replied, "Sparky, I don't give a shit."

The Yankees in their drift and the Red Sox in their surge met for the first time in the 1978 season on June 19th, the day after Bill Lee re-joined the Sox following his walkout. The Red Sox-Yankees rivalry is of such great import in Boston that, on June 18th, the day before that first meeting, it was considered more newsworthy than the game the Sox played the day before, a 3-2 loss to the Seattle Mariners. Lee's return did not mark a change in his disposition, as he lashed out at management with a comment that may have offended some teammates. "They trade away all the genuine personalities and surround themselves with Kapstein plastic," said Lee, referring to the departed Carbo but reflecting on a large group of individuals on the Sox represented by Jerry Kapstein, a players' agent who had come to understand the principles that would govern the new era of free agency sooner than most. That group included personalities as diverse as Fred Lynn (laid-back Californian), Carlton Fisk (principled New Hampshire yeoman), Jerry Remy (Massachusetts born and bred, favorite of the working-class "townies" who filled Fenway's bleachers) and Rick Burleson (who loved to win in the same way that Norman Bates of Alfred Hitchcock's *Psycho* loved his mother). While Lee didn't use an agent, few noted the inconsistency in his position; the self-proclaimed enemy of authority had criticized teammates who employed a professional in order to protect their interests against management.

The first encounter between the Sox and the Yankees in 1978 went to Boston, but only after starter Luis Tiant was lifted in the fourth inning trailing 4-1. The Sox tied the game in the fourth and scored 6 runs in the eighth inning to win 10-4. Dwight Evans threw out Fred Stanley in the fifth as he tried to go from first to third on a single by Roy White. If Stanley had made it to third, the Yankees would have had men on first and third with none out and the second, third and fourth batters in the lineup set to bat. Instead, they had a man on first with one out, and no harm was done.

The next day the score was reversed as Don Gullett pitched his first complete game of 1978 and the Yankees won, 10-4, on a grand slam by Fred Stanley, his first runs batted in of the season. It was Gullett's second win of the season giving him a career record of 107-48, the best of any active pitcher in the major leagues. Reggie Jackson had a three-run homer which, with a double the day before, seemed to indicate that he was breaking out of a recent slump; he was 0 for 12 in the Yankees' most recent series against the California Angels, and had struck out four times in one game. For the season, he had a .272 average, 10 home runs and 37 runs batted in. "I know I haven't started my rise," he told a reporter. "I'm concerned about that but not worried. I know the team hasn't played good ball and we'd better get started soon. Course if the Red Sox keep playing the way they've been playing we won't catch them with a motorcycle." Dennis Eckersley pitched for Boston in the closing game of the series and won, as the Sox pushed the Yankees eight games out of first place with a 9-2 win.

The loss of the series caused the murmurings about Martin's job prospects to grow louder. Knowledgeable speculation predicted that Martin would not survive until the All-Star break, when he was scheduled to lead the American League team as manager of the previous year's league champions. The rumors caused Martin's paranoid inclinations to predominate. He kept a tape recorder in his desk and let it be known that he turned it on when approached by writers he didn't trust. "I don't want to be fired because of a misquote," he said. "Have you ever been burned by the press?" a reporter asked. "More than Joan of Arc," came the reply. Nonetheless, he began to indulge in more braggadocio than usual, perhaps because of (and not despite) his sense of insecurity over his job. "All we've got to do is win our own ball games," he confidently told one reporter. "If the Yankees start winning like we can, and we will, we won't have to worry about the Red Sox. Pitchers in the long run will be their downfall," he predicted. "I said that before, but I said it when we had a healthy pitching staff."

When the Yankees left Boston the Orioles came to town, winners of 18 of their last 21 games. Bill Lee, pitching for the first time since his return, beat Jim Palmer in the first game 5-2, his first victory since May 26th. After the game he showered and went to a rally against nuclear power, not tarrying long enough to hear Don Zimmer praise him. The Yankees beat the Tigers the same day, as Sparky Lyle picked up a fortuitous win, relieving Ed Figueroa in the fifth inning when the starter couldn't continue despite a lead built on a grand slam home run by Chris Chambliss in the first inning. The win gave Lyle a 5-1 record that he felt he didn't deserve. "You're five and one?" asked Graig Nettles. "Keep quiet about it," Lyle told him. "I don't want anyone to know I'm doing so well pitching so badly."

Luis Tiant followed Lee's win with his seventh consecutive victory of the season and his eleventh straight win going back to August 30th of 1977. Mike Torrez won the next day to complete the sweep of the series with Baltimore—Torrez was 11-3, the winningest right-handed pitcher in the major leagues. Carlton Fisk and Rick Burleson, who had started the season in slumps, were beginning to hit, and George Scott, who usually struck out twice as often as he walked, had walked twenty times over the course of the season while striking out only seventeen times. The Sox were now eight and a half games ahead of both Baltimore and New York, but Boston's history and their apparent need to fail caused skeptics to begin to offer predictions about their eventual demise. Baltimore manager Earl Weaver: "They can't play all year without playing poorly. They're going to hit a stretch when everything goes against them, as individuals and as a team." To which Zimmer responded, "I don't think we're going to win every game, but we're not going into any tailspin. We're twenty-nine games over five hundred, and that means we could play five hundred ball the rest of the season and still have ninety-five wins. Maybe that won't be enough, but I guarantee you we won't play five hundred ball the rest of the way either."

The Yankees won the last game of their series with Detroit as Don Gullett got his third win of the season, giving the Yankees three wins out of four chances. Reggie Jackson declined to provide his services in the final game after being moved from fourth place in the batting order—the honorific "cleanup" position—to sixth. "There was no physical reason why he didn't play," Martin responded tersely to a reporter. By a quirk of scheduling the Yankees prepared to play their next two games against the Red Sox in New York.

In a show of support for Martin in light of the rumors of his imminent firing, Yankee fans greeted him with a two-minute standing ovation when he walked to home plate with his lineup card. The first game of the series went to the Sox, however, as Dennis Eckersley, who had failed to beat the Yankees in his three years in Cleveland, got his second win over New York in five days, beating Andy Messersmith 4-1. Messersmith had now gone without a victory since June 25, 1977. The next night Martin emerged from a meeting with Steinbrenner, Al Rosen and Martin's agent and heard Steinbrenner read a statement that Martin would be manager for the rest of the season "no matter what." Clubhouse book-makers accordingly issued a morning line offering even money that Martin would be gone in two days, with longer odds available for each additional day a plunger was willing to wager the manager would survive. That night Ron Guidry, whose twelve wins to start the season was approaching the major league record of thirteen, was chased from the mound by the Sox at the earliest point in a game thus far in 1978. Gossage held Boston from the seventh through the eleventh innings, when Lyle came in and pitched three innings, giving up only one hit. Graig Nettles homered off Dick Drago in the bottom of the fourteenth inning for a 6-4 Yankee win.

The next night New York dropped a double header to Milwaukee as Thurman Munson began a three-game suspension for bumping an ump in Detroit the week before. On the last day of June, Luis Tiant lost his first game of the year to Baltimore, 3-2, after pitching eleven innings and giving up only five hits. The Sox had won 18 and lost 7 in June and ended the month eight and a half games ahead of second-place Milwaukee. On the same day the federal government agreed to guaranty up to $1.5 billion in long-term loans to New York City, thereby enabling the city to avoid bankruptcy. For the month, the Yankees showed a slightly smaller deficit, managing 14 wins against 15 defeats, but they were in third place, trailing Boston by nine.

The Spaceman

The day is Sunday, July 2, 1978. The place: Baltimore's now-demolished Memorial Stadium. The Red Sox are scheduled to play the Orioles in an afternoon game, but it is raining, lightly at first but then harder. A Boston player emerges from the dugout, bat, ball and glove in his hands. He drops the glove and hits a pop fly. He picks up the glove, runs after the fly and catches it. He repeats this sequence, warming to a rhythm after a while, in some cases making diving catches on the outfield grass. The player is Bill Lee, and the delight he displays in the sheer joy of hitting and catching a baseball, dirtying his uniform with belly-flopping catches on the mud-luscious field, will cause the observer to put the Red Sox pitcher in one of two categories, depending upon his or her larger view of life: either Lee is an eternal child in the midst of grown men more concerned with their money than the game they play, or he is someone who doesn't have the good sense to come in out of the rain.

A player who regularly and emphatically claimed that he played baseball for the fun of it, that baseball was only a game and that people took it too seriously, William Francis Lee, III, who *The Complete Record of Red Sox Baseball* notes was also known as "Spaceman", nonetheless had a virulent dislike for one particular opponent and its owner and manager—namely, the New York Yankees, George Steinbrenner and Billy Martin. When it was rumored that the Red Sox might trade Lee to the Yankees after the 1971 season for Danny Cater, a first baseman who had always hit well in Fenway Park, Lee claimed he would have left baseball if the deal had gone through. "Having grown up hating [the Yankees'] cold, corporate image and their strutting glorification of elitism, there was no way I would have put on pinstripes," Lee explained later. "I would have headed for Japan." After his shoulder injury at the hands of Graig Nettles of the Yankees in 1976, Lee met with the press and called Steinbrenner and Martin "Brown Shirts," saying there was an element of fascism in Martin's approach to the game and that the Yankee manager probably thought Mussolini was just a nice guy whom Hitler had led astray. Lee's characterization of Martin as a fascist got under the Yankee manager's skin, and Martin paid a clubhouse boy to put a dead fish in Lee's trousers shortly after the comment reached his ears. The clubhouse boy brought the fish to Lee, saying, "You don't need this in your pants, do you?" Lee was later told that Martin had attached a note to the fish that said, "Stick this in your purse, you no-good pussy." "I doubt it," Lee said. "Billy doesn't know how to spell 'pussy'."

The Spaceman

This dual personality—none dare call it schizophrenia—exemplified a division of the mind of Bill Lee, born December 28, 1946, into two opposing camps. One faction adopted as its colors the easy mysticism that imbued the youth movement of his college years—the 1960s—with some of its deeper hues; the other wore the uniform of Lee family tradition, which extended in baseball terms back at least 70 years to his grandfather, an accomplished semipro infielder in Los Angeles; his aunt Annabelle Lee, who had a lifetime earned run average of 1.17 and pitched the first perfect game in the history of the Chicago Women's Semi-Pro Hardball League; and his father, who coached him and taught him how to throw a curveball and a knuckleball when the son was eight. This latter strain of his temperament gave Lee a contentious aspect and a perfectionist cast that made him both a fierce competitor and intolerant of those he deemed baseball's fools; the former provided him with a convenient and high-falutin' wrapper in which to package a laid-back and hedonistic philosophy that is thought to be endemic to his native Southern California, but which is anathema to that portion, however large, of a typical big-league manager's personality that partakes of the disciplinarian.

When Lee first joined the Red Sox he was assigned number 37, which had formerly been worn by Jimmy Piersall. Piersall was a Sox outfielder whose autobiography *Fear Strikes Out*, written with the assistance of Al Hirshberg, described his descent into mental illness and a seven-month stay in the violent room at a state hospital in Westborough, Massachusetts. (It was later made into a movie with Anthony Perkins in the role of Piersall.) Lee would exhibit some of Piersall's more genial eccentricities, but he seemed to find in drugs and a superficial mysticism the solace that eluded Piersall. Lee's metaphysical side was in turn composed of equal parts ironical put-on and genuine, if credulous, belief. He admitted that he "developed a way of answering questions that had little to do with the question being asked." This interlocutorial style developed partly out of defensiveness—Lee claimed to have been misquoted often during the early part of his career, and he took pleasure in gulling reporters into, for example, taking down his fanciful explanations of pitch selections based on Einstein's theory of curved space. It also stemmed from a desire to mock the seriousness with which some sports reporters approach the game. "I wasn't yanking anybody around," Lee said. "I was trying to make a comment on the game: 'Let's not take any of this too seriously. The game is supposed to be fun.'"

Lee's capacity for whimsy, and his ability to express that sentiment in his pitching, was probably best expressed by his fondness for a latter-day variation of the "eephus" pitch, a slow arching curveball that crossed through the strike zone on a downward slope after having been launched skyward as in slow-pitch softball. Lee revived this novelty, made famous by Truett Banks "Rip" Sewell, a Pittsburgh Pirates pitcher of the '40s, and remodelled it as his "Leephus" pitch or "Mooncurve". In the seventh game of the 1975 World Series, Lee had thrown three such pitches successfully before facing the Reds' first baseman Tony Perez in the top of the fifth inning with a 3-0 lead. Lee had been told by the Red Sox' scouts not to throw any slow pitches to Perez, a power hitter who, like Willie Mays in his prime, could reset his batting clock with an internal snooze alarm anytime he saw a slow pitch coming. Perez had taken a called strike on one of Lee's earlier Mooncurves, however, and Lee—heeding no scouting report other than his own internal compass—decided to risk another one. (Had Lee's mastery of Fenway history been stronger, he might not have; Ted Williams hit the first home run ever off an eephus pitch facing Sewell in the All-Star Game held there in 1946.) Perez was expecting a fastball or a hard screwball, not a blooper, but Lee's fastest pitches could be captured by technology less sophisticated than a radar gun, including a reasonably efficient courtroom artist. Perez looked at Lee's offering and recoiled, and when he released his spring Boston sportswriters were offering lessons in local geography to visiting journalists who needed to describe where the ball might have landed—the Massachusetts Turnpike, Cambridge, or in the furthest arc of hyperbole, New Hampshire. Boston 3, Cincinnati 2. Lee was gone an inning later after developing a blister that caused him to lose his control and walk Ken Griffey. The Reds won the game and the series when Joe Morgan hit a bloop single to shallow left-center field off rookie reliever Jim Burton with two out in the top of the ninth.

The more sincere component of Lee's mysticism was inspired at least in part by his experience with drugs. He first tried hashish in 1972 while in Cleveland for a series with the Indians. The next day, feeling cleansed by the drug, he wandered around the city until he came to the public library, where he was led, as he recalled, "by invisible forces" to the philosophy and religion stacks.[*] There he perused the works of Gurdjieff, Ouspensky and Paramahansa Yogananda, beginning an autodidact's exploration that led him to become involved in charitable causes far removed from, and more fashionable among countercultural types than, the typical baseball player's visit to a dying child in the hospital, to the displeasure of some older sportswriters and fans. The metaphysical writings Lee explored made him realize that, in his words, "although I loved the way I made a living and had no wish to stop, playing ball satisfied only my needs. It did not contribute to the earth's well-being. I decided to change what had been a selfish existence by donating my free time to other people and their worthwhile causes."

Regardless of whether Lee's mysticism was affected or genuine, at some point we are what we do. Repeated efforts to put a label on Lee that would capture the otherworldly character of his discourse eventually resulted in the adoption in general currency of the nickname "Spaceman", which was apparently first used by a Red Sox teammate, infielder John Kennedy. This moniker stuck where several prior proposals—including "Space Cowboy" and "Ace of Space"—from the chorus of journalists whose job it is to explain the drama of baseball to the world had not.

However deeply felt Lee's convictions may have been at

---

* Thereby indulging in another form of conspicuous leisure identified by Veblen in addition to the consumption of inebriants noted before: "So, for instance, in our time there is the knowledge of the dead languages and the occult sciences. . . .In all these branches of knowledge the initial motive. . .may have been something quite different from the wish to show that one's time had not been spent in industrial employment; but unless these accomplishments had approved themselves as serviceable evidence of an unproductive expenditure of time, they would not have survived and held their place as conventional accomplishments of the leisure class." Veblen, *The Theory of the Leisure Class*, Book of the Month Club edition, 1981, p. 45.

bottom, the image he chose to reveal to the world was part court jester and part shop steward, a man who represented the interests of himself and those of his teammates he considered soulmates by continually jousting with management on issues both large and small. On the minor issues, Lee's resistance resembled that of the harmless high school rebel who wants to demonstrate his intellectual superiority to the dull pedants charged with holding him in educational stir until he is ready for college. When Don Zimmer imposed a rule that players had to wear sports jackets on a team trip to Puerto Rico, Lee wore a jogging top; when Zimmer told him he wasn't properly dressed, Lee replied, "This is a jacket and jogging's a sport."

Lee's iconoclasm and sense of humor endeared him to the majority of Boston's sportswriters, who were for the most part close to him in age and outlook. The attitudes of the remainder of the Boston press corps towards Lee covered a wide spectrum: There were older men who saw in Lee a latter-day Dizzy Dean with a nice intellectual patina, one of the most interesting baseball personalities they had encountered in a generation. The affection these writers and some of their younger counterparts felt towards Lee was partly genuine and partly the result of enlightened self-interest, since Lee was funny and thus made for good copy and easy stories. And there were those who viewed their mission as journalists to have been best expressed by Finley Peter Dunne's Mr. Doolittle; namely, to comfort the afflicted and to afflict the comfortable. In the case of organized baseball in the 1970s, the old notion of the ballplayers as blue-collar workers and the owners as greedy bosses hadn't yet been eroded by the passage of time since the

Messersmith/McNally decision, although the analogy became less accurate with each passing day. Eighteen years later, it was to be dispelled for good by a strike in which millionaire players proposed to hire real working stiffs to walk the picket line for them.

Sympathetic sportswriters made for favorable coverage, and, as with the envy that Billy Martin came to feel for Reggie Jackson, favorable coverage of the player gave rise to resentment on the part of the manager. Zimmer began to collect a file of press clippings on Lee midway through the '78 season consisting of articles and interviews in which Lee had referred to Zimmer as a "gerbil." The rodent metaphor Lee formed out of his impressions of Zimmer was originally crafted in response to a reporter's question; namely, if Billy Martin is a rat, what is Don Zimmer? "Don is a gerbil," Lee answered, "a cute, puffy-cheeked creature." This metaphorical transmogrification would probably pass some sort of objective test as to both managers; yon Martin had a lean and hungry look and a competitive streak that bordered on the feral, while Zimmer, with his chaw, was certainly puffy-cheeked and, to a sympathetic audience like that he later found as the manager of the Chicago Cubs, he must have seemed cute.

In the battle between Lee and Zimmer, Boston fans overwhelmingly sided with Lee for reasons that had more to do with local color than inside baseball. Boston fans and sportswriters participate in an exercise in self-congratulation that is followed in nearly every city in America with a major league sports franchise, including New York; namely, the assertion that its fans are the most knowledgeable of any city in the league. In Boston's case, this popular delusion springs in part from the city's reliance on its academic industry as a source of local self-esteem; in New York's case, it flows from the widely-held sentiment among residents that, despite its many imperfections, that city is the greatest in the world. The ubiquity of the claim, and the impossibility of its truth in the case of more than one city, leads one to view it with the same skepticism normally reserved for signs in restaurants that boast "Best cup of coffee in town."

Why Bostonians would have preferred Lee over Zimmer is not difficult to understand. The self-consciously eccentric Lee was clearly favored over the square and stocky Zimmer by fans drawn from Boston's perennially youthful population who were in the midst of efforts to find or fashion themselves similar to those that Lee was so obviously engaged in. As for those whose student days were behind them, Boston's labor force includes a disproportionate number of workers who toil primarily in the vineyards of the written word, and for them Lee's verbal sallies were a far richer source of entertainment than Zimmer's stolid but professional responses to the working press. For Red Sox fans who punched a time clock, Lee represented a vicarious revolt against management; the great mass of Red Sox followers probably wished they had the opportunity that Lee had to tell off his boss in public every day, even if they sometimes cringed at the foolhardy courage he displayed in doing so. Thus, when Lee was dropped from the starting rotation in 1978, he received a standing ovation as he made his way to the bull pen to start his stint as a reliever, and a standing ovation when he made his first appearance in relief; Zimmer, as Lee told a magazine interviewer, received "corresponding standing boos."

The Year of the Gerbil

Lee generally came out on top in his battles with the Yankees as well, with the notable exception of his run-in with Mickey Rivers and Graig Nettles in 1976. "I always pitched well against the Yankees," Lee would recall. Lee believed that the Yankees had built their teams around left-handed power due to the dimensions of Yankee Stadium, with its short right field, just as the Sox had historically overloaded themselves with right-handed power hitters to take advantage of Fenway Park's short left-field wall. When pitching in Yankee Stadium, Lee said, he "would throw a lot of soft stuff in their kitchens. They would try to pull it over the right-field fence, and the result would be a lot of bloopers to my second baseman. When they came to Fenway, they'd shoot for the Wall. I'd nail them with hard sinkers inside. They never were able to adapt, and after a few wins against them, I felt like I owned them." In fact, Lee ended his career with a won-lost record against the Yankees (12-5) that was the third best in baseball history, behind only Dickie Kerr of the Chicago White Sox (14-4) and, ironically enough, Babe Ruth during his Red Sox years (17-5).

Since Lee had his philosophical side, his feelings towards the Yankees had an intellectual underpinning as well. "They were an elitist corporation with a self-promoted public image of cold arrogance that went against my grain. The Yankees represented the political right in baseball, while the Red Sox were their opposite number. We were composed of the stuff that had made this country great. We were like a bunch of modern-day Pilgrims." Lee's heroic view of the Red Sox is difficult to square with the contemporaneous accounts of other players who shared his years with the team. The Pilgrims were known for their sense of community and submission to a common goal, as expressed in The Mayflower Compact, in which they declared as follows:

> We. . .Do by these Presents, solemnly and mutually in the Presence of God and one another, covenant and combine ourselves into a civil Body Politic, for our better Ordering and Preservation. . . and by Virtue hereof to enact, constitute, and frame, such just and equal Laws, Ordinances, Acts, Constitutions and Offices, from time to time, as shall be thought most meet and convenient for the general good of the Colony; unto which we promise all due Submission and Obedience.

While the Red Sox were previously known as the Boston Pilgrims, the Plymouth Rocks and the Boston Puritans, the similarities between the team and the early American colonists ended with these names. Frank Duffy, who joined the Red Sox from Cleveland in the trade that brought Dennis Eckersley to the team, summed up the self-centered spirit of the Red Sox with the observation that after each game the team scattered, "Twenty-five players, twenty-five cabs." If the Pilgrims had indeed resembled the Red Sox, one would have expected a precursor of Duffy standing on the dock at Delfs-Haven to mutter as the religionists set sail, "A hundred and one Pilgrims, a hundred and one ships."

The Fall

There had, of course, been spectacular crashes by major league teams before the fall of the 1978 Red Sox. In 1915 the New York Giants held a fifteen-game lead on the 4th of July but finished ten and a half games behind the pennant-winning Boston Braves. In 1964 the Philadelphia Phillies had a six and a half game lead over the St. Louis Cardinals with twelve games left in the regular season; they lost ten straight games and the Cardinals took the pennant and went on to beat the Yankees in the World Series, four games to three. In 1951, the Brooklyn Dodgers had a thirteen and a half game lead over the New York Giants on August 11th, were tied on the last day of the season, and lost a three-game play-off and the pennant to the Giants in the ninth inning of the last game of the series on Bobby Thompson's home run.

The Sox themselves have suffered enough late-season col-lapses to cause one wag to suggest that they move to the

Philippines and change their name to the Manila Folders. For instance, the Sox lost three pennants in five years during the late 1940s by a total of only three games. In galling particular, they lost a pennant to the Yankees on the last day of 1949, playing their last two games in Yankee Stadium and needing to win only one to move on to the World Series. They lost both. In 1974 the Sox held a six and a half game lead over the Yankees on September 1st; the Yankees overtook them in early September, and the Baltimore Orioles surpassed them both, leaving the Sox in third place.

The conventional wisdom is that the Sox' fall from their early-season pinnacle in 1978 began in July, when, in the last game before the All-Star break, shortstop Rick Burleson hurt his ankle sliding into second base in a game against Cleveland. Prior to that injury, the Sox were 5-3 for the month, including Eckersley's third win in 12 days over the Yankees, a 9-5 victory on July 3rd in Boston in which Carl Yastrzemski got his 2,800th hit. The next day's game was rained out at a time when the Yankees' pitching staff was so depleted that Jim Spencer, a free agent first baseman, had been seen warming up in the New York bull pen on at least two occasions since July 1st. The middle of the Yankees' infield consisted of Damaso Garcia and Fred "Chicken" Stanley, as both Willie Randolph and Bucky Dent were injured. Rawley Eastwick and Ken Holtzman had been traded, Andy Messersmith, Catfish Hunter and Ken Clay had arm injuries, and minor league pitchers unknown now to even the most learned of Yankee fans—Kammeyer, Rajsich, McCall and Semall—were being shuttled in to Broadway from summer stock at the club's farm team in West Haven, Connecticut, and back to the provinces again when they folded after opening night, or day. As Billy Martin put it that day, "The rain's come at a good time."

Burleson would be out for the next seventeen games, and the Sox would lose ten of those games with utility infielder Frank Duffy taking his place. The Sox starters weren't known as a group that welcomed temporary replacements from the chorus line for injured members of the original cast, and no exception was made in Duffy's case. The pecking order that prevails on most professional baseball teams represents an atavistic relic of the predatory aspect of the sport, and is expressed in hierarchies that are applied to matters both great and small. In baseball, as in other competitive endeavors, you eat what you kill, and if you kill enough to be a starter, you eat first. On the '78 Red Sox, this rule was conveyed to backup infielder Jack Brohamer one day in spring training as he moved towards the buffet laid out by the clubhouse attendant. "You can't eat the spread until the regulars have had it," rightfielder Dwight Evans brusquely yelled at him. Lateral acquisitions from other clubs have noted that the Sox' batting practice pitchers use clean, new balls when pitching to regulars and scuffed balls when pitching to benchwarmers. Sox starter Mike Greenwell would get into a physical confrontation with a heavyset rookie named Mo Vaughan some years later when Vaughan dared to line up for batting practice ahead of Greenwell. Greenwell, who would compare unfavorably to Vaughan in what boxing writers call the "Tale of the Tape", suffered a black eye and wounded dignity in the altercation, as he failed in his attempt to move up in weight class. Some hierarchies are more objective than others.

The Year of the Gerbil

On the 1978 Sox, even Bill Lee, a man who seemed to think of his teammates as noble Communards collectively resisting a corrupt aristocracy, was capable of making a class distinction between the regulars and the reserves, who were referred to by the starters and other money players as the "F Troop", after the incompetent cavalry company in the television series of the same name. "Duffy was unable to do the job at shortstop," Lee told a writer some years later, but the objective evidence for the claim that the Sox faltered because Burleson was out and Duffy was in is somewhat questionable. Duffy had a better season at the plate than Burleson in 1978, batting .260 to Burleson's .248, and he was a more than serviceable utility infielder; that year he had a fielding percentage of 1.000 at second base (12 games) and a .960 percentage at third (22 games). Unfortunately, he achieved only a .929 average in 21 games at shortstop, making seven errors, while Burleson had a .981 average over 144 games. Three of Duffy's errors came in his first start at shortstop, following a game in which he made three exceptional plays at second base. His skills were apparently better suited for the shorter range and throw required from the right-hand side of the diamond.

Wherever the truth may lie along these yardsticks for measuring a shortstop's performance, the Sox began to unravel after the All-Star break. They lost nine straight games beginning with an 8-6 loss to Milwaukee on July 20th; during this stretch Boston allowed Kansas City, Minnesota and Texas each to sweep a two-game series from them. Burleson's absence may have had something to do with it.

Burleson was the type of player often metaphorized by sportswriters as a spark plug, and without his ignition the

Red Sox stalled. His throws to first from his position at short were known for their sting, and he was as hard on himself after a bad game as he was on his teammates when they performed at a level below their best. Burleson was nicknamed the Rooster and aptly so, since no player on the team (or perhaps the major leagues as a whole) had such a proprietary approach to his particular portion of baseball's barnyard as Burleson exercised over the ground he crossed in order to make the throw to first to complete a double play. He was in many ways a latter-day version of Billy Martin, and although he was as quick to take offense at a perceived slight as Martin, he was able to limit his outbursts to the clubhouse and the playing field and thus avoid the sort of off-field trouble in which Martin perpetually found himself, from a 1957 brawl at New York's Copacabana Club to a 1979 altercation with a marshmallow salesman in the lounge of Bloomington, Minnesota's Hotel de France, where Gallic rudeness apparently prevailed. It was hard to let up with Burleson around, since his depression in defeat seemed to border on the suicidal, if not the homicidal. Other Red Sox were as serious about the game as Burleson, but none of them possessed Burleson's brooding will to win. Burleson is probably the only player in baseball history with "rabbit ears", the condition that causes players to take offense at taunts from the grandstands, big enough to get mad at a lighting fixture; when the Yankee Stadium scoreboard fed New York fans with cheers for Reggie Jackson during a game in 1977, Burleson actually turned around and yelled at it.

The Sox troubles didn't initially give rise to panic for two reasons; first, because they were so far ahead. One writer for the Boston *Globe* pointed out that 54 of 78 teams in first place on July 4th had won a pennant in the previous thirty years. The Sox had won their league championship twice out of three chances when they had found themselves in that position, namely, in 1946 and 1975, the other time being 1974, when they went from seven and a half games up on August 23rd to seven and a half games behind the Baltimore Orioles on the last day of the season.

The other reason the Sox appeared calm even as their fans began to experience a sense of foreboding was that the Yankees weren't gaining any ground on them. The Yankees stumbled through the first few weeks of July, winning only four of their first thirteen games. On July 2nd Ron Guidry tied the major league record of 13 wins to begin a season. He had equaled the Yankee record of 12 consecutive wins to begin a season on June 22nd against Detroit, a record that he shared for a week with Tom Zachary, who performed the feat in 1929, and one Richard Atley "Swampy" Donald, the scout who had signed Guidry in the third round of the 1971 draft for a $10,000 bonus, two rounds after the Sox had signed Jim Rice. The Yankees in their wisdom decided not to renew Swampy Donald's contract in 1974. Guidry, the only starter on the Yankees' staff who had avoided injury or arm trouble since opening day, suffered his first defeat of the season in his next start, a 6-0 loss to Milwaukee in which Larry Hisle hit two home runs; the stoic Cajun apparently wasn't invincible after all.

On July 6th, Luis Tiant, who hadn't lost a game until June 30th, pulled a muscle in his right groin, the fulcrum from which he obtained the leverage that enabled him to push towards and turn away from the plate in his maddening gyre, but the Sox' pitching still seemed adequate. On July 8th Dennis Eckersley improved his record to 10-2 with a 12-5 win over Cleveland in the opener of a doubleheader the Sox swept, giving him 50 wins in three and a half years in the major leagues. The cynic's view of the Sox' pitching staff was that the larger ecosystem of the Sox had not been harmed by the forced migration of the Buffalo Heads, but the news from the more hospitable climes that members of the herd now inhabited was cause for some small measure of regret; Reggie Cleveland had 9 saves for Texas, where Ferguson Jenkins had 8 wins. In Chicago, Jim Willoughby had 10 saves. Only Rick Wise, in Cleveland, had failed to thrive in his new surroundings, registering a 6-11 record without much support on his way to a dismal 9-19 record for the year.

On July 8th Goose Gossage gave up a pair of home runs to Hisle for the second time in the season and the Yankees fell again to the Brewers, 8-4. On the day before, Bucky Dent had returned to the starting lineup at shortstop for the first time since early June; he promptly reinjured his hamstring and was again placed on the disabled list. Thus, New York limped into the All-Star break with Willie Randolph and Dent out of the lineup and four possible starters—Ken Clay, Don Gullett, Andy Messersmith and Catfish Hunter—out of action. Guidry wouldn't lose in his next turn in the pitching rotation on July 14th, but only because Cliff Johnson hit a pinch-hit home run in the bottom of the ninth inning to tie the score. Reggie Jackson led off with a double in the bottom of the eleventh inning and came home on a single by Graig Nettles to score the winning run in a 7-6 victory over the White Sox.

Frustrated by the Yankees' lack of progress, owner

George Steinbrenner used the occasion of the team's state of collective recuperation to put into place some changes that Martin undoubtedly bristled at in principle but which, in view of the team's sluggish performance, he could hardly object to. Jackson would become designated hitter, rookie Mike Heath would replace Thurman Munson as catcher, Munson would move to right field and Gary Thomasson would play left field. While Steinbrenner could give these directions from on high in the owner's box, he could not, without risking a Whiskey Rebellion from Martin, force the manager to implement them on a day-to-day basis. Thus while Steinbrenner, at Jackson's prompting, urged Martin to bat Jackson fourth, Martin responded by allowing Jackson to slide lower in the batting order until, when the Yankee line-up card was handed in on July 14th, he had slipped to sixth place, preceded by Chris Chambliss batting fourth and Graig Nettles coming next. It was a chafing spot for a tender ego, and Jackson announced to the press that he was no longer available for interviews. Since Jackson had earlier ceased to talk to the majority of his teammates, he was now cut off from even indirect communication with his ball club, and began to stew in his own bilious stock.

On July 15th Sparky Lyle reached an agreement with Yankee owner George Steinbrenner that adjusted Lyle's salary upwards over a three-year term from $135,000 to $200,000 a year. By the standards that Steinbrenner had set over the preceding winter it wasn't much; Lyle's raise of $65,000 could probably be found behind sofa cushions at the homes of Reggie Jackson ($2,930,000 a year) and Goose Gossage ($2,750,000). Nonetheless, Lyle was satisfied, thus easing one source of tension on a team troubled by personality clashes.

Martin would bench Jackson and start Cliff Johnson, a right-handed batter, against the Kansas City Royals' left-handed pitcher Larry Gura on July 16th, and as a result Jackson had another reason to pout, but he represented a minority of one on this issue. His teammates viewed him as a defensive liability who wasn't hitting the ball or even challenging pitchers at the time, thus making it more difficult for players near him in the batting order to gain an edge when they came to the plate. The Yankee owners were paying Jackson a lot of money, however, and Steinbrenner didn't feel they were getting a proper return on their investment when Jackson sat on the bench. Thus Jackson would play, his teammates would begrudge him the playing time he would get, and Jackson would silently sulk at the slight to his talents, which were formidable (he led the team in runs batted in and was second in home runs) though inconstant (he was 2-for-16 since the All-Star break).

The Yankees would fall to the Royals that night, 3-1, on the strength of a two-run homer by Amos Otis in the first inning and the pitching of Gura, a former Yankee who, traded twice by Billy Martin in his career, disliked his former manager intensely and relished his first victory over his former teammates. "The Yankees are in a slump right now," he said in answer to the inevitable question from a reporter, "but it's great to finally beat them. I hope it's the beginning—I owe them about three or four more." The loss was the eighth in ten games for the Yankees, and it put them in fourth place—behind the Sox, the Brewers and the Orioles, in that order—for the first time since April 13th. Not since 1975 had New York been so far from first place—13 games—and not since 1974 had they been in fourth place so late in the season.

One reason for the Yankees' misfortunes was that Mickey Rivers wasn't hitting or stealing bases in the style to which New Yorkers had become accustomed; at this point in the season he was hitting .250 with 10 stolen bases, while he had hit for averages of .312 and .326 in the two preceding seasons, and had stolen 43 and 22 bases in those years. He was hobbled by a sore leg and had suffered a hairline fracture of his right hand when he was hit by a pitch by Detroit's Dave LaRoche. The peculiar form of afflatus that inspires sportswriters for New York papers causes them to suppose that, because New York's intelligentsia views the city as the largest vat for the nation's intellectual ferment, the teams that they cover must be portrayed as thoughtful, ratiocinative types, even in the face of abundant evidence to the contrary. This style was lampooned in the early 1970s in a *New Yorker* article that portrayed the New York Knicks, the "thinking man's basketball team," swapping quotes from Sartre while they snapped each other's butts with towels. Exposure to this school of writing caused one reporter to lead a story about Rivers's woes during this period with the following psychoanalysis: "Of George Steinbrenner's vast and varied collection of large and sensitive egos, Rivers is one of the smallest but one of the most sensitive." Rivers himself was then quoted on the subject of his aching hand and his teammates' unfeeling attitude towards his plight: "I wrapped it up and taped it up, and nobody care how I feel or did but Billy and a couple of other players," he complained. "Nobody else didn't care."

Martin tried to create a happier workplace by returning Reggie Jackson to his treasured cleanup spot the next night, even though the Royals' starting pitcher—Paul Splittorff—was the left-hander whose supposed dominance of Jackson had caused Martin to bench his slugger in the deciding game of the previous year's American League Championship Series. "The way we're going now, maybe hitting fourth will make him happier and if it helps him and makes him happy, maybe he'll hit better and we'll win some games and make me happy," Martin reasoned, aligning his own and the team's self-interest with Jackson's self-absorption. Martin's explanation had the air of a rationalization about it, however, since it followed an hour-long meeting between Steinbrenner and Jackson that the player had requested, presumably to complain about his declining placement in the Yankees' batting order.

Martin contrived to annoy another of his players at the same time that he was mollifying Jackson, however, as if he had a fixed portion of spleen to vent every day that would be wasted if he didn't antagonize someone, anyone. The target on this occasion was Sparky Lyle, who was told by his manager that he would be pitching the sixth and seventh innings to set things up for Goose Gossage. Catfish Hunter started his first game since May and pitched well, leaving with a 5-3 lead after five and a third innings. Lyle came in, got out of the fifth and shut out the Royals in the sixth. He then left the mound and began to walk up the runway, saying, "That's my two innings." When pitching coach Art Fowler came after him, he construed Martin's offer strictly against the manager. "I'm not a long man, and you're not going to put me in that job. Two innings are two innings, and now the other guy can take over." He showered, dressed and got in his car.

What he heard on his car radio as he listened to the game on his way home was an act of industrial sabotage by Jackson. Incredibly, Jackson had chosen the night on which Martin had moved him to his desired spot in the batting order to give tangible expression to his long-simmering resentment against the manager. With the score tied 5-5 in the bottom of the tenth inning, Jackson was asked to bunt to move Thurman Munson, who had opened the inning with a single, over to second. Jackson, offended by the request to hold his fire with a duck on the pond, reluctantly squared to bunt on the first pitch by Al Hrabowsky, the Mad Hungarian reliever who would explode from a self-induced trance to a state of rage before every pitch. Hrabowsky's first pitch was inside and Jackson took it for a ball.

With the infield now drawn in, Martin took the bunt sign off, a fact that was communicated to Jackson by thirdbase coach Dick Howser. Nonetheless, Jackson turned to bunt again and missed for strike one. Martin flashed and Howser relayed the hit sign again, but Jackson bunted again, this time connecting for a foul ball and strike two. Enraged at Jackson's insubordination, Martin considered calling time to put in a pinch hitter but couldn't achieve the calm necessary to do so. Hrabowsky took the mound and threw, and Jackson again bunted foul, striking out. In the eleventh Thurman Munson dropped a fly ball, the Royals loaded the bases and Gossage walked in a run and was thrown out of the game when he protested the call. The Royals got two more runs on a single by Fred Patek and the two runs the Yankees scored in the bottom of the inning accordingly went for naught. New York was fourteen games behind the Red Sox, their biggest deficit of the season.

Martin reacted with his characteristic rage and Jackson with his usual aplomb, telling the credulous press that he was only trying to advance the runner. "How can they say I'm a threat swinging the bat," Jackson asked disingenuously, "when I'm not even playing every day. I'm a part-time player." Martin met immediately with Cedric Tallis, New York's general manager, who then conferred by phone with Steinbrenner and Al Rosen. Martin emerged from his office to announce the club's decision to suspend Jackson immediately without pay.

The Yankees left for a road trip that began with two games against Minnesota, while Jackson went home to Oakland for a one-week hiatus. The effect on Martin was immediate and purgative. He seemed relaxed and the team, perhaps sensing that the club would be run from the bench and not the owner's box for a time, responded with five straight wins. The first two were complete game shutouts by Figueroa and Guidry over the Twins, the first time Yankee pitchers had finished what they started in consecutive games since the end of May, and then three straight games from the White Sox, including five and two-thirds innings of shutout pitching in the opening games of the series from Catfish Hunter. Tacked on to the back-to-back shutouts from Figueroa, Hunter's tally produced 23 consecutive scoreless innings for the team's pitching staff. Still, Boston was 12 games ahead of New York, and Ray Fitzgerald, the Boston *Globe*'s senior sportswriter, produced a column of suggestions for Red Sox fans on ways to avoid boredom.

Billy Martin had, with a few exceptions, always inspired

loyalty in his players, and the visible sign that Steinbrenner wouldn't permit a personal favorite to challenge his manager's authority indicated that the revolution in player relations that Jackson's attitude seemed to represent had not yet arrived. Jackson's teammates generally took Martin's side in the dispute over the bunt. Chris Chambliss pointed out the obvious flaw in the apparent logic behind Jackson's behavior: "The man's batting fourth, we needed runs. He'd always wanted to bat fourth." Others wanted nothing more than peace. Ed Figueroa, starting the next night against the Twins, said simply, "I feel like I like to get out of this club. Not next year, this year. Too much junk going on." Rivers offered a minority report: "We need a big bat in the lineup right now. They should just fine him and let him play." The suspension in time, in Poor Richard's fashion, did cost Jackson money; the time he spent missing five days of play was money to him, $9,000 and change.

A sportwriter for a New York daily, on the other hand, compared Jackson's suspension to the Yankees' decision to overlook Sparky Lyle's arguably comparable act of disobedience and found evidence of racism on the part of team management. Martin hadn't taken issue with Lyle's decision to leave the park, however, and there had been no running feud between the pitcher and the manager to give Lyle's offense the aspect of premeditation. Lyle found fault with the article's tone and its substance, and he expressed his concerns to the author, New York *Post* reporter Henry Hecht, in person. "If you ever write another thing about me," Lyle offered by way of helpful criticism, "I'm going to kick your ass." There but for the grace of Steinbrenner the matter would have rested; the owner had read Hecht's piece and questionned his reliever about the incident. "Did you say to Billy on the bench that you're not a long man and you're not pitching anymore?" was the inquiry. "No I didn't," replied Lyle, reasoning, Jesuitically, that he had said it to Art Fowler in the clubhouse.

On Sunday, July 23rd, Reggie returned and as predicted served as the swizzle stick for the high-proof glass of Long Island Iced Tea that the Yankees had become. When asked by a reporter what had occupied his mind during his exile from Jacob Ruppert Avenue, he thought for a while and then said calmly, "The magnitude of me." He gave no apology for his self-coached approach to a team game, and told the reporters who assembled around him (when his teammates refused to comment on his return) that he had done no wrong. Martin heard him and, inevitably, responded. "It's like a guy getting out of jail and saying he's innocent after killing someone," Martin said out loud. Then he turned to Jackson: "We're winning without you," Martin exploded. "We don't need any more of your crap." And then, in a stage whisper to the assembled multitudes in the clubhouse: "If he doesn't shut his f___ing mouth, he won't play, and I don't give a damn what George says. He can replace me right now if he doesn't like it."

After the Yankees' victory over the White Sox that day, Martin began to drink, downing four scotches in the press room at Comiskey Park and taking more with him in a paper cup went he went to the team bus. After reading some of Jackson's comments in a story to be filed by a New York *Daily News* reporter, Martin became agitated at the fact that Jackson's remorseless attitude would soon be broadcast to the public beyond the Yankees' clubhouse door. He told Murray Chass of the New York *Times* he wanted to talk with him when the bus arrived at O'Hare Airport. Once there, he renewed the diatribe against Jackson and Steinbrenner he had begun in the clubhouse that day. "I'm saying shut up, Reggie Jackson. If he doesn't shut up he doesn't play and I don't care what George says. He can replace me right now."

Martin, clearly in his cups, was given what amounted to a fair-minded journalist's Miranda warning, namely, that Chass considered their conversation to be "on the record" and therefore both quotable and attributable. Martin replied that everything he said was on the record. Chass left to go to a phone to call the paper and tell them he would have a story for the next edition. When he returned, Martin continued with a litany of instances in which Jackson had been given preferential treatment; Steinbrenner had allowed him to report late to spring training and to travel to exhibition games in his Rolls Royce—"that damn Rolls," in Martin's resentful phrase—rather than riding the team bus.

Jackson, said Martin, was a liar; most recently, Jackson had claimed when he returned to the team after his suspension that Martin hadn't talked to him in the year and a half they had been together, a claim that was refuted by any number of photographs showing them together, in some cases horsing around and smiling. Jackson, Martin said, was a born liar. "The two of them," meaning Jackson and Steinbrenner, "deserve each other." Borrowing a phrase that he had heard a Yankee player use recently, Martin then uttered the words that would cost him his job. "One's a born liar and the other's convicted." Martin was referring in the latter instance to Steinbrenner's 1974 guilty plea to charges that he had made illegal corporate contributions to the 1972 presidential campaign of Richard

Nixon and had subsequently obstructed an investigation into the wrongdoing that he had perpetrated. Technically speaking, Steinbrenner was thus not a convicted liar, but Martin had landed a blow to the one thin spot on his boss's otherwise thick skin. Steinbrenner had ultimately paid a $15,000 fine in 1974 and was pardoned by President Ronald Reagan in 1989 in one of his last acts in office, but the criminal conviction proved to be a continually fresh brush with which antagonistic sports journalists could tar Steinbrenner, both darkly and accurately.

Chass, doing his duty, phoned the *Times* with Martin's quote and then called Steinbrenner for a reaction. Steinbrenner, normally voluble, was so struck by Martin's crack that he had no response. He called Al Rosen, president of the Yankees, to tell him what had happened and to order him to get out to Kansas City, where the team was headed from Chicago. Rosen in turn called Mickey Morabito, the Yankees' publicity director, and a round-the-horn series of phone calls from Steinbrenner to Rosen to Morabito continued into the night. The last call, in the early morning of July 24th, went to Bob Lemon, Rosen's former teammate on the Cleveland Indians team that beat the Red Sox in a one-game playoff for the 1948 American League pennant. Earlier in the season Lemon had been fired by Bill Veeck from his job as manager of the Chicago White Sox. At that time, Rosen had called to say "Keep yourself in cold storage, meat. Sooner or later I want you in the Yankee organization." Now, at approximately 1:00 a.m., Pacific time, Rosen reached Lemon at his home in Long Beach, California. After saying hello, Rosen added simply, before quickly hanging up, "Just wanted to know if you were home. We might be making a change."

Billy Ball

At the end of his 1949 season with the Oakland Oaks, his last in the minor leagues, Billy Martin was sold to the New York Yankees. In those days, before nationally-televised baseball games, minor league teams in smaller metropolitan areas like Oakland were the principal object of sports enthusiasm for fairly large regions of the country, and the big leagues were understood to exist in a wholly different time and place. A minor leaguer's promotion to the majors was thus a significant occasion; it both bestowed reflected honor on the minor league team and its community, and it gave the team's fans a connection to others in a bigger city through the sympathies they shared for the player who was once one of theirs. It was thus remarkable, although not inexplicable, that on the night Billy Martin was sold to the Yankees, an advertising blimp flying over Oakland's stadium communicated the message "BILLY MARTIN SOLD TO

YANKEES" to the fans below. Martin had made it to the big show.

But Martin was only part of the transaction. Going with him would be Jackie Jensen, the Most Valuable Player in the Pacific Coast League and an All-American football player during his days at the University of California. Martin was thus something of a garnish on the special of the day, albeit one whom Casey Stengel, his former mentor at Oakland and now Yankee manager, had insisted on as part of the deal. Martin's subordinate role in the transaction was emphasized by the fact that Jensen would receive $60,000 to sign with New York, an extravagant sum for a rookie in those days. Martin had been making $9,000 a year with the Oaks, while the Yankees would pay him only $7,500 for the privilege of wearing their pinstripes, and that much walking-around-money would have to fuel Martin's meanderings in New York City, a more expensive stroll than Oakland.

Of all the acts and omissions that made up the man who was Billy Martin, an obscure one stands out. With his elevation to the big leagues coming alongside that of Jackie Jensen, Martin's insecurities about his talents, his background and the life that lay ahead of him would be magnified. Jensen, the California golden boy, was touted by the Yankee press machine as a future star. Who, reporters asked Stengel, was the new fellow—Alfred Manuel Martin—the Yankees had added to their roster? "A hard-nosed, big-nosed player," answered Stengel, mixing the literal with the figurative, since Martin was both competitive and the owner of a nose most charitably described, with a nod to his Italian heritage, as "Roman". When the team assembled the next spring in St.

Petersburg, Martin's nose had undergone a transformation. In the euphemism of the day, it had been "bobbed". Billy Martin, a scrapper by instinct, had enough vanity in his truculent, tough-guy persona to require a nose job before he set foot on what was then the grandest stage for the performance of baseball's arts.

Martin had joined the Oakland team in September of 1947, where he was under the supervision of one Charles Dillon Stengel, known to the world as "Casey", the man who would manage the Yankees during the glory years of the 1950s. Stengel, who was notoriously critical of his players as a major league manager, was fond of Martin for the same reason that a teacher responds to a serious student. Although Stengel was blessed with teams that some New York fans considered incapable of losing, no one ever doubted that Stengel, despite his fractured syntax and grammar, was a scholar of the game. And while Stengel would manage players who had, for the most part, surpassed him in terms of formal education, he would never meet a player who was more eager to learn the game than Martin. "He was anxious to learn and he was very smart but not too smart that he couldn't listen and pick it up if you gave it to him," Stengel would observe some years later in a comment that displayed both his affection for Martin and his capacity for linquistic virtuosity. Even then, as a rookie, Martin was thinking of someday becoming a manager. In a New York *Post* column written barely a month into Martin's first season, Jimmy Cannon quoted Martin as asking him, "Do you think I can manage? I have all the credentials, you know. I can really run a game, run a team. I'll do it some day, you'll see."

While Martin was, like Zimmer, a player with merely

average skills, he displayed flashes of brilliance in clutch situations for the Yankees that fans remembered long after he left the club for the Kansas City Athletics. He began his major league career auspiciously, hitting safely twice in the same inning in his first two at bats, a record-keeping oddity that wasn't duplicated until August of 1996 (by the Chicago White Sox's Greg Norton), and one that is recalled with a trace of bitterness by Red Sox fans. The year was 1950, and the Yankees and the Red Sox met on Opening Day in Fenway Park. The Yankees had won the 1949 American League pennant as the Sox blew a game-and-a-half lead they had held going into the last weekend of the season. The Red Sox got off to a 9-0 lead on opening day of 1950, and the fans at Fenway were drunk with a mixture of intoxicants consisting of the excitement of Opening Day, the prospect of a victory over the Yankees, and revenge for the pennant that New York had stolen from them on the last day of the preceding season. The Yankees, with Martin replacing Jerry Coleman at second base, started to come back, however. They got four runs in the sixth inning, and in the eighth inning, after Yogi Berra singled leading off and Billy Johnson walked, Martin sent a 1-1 pitch from Red Sox starter Mel Parnell to Fenway's left-field wall for a double in his first major league at-bat. When Martin came up for the second time in the inning, he drove in runs eight and nine on a line single to left field, and the Yankees won 15-10.

As a fielder, Martin was considered to have quick hands and an economical style, but his star was eclipsed by the acrobatic grace of Jerry Coleman, the incumbent Yankee second baseman who at that time set the mark against which other players at the position were measured. Martin's World Series exploits have for the most part been forgotten outside of New York City, but he was, in his day, the predecessor to the Mr. October that Jackson would later become, a fact that Martin would call to Jackson's attention when the two met not as team-mates but as opponents in the 1981 American League Championship Series, in which Martin managed the Oakland Athletics and Jackson played his final year as a Yankee. "We'll go right at him," Martin said of Jackson at the time. "We're not afraid of him—'Mr. October,'" he added with a supercilious tone. "Hey, check my record. I was a better October hitter than him."

While Martin's assertion was not quite true (Jackson averaged .360 to Martin's .333 in World Series play), his World Series heroics included memorable play both at the plate and in the field. In the 1953 World Series against the Dodgers, he batted .500 and won the Babe Ruth Award as the outstanding player after his line drive single to center field won the final game. He batted .320 in the 1955 series and .296 in the 1956 series (both times against the Dodgers). Jackson's claim to greatness was based primarily on his ability to pro-duce runs in clutch situations, but Martin was his equal, if not in power at least in results. In the field, of course, Jackson never pretended to be anything other than a defensive liabil-ity, while Martin is remembered for at least one stirring play with his glove. In the seventh inning of the seventh game of the 1952 World Series with the Yankees leading 4-2, the Brooklyn Dodgers loaded the bases with two out, bringing up Jackie Robinson. Robinson hit a pop fly just slightly behind the pitcher's mound but into the sun. The dinky little hit, which would have been a routine out in a situation with less pressure on the defense, froze the infielders while Dodger runners scurried around the bases. It was Martin who, seeing that no one was taking the play, broke towards the mound and caught Robinson's fly just before it fell to the grass. The Yankees won the game and the series.

The drive that fueled Martin's will to win on the baseball field also found expression in his tendency to resort to fisticuffs as a method of dispute resolution. A partial listing of his bouts through the end of the decade under consideration here would include the following highlights:

YEAR	OPPONENT/AFFILIATION	DECISION
1950	Unidentified civilian	Won, fined $2,658 by U.S. Army
1952	Jimmy Piersall Boston Red Sox	No decision
1952	Clint Courtney St. Louis Browns	Won, fined $150 by American League
1953	Clint Courtney St. Louis Browns	Won
1953	Matt Batts Detroit Tigers	Draw
1956	Tommy Lasorda Kansas City Athletics	No decision
1957	Minnie Minoso Chicago White Sox	No decision, fined $150 by American League
1960	Gene Conley Philadelphia Phillies	Loss
1960	Jim Brewer Chicago Cubs	Won, $10,000 settlement paid
1966	Howard Fox Minnesota Twins (management)	Won
1969	Dave Boswell Minnesota Twins	Won

Billy Ball

Year	Opponent/Affiliation	Decision
1972	Jack Sears Detroit Tigers fan	Won
1974	Burt Hawkins Texas Rangers (management)	Won
1978	Ray Hagar Nevada State *Journal* reporter	Won, $7,500 settlement paid
1979	Joseph Cooper Marshmallow salesman	Won
1979	Cabdriver, Lake Shore Drive, Chicago	No decision

Martin fought with various bar patrons from the soft-shell crab-blessed waters of Baltimore to the citrus-fragrant groves of Anaheim. He fought his own players (pitchers Dave Boswell and Ed Whitson) and Reggie Jackson in the infamous No-Decision in the Dugout at Fenway Park in 1977. He fought whenever and wherever the mood suited him, or didn't. In short, he lived by the credo instilled in him by his mother. "Don't," she told him, "take no shit from nobody."

In addition to these bouts, Martin was also involved in more than a few battles royal, including a melee on ten-cent beer night in Cleveland during his tenure as manager of the Texas Rangers, and a group conflict at a topless bar called "Lacy" in Arlington, Texas. In the police report he filed after that altercation, in which he was set upon by a bouncer and another unknown "w/m" (white male), Martin indicated his willingness to prosecute the miscreants, giving his address as "Yankee Stadium" and his occupation as "Manager". For purposes of follow-up phone calls, he characterized his work hours with the word "Vary".

The Year of the Gerbil

The fight that had the greatest impact on Martin's career as a player was an altercation in New York's Copacabana Club that was the occasion, or perhaps more precisely the excuse, for his forced departure from the Yankees. The Copacabana incident occurred in the spring of 1957, following the Yankees' World Series victory of the preceding fall. Martin's birthday and Yogi Berra's fell within several days of each other, and Martin had organized a joint party for the night of May 15th, an open date for the Yankees. The game the night before was rained out, however, and it was rescheduled for the night of the party. Martin, a shy and unworldly youth before he left Oakland for New York, had become a more assiduous partygoer than teammates whose exposure to nightlife began at an earlier age, in much the same way that religious converts pursue their devotion with greater fervor than those baptized as babes. Since Martin's personality compelled him to seek the company of others and the relief of drink, the party would go on.

The Yankees started with dinner at Danny's Hideaway, moved on to the Waldorf-Astoria bar for drinks, and planned to end the night with a show at the Copacabana. In attendance were Martin (without a date), and Berra, Mickey Mantle, Whitey Ford, pitcher Johnny Kucks and Hank Bauer, with their wives. Singer Sammy Davis, Jr. was the attraction at the Copa. The players were seated next to a table of seventeen bowlers and their wives, who made racist remarks about the singer, an African-American who had converted to Judaism and married a white woman. At one point Bauer, who had experienced racial integration both as a solder in the army in World War II and as a Yankee, told one of the bowlers to shut up. Bauer's sensitivity—he was a close friend of Elston Howard, the Yankees' first black player—caused the group of bowlers to persist with their comments until Davis stopped the music, walked to the front of the stage and told them to keep quiet or leave. Bauer and the bowlers exchanged some more words, with Bauer telling the bowlers to shut up or get out. One Edwin Jones, a delicatessen owner, replied to Bauer with the words that have ignited a million fistfights—"Why don't you make me?"

Bauer accepted the challenge, and the two men rose from their seats and headed for a small alcove next to the men's room. Yogi Berra and Johnny Kucks temporarily restrained Bauer, while Martin and Leonard Jones, the delicatessen owner's brother, exchanged words. Martin and Leonard Jones negotiated a cease-fire, with Jones reportedly saying, "You take care of Bauer and I'll take care of my brother. We don't want no trouble." Like the Battle of New Orleans, the Battle of the Copacabana was fought after this official truce had been declared, as Edwin Jones was found lying on the nightclub's floor with a concussion, a possible fractured jaw and other injuries. "I didn't hit anybody," Bauer said. Several bouncers employed by the club had been seen in the area, and Bauer claimed that they must have inflicted the injuries upon the deli owner.

Bauer and his wife left the premises in a hurry and the other Yankees disappeared shortly thereafter, but a gossip columnist from the New York *Post* who was in the lounge of a hotel nearby heard a report of the brawl and hurried to the scene. The headline in the *Post* the next day was "Yankees Brawl in Copa," and each of the Yankees was summoned to appear before Dan Topping, the team's owner, to give his account of the story. Those stories were all variations on a theme expressed most elegantly by catcher Yogi Berra as "Nobody did nothin' to nobody." That version of the evening's events—namely, that someone other than Bauer was guilty of the battery—prevailed among the Yankees' owners and management, but general manager George Weiss still held Billy Martin accountable for organizing Mantle's birthday party in the first place. Weiss was notorious for his niggardly approach to player salaries and was paid a bonus by Yankee owners Del Webb and Dan Topping for keeping the club's payroll below a certain maximum level each year. He used the occasion of the Copacabana brawl to try to trade Martin and to install Bobby Richardson, whose skills were coming into sharper focus at the same time that Martin's were beginning to fade, at second base. Martin had also angered Weiss by his manner, which Weiss found abrasive and not in keeping with the Yankee tradition embodied in the demeanor of players such as Lou Gehrig and Joe DiMaggio— quiet, self-effacing and gentlemanly. Weiss was irritated by Martin's taste for nightlife, in one instance confronting him when a woman wrote to Weiss to complain that Martin had taken her daughter to a nightclub in the off-season. In a sentence whose overtones resound with the harmonies of a more innocent time, the woman wrote, "I didn't know ballplayers are allowed to go to nightclubs."

As the trading deadline of June 15th arrived in the summer of 1957, the Yankees were in Kansas City. Martin was on the bench, Richardson was at second, and Weiss was negotiating with the Kansas City Athletics, perennial occupants of last place in the American League and at that time as far removed from the lights of New York as a player could be and still call himself a major leaguer. Casey Stengel, Martin's mentor from his days in Oakland, found himself unable to bear the burden of the bad news and asked minor league director Lee MacPhail, later president of the American League, to convey to Martin the name of his new team. "Where am I going?" Martin asked MacPhail when he knocked on Martin's door that night. "Kansas City," MacPhail said. And so Martin's career as a Yankee was over.

Martin would last four more years in the majors, moving from Kansas City to Detroit to Cleveland to Cincinnati to Milwaukee to Minnesota. It was as if a man who had lost the deepest love of his life was incapable of committing himself to another. While Martin still had the will that had made him a tough out and a formidable competitor in New York, it had been diluted by his rejection at the hands of the Yankees, and his frustrations rose more quickly to the surface. Without the moderating influence of his surrogate father (Stengel) and brothers (Mantle and Whitey Ford), he began to explode at his managers, his teammates, his opponents and umpires with a frequency and severity that was out of proportion even for Martin.

Martin retired as a player in the spring of 1962, replaced by a younger man at second base for the Minnesota Twins. He was hired by the Twins as a scout and in 1965 became third base coach for the team. The years between his retirement as a player and his elevation to on-field management marked a period of relative calm for Martin, with no notable fistfights for four years. Martin would get his first chance to manage in

1968, when Twins owner Calvin Griffith asked him to run the club's Denver farm team. Griffith persuaded a reluctant Martin to take the job, and Martin accomplished two things that made a favorable impression on the Twins' upper management: he improved the team, moving them from sixth place to fourth, and he drew crowds, with attendance rising by 100,000 fans more than the previous season. Since the number of people attending Twins' games had declined and the team was struggling under manager Cal Ermer, Griffith decided to take a chance and gave Martin charge of the parent club, his first major league assignment.

Martin's performance in the big leagues mirrored his results in the minors. The Twins won the pennant (but lost the first American League divisional championship to the Orioles, who swept them in three games), and home attendance increased by 200,000. Yet he was gone almost as soon as the season had ended as a result of a combination of character traits, some previously apparent, some newly revealed, that would manifest themselves at every future stop in his career as a manager. First, Martin criticized the front office for decisions about players, going public when a young pitcher he favored was sent down to the Double A level of the minors rather than Triple A, where Martin felt he belonged. "Those guys don't know anything about players," Martin told a local columnist. "Why didn't they ask me?" The decision had been made jointly by Calvin Griffith, who liked to act as his own general manager, Griffith's brother-in-law and another member of the Twins' management, so Martin had managed a hat trick on the first slap shot at the executive suite in his professional career.

The second incident came in August, with the Twins on the road in Detroit and the pennant yet to be won. Martin was unique in his willingness to fraternize with—and drink with—his players, and he interceded in a fight that broke out between veteran outfielder Bob Allison and a young pitcher named Dave Boswell whom Allison had taken under his wing. Boswell objected to what he considered Allison's overly solicitous tutelage, told him he didn't want any more advice, and invited him to step outside when Allison took umbrage at Boswell's declaration of independence. The two players quit the Lindell A.C. (a bar near Tiger Stadium later frequented by Bill Lee and the Buffalo Heads, among others) to settle their differences. When Martin heard what was going on he joined the fracas and decked Boswell, the less valuable of the two players, with a flurry of punches. Calvin Griffith's approach to baseball management was more businesslike than that of most major league owners, and could be summarized as Sparky Lyle did some years later, namely, "Bring as many people into the park as inexpensively as possible." As such, while he was upset by the fact that Martin had been drinking with his players, he was outraged by the fact that his manager had deliberately damaged a piece of his inventory, even if he had used last-in, first-out accounting in choosing which item to scrap. The Twins were in the middle of a pennant race, however, and Griffith let Martin remain as manager.

The third incident came in the last game of the playoffs, when Martin chose to pitch Bob Miller, a mediocre pitcher, over Jim Kaat, the mainstay of the Twins' staff for many years. After Miller lost the game to end the series, Griffith criticized

Martin's decision both publicly and in a postseason interview with Martin. "Why Miller," Griffith asked Martin. "Because I'm the manager," Martin answered. Thus, while Martin reserved the right to criticize decisions made by management, he resented any intrusion on his prerogatives. In other words, as with the bargaining style supposedly adopted by the former Soviet Union, what was his was his, and what was someone else's was negotiable.

Martin, who was working on a one-year contract with the Twins, learned that he had been fired by hearing it on the radio while driving in Nebraska. Griffith had told reporters at the World Series in New York that he would be calling Martin soon with his decision on whether to renew the contract, and that it would not be to tell him he'd be managing the Twins the next year. What Griffith cited as the reason for his decision was Martin's insubordination; Griffith had asked Martin to consult with him on certain issues and to meet with him on particular occasions, and Martin, in Griffith's version of their relationship, had failed or refused to do so. Billy's prideful account was slightly different: "Calvin Griffith wanted me to go up to his office every day and tell him what I was doing on the field. The first day I went up he was on the phone and couldn't see me. The second day his secretary told me he was taking a nap. That was it—there was no third day." Griffith's decision was both counterintuitive—Martin had produced a winner—and unpopular for less tangible reasons, since Minnesota fans felt an affinity with Martin's win-at-any-cost attitude that the notoriously frugal Griffith could not inspire.

Martin was out of baseball for one season after leaving Minnesota, but was hired to manage the Detroit Tigers in

October of 1970. The Tigers had won the World Series in 1968 but had slipped to second in their division the next season and to fourth the following year. Martin brought the club back to second place in 1971 and to first place in their division in 1972, after which they lost the American League Championship Series three games to two to the Oakland A's. Martin, embittered by his failure to win the pennant in his second championship series in four years, began to drink more heavily than usual and to relate to his players in a more caustic manner, a pattern of behavior he would repeat at his subsequent managerial posts, moving from early and perhaps excessive enthusiasm to later frustration and then to bitterness. The same inner drive that enabled Martin to motivate his players and produce winners caused him to turn on them when, as might be expected, they turned out not to be the Yankee dynasty in which he had come of age.

Martin's departure from Detroit came late in August of 1973, his third year with the club. Martin had already resigned once that season after arguing with Tiger general manager Jim Campbell over the lackadaisical play of Willie Horton, and the Tiger clubhouse had been tense throughout the season. In August, two Detroit pitchers announced that they would throw spitballs in a game against the Cleveland Indians' Gaylord Perry, who had admitted to throwing a spitter in his book *Me and the Spitter*. Martin had attacked American League president Joe Cronin and baseball commissioner Bowie Kuhn the previous season for not punishing Perry, but he denied ordering his pitchers to lubricate the ball, a claim that was discounted heavily in sport's marketplace of opinion. Cronin could take no more, and informed Martin and his general manager on August 31, 1973, that Martin would be punished by a three-day suspension for flouting the rules of the game. Campbell, a man who disliked controversy, fired Martin two days later. Again, the team's move was perverse—Martin had turned the Tigers around—and unpopular; Martin was the subject of an admiring profile on Detroit television shortly after he was dismissed, and left town in a glow of municipal affection of the sort that usually warms the departing rear end of a successful manager who retires, not one who is dumped.

This time Martin wasn't out of work long. In a rapid series of managerial switches, Yankee manager Ralph Houk resigned because he couldn't work with George Steinbrenner, and was promptly hired by the Tigers; Whitey Herzog was fired as manager of the Texas Rangers on September 7th, and Martin was hired as the new manager of the Rangers the next day by Bob Short, a Minneapolis hotel owner whom Martin had once served as fund-raiser when Short ran for governor of Minnesota. Again Martin began by converting a team that had been stagnant into a group of aggressive ballplayers. The Rangers had finished sixth in 1973 but improved to second place in 1974. In 1975, Martin began to get into disagreements with the team's management over personnel, particularly David Clyde, a highly-regarded Texas high school pitcher, just as he had in Minnesota over Jim Kaat and in Detroit over Willie Horton. The team didn't improve that year, unlike the previous two seasons, and Martin again became bitter. His friend Bob Short sold his majority interest in the team and Martin was left to deal with new owner Brad Corbett, who was younger than Martin and had ideas of his own about the players who would wear his team's uniform. Martin, who

was prone to excuse his losses in the best of times, commiser-
ated to a reporter that he couldn't win with the players that
Corbett was forcing on him. Martin was fired for what Corbett
characterized as disloyalty. "One thing I'm not," Martin told
reporters, "is disloyal."

Martin had now been fired by Minnesota, Detroit and
Texas, and to some observers, including Yankee general manager Gabe Paul, was virtually unemployable. "That's the end
of Billy Martin," Paul is reported to have said to Bob Short,
the former Texas owner, whom Paul was visiting when he
heard the news that Martin had been fired by the Rangers.
"No one else will hire him now." "You've got to be kidding,"
Short said. "There will always be someone in this game to
hire someone like Martin," and he offered to bet Paul $500 on
the proposition. "He'll be hired within ten days," Short predicted, and offered to make a further bet on which team
would hire the three-time reject. Paul was curious, but not
ready to increase his risk. "Tell me," he said to Short. "The
Yankees." Paul said Short was crazy. "I know Steinbrenner
better than you do. George would never hire him." Short proposed fairly long odds, 10 to 1, $500 for Paul to win $5,000.
Short's confidence reflected inside information that made his
apparent gamble a sucker bet. Short knew Steinbrenner's
mind, a difficult task for the most clairvoyant of seers,
because George had asked for his help in signing Martin to
manage the Yankees. Short claimed that Paul had accepted
the wager. Paul said he hadn't, and refused to pay up. It is
unclear whether Paul was sincere in his denial or whether he
was simply displaying a tendency to parsimony that he had
acquired as a result of his long years in baseball management.

Paul had been traveling secretary for the Cincinnati Reds when a catcher named Willard Hershberger committed suicide by slitting his wrists in a Boston hotel. According to the joke that circulated among the players, when Paul arrived at the scene the first thing he did was search the room for the catcher's remaining meal money.

Martin had been Yankee manager for nearly two full seasons before Reggie Jackson joined the team. Steinbrenner pursued Jackson without consulting Martin and, once the manager learned of Steinbrenner's plan, against his wishes; Martin wanted to hire Joe Rudi, who like Jackson had chosen to become a free agent. Jackson was paid six times what Martin made, and, by virtue of the courtship ritual of free agency in which he had yielded to the suit of the Yankees' owner, was immediately on terms of intimacy with George Steinbrenner that Martin would never achieve; "I'm very happy to be coming to New York to play for George Steinbrenner," Jackson announced after he had signed with the Yankees, and Martin read that quote to mean that Jackson thought he didn't have to answer to his manager on the bench.

Jackson, for his part, did little to soothe the irritation that his preference in the owner's eyes caused Martin. When the Yankees assembled in Fort Lauderdale, Florida, for spring training in 1978, Jackson was absent, angering Martin. Steinbrenner, who seemed to confuse impetuosity with decisiveness, first supported Martin and then reversed himself, saying he had given Jackson permission to arrive late. "George understands me," Jackson said. "He's a businessman. I had business to take care of. Billy doesn't understand that. He's only a baseball manager."

While Martin in his time had been, like Jackson, an audible and frequent adversary of his managers, his opposition was always expressed as a disagreement on issues of baseball because baseball was all he cared about. He would never have thought to challenge his mentor, Casey Stengel, or any of his other managers on the grounds that baseball should be considered subordinate to some other pursuit. To do so would have called into question the notion of hustle, which was the principal reason for Martin's success as a ballplayer. Martin's mother once sent him a clipping with a quote by Ty Cobb from a San Francisco newspaper. The Detroit Tiger great, who was a cruel man and a racist but an undeniably great player and fierce competitor, said this about Martin:

> If I were managing a ball club I certainly would do everything within my power to keep from losing a player like Martin. He's a winner. I think of him as a throwback to the old days when players were supposed to fight for every advantage. Sure there are better hitters, better fielders, but for fight, spirit, and whatever it takes to win a game, Martin is something special.

The thing about Reggie Jackson that irritated Martin the most was consequently his apparently blasé attitude about winning and losing. While Jackson and Martin were both egotists of the first water, Jackson preferred to display the brilliant gem of his talent like the Hope diamond, when and where he felt like it, taking himself out of games if he didn't feel like facing the opposing pitcher or simply didn't feel like playing.

Martin wore the stone of his obsession in a pinky ring, ostentatiously and more frequently than good taste would have suggested. Casey Stengel would bench Martin at various times throughout his career whenever he felt that another player could help the team more. "In games like that," Yankee shortstop Phil Rizzuto would remember later, "Billy sat next to Casey and picked his brains—'Why did you do that, why did you do this?' He was always thinking baseball." The idea of Billy Martin taking himself out of game was thus beyond the power of his contemporaries to conceive. Jackson not only chose not to play on occasion, he was often dishonest about the cause of his bench-sitting. George Steinbrenner once asked him during Martin's tenure as manager why Jackson hadn't played after the outfielder had scratched his own name from the lineup because of the pitcher he would have had to face. "Beats me," said Jackson, deflecting the blame to an unsuspecting Martin.

But it was Jackson's insubordination and his lack of repentance over his petulant decision to keep bunting after Martin took off the bunt sign in Chicago that finally drove Martin to his self-destruction at O'Hare Airport. The fact that Steinbrenner supported Martin on that occasion did not, in Martin's mind, exonerate him from creating a relationship that Jackson believed gave him license to deal directly with the Yankees' owner rather than Martin. Once he was sober, however, Martin realized the gravity of his words, and called his agent to tell him he was thinking of resigning. The game that Monday night, July 24th, would be televised nationally, and Martin's sense of pride as a member of the Yankees since the days when Jackson was a toddler would compel him to give up the status he prized more than anything in his life rather than be fired in such a setting.

Martin wrote a short statement on a notepad bearing the insignia of Kansas City's Crown Center Hotel, just as Jackson had first expressed his intent to play with the Yankees less than two years earlier on stationery from Chicago's Hyatt Regency Hotel, the hotel nightstand serving as the escritoire for most spontaneous literary efforts by employees of major league baseball. Mickey Morabito, lately dispatched from New York by Steinbrenner along with Al Rosen, arrived in Martin's room to tell him that Rosen wanted to see him. He saw the notes in Martin's hand. "I'm quitting," Martin said. Morabito, pointing to Martin's notes, said, "You'll have to be able to read that," and offered to type it up. Martin agreed on the condition that Morabito had to return within ten minutes or Martin would make his announcement extemporaneously and without Yankee management represented. Morabito went back to his room and reduced Martin's six pages of handwritten notes to less than one typewritten page. Then he, Rosen and general manager Cedric Tallis returned to Martin's room and gave him the statement. "Keep in touch," Rosen said.

Morabito then arranged a hasty press conference, hiding Martin behind a fig tree until the reporters following the team could be alerted. Martin announced that he would read the statement but would not answer questions, saying, "I am a Yankee and Yankees do not talk or throw rocks." (A reasonably alert reporter might have wondered what Yankee besides Elston Howard Martin could possibly have had in mind.) "This team has a shot at the pennant and I hope they win it," he continued.

I owe it to my health and my mental well-being to resign. At this time I'm also sorry about those things that were written about George Steinbrenner. He does not deserve them, nor did I say them. (With this assertion, Martin had passed from the realm of hyperbole to that of fiction.) I'd like to thank the Yankee management, the press, the news media, my coaches, my players, the fans and most of all. . .

Martin then burst out crying and was touched by the hand of Phil Rizzuto, his friend and former teammate, who reached out to him from the assembled onlookers. They walked away from the crowd together, Rizzuto's arm around Martin's shoulders, remnants of an era when teams were made up of teammates and not free agents. As the reporters dispersed to file their stories, Reggie Jackson stood alone in the hotel lobby, staring down at his shoes.

Third base coach Dick Howser was dragooned into managing the team while Bob Lemon, their new commander, flew to the field of battle from his California home. The Yankees' disarray was epitomized that night when, with a two-run lead and two out in the home half of the seventh inning, ersatz outfielder Thurman Munson dropped a line drive by the Royals' Steve Braun and kicked it away, allowing two runs to score. Sparky Lyle was ineffective in relief and the Royals scored three more runs to win, 5-2. The Yankees had one more game to play in Kansas City and Ron Guidry made Lemon's debut as Yankee manager an easy one, striking out eight and shutting out the Royals on six hits, 4-0, with Reggie Jackson still on the bench as Paul Splitorff pitched for the Royals. It was Guidry's second consecutive shutout, and his record stood at 15-1 while his earned run average was 1.99.

On July 26th, back in Yankee Stadium, Lou Piniella homered in the bottom of the ninth to beat Cleveland's Rick Waits, 3-1, as Jackson again didn't play, prompting speculation that Lemon was afraid of the reaction Martin's nemesis would receive before the home crowd. Jackson returned to the lineup the next day, hitting a home run and two run-scoring singles in the opening game of a doubleheader as the Yankees won 11-0 behind Ed Figueroa, and going two for five in the second game, which the Indians won 17-5, knocking out Catfish Hunter in the first inning. It was the first time in Hunter's career that he had failed to retire a batter.

The personality of the man who replaced Billy Martin as manager of the Yankees can be drawn with three quick strokes; he was a tea drinker, he read *Reader's Digest*, and he wore bifocals. In short, the image he projected was that of a comfortable old man sitting in his easy chair, rather than a prideful, hard-drinking baseball lifer resentful of the fool of an owner that he had to work for. In what must surely rank as the greatest understatement in Yankee history, Lou Piniella compared Lemon to Martin by saying, "Bob's a little more placid." The Yankees proceeded to win eight of their first nine games under Lemon, and Piniella, for one, attributed the results to Lemon. "We're playing a little better now," he said. "The team is more relaxed," because, he thought, Lemon's personality was easier to deal with.

Robert Granville "Bob" Lemon was, like Billy Martin and

Don Zimmer, a career baseball man. Unlike either of them, however, it was said of Lemon that, like the converse of Will Rogers, he'd never met a man who didn't like him. He had broken into the major leagues with Cleveland as a utility infielder, but he was soon converted into a pitcher and won twenty games six times in seven years over one stretch, numbers exceeded among Red Sox pitchers only by Cy Young. He had first managed in the major leagues with Kansas City in 1970, and then again with Chicago in 1977 after a series of subordinate positions. He was fired by the White Sox on June 29th of 1978 in favor of Larry Doby, the first African-American to play in the American League. At one point in the season a swap of Martin and Lemon had been discussed by Steinbrenner and White Sox owner Bill Veeck, but it had not been consummated. Now Lemon, who had barnstormed with Martin through Japan on a team of American all-stars and who claimed to like him, was charged with cleaning up the mess that his predecessor had left behind, in much the same way that the treasurer of a fraternity has to make sure that the kegs are returned for the deposit after the party is over. "I don't think Boston has won it yet," was all he would say when asked about his team's chances.

Lemon's palliative influence appeared to be spreading by osmosis through the Yankees' hardened membranes. Even a player as irredeemably embittered as Sparky Lyle seemed to benefit from his calming influence. "The best thing they did was hire Lemon," he said after the season was over. "The guy is so easy to play for." Lemon was capable of communicating at a lower pitch than Martin's three frequencies of exhortation, sarcasm and anger, and Lyle appreciated knowing when he would be used and for what purpose. Lyle had liked Martin at first but had become cynical as a result of the erratic announcement, selective enforcement and ultimate abandonment of trivial rules such as a requirement that players wear coats and ties when traveling. Lemon, he noticed, asked only one thing of his players: that they hustle. If one of them didn't, the manager sat the man down until, in Lemon's words, "he walks through my office door and tells me he's ready to play."

While Lemon's arrival acted as a salve to soothe hurt feelings in the Yankee clubhouse, Martin's abrupt departure remained an irritant to the occupants of the bleacher seats at Yankee Stadium. Whatever else can be said about Billy Martin, it was always and everywhere true that he was loved by the fans of baseball teams that he managed. This sympathy was enhanced, in the case of Yankee fans, by Martin's intensity of play during his career with the team during the years from 1950 to 1957 when they won seven pennants and five World Series. The resignation of Billy Martin on July 24th was thus received by Yankee fans with a higher level of dudgeon than had been the case when he was fired in Minnesota, Texas and Detroit. What most irked the team's followers was the lenity of the punishment imposed on Jackson—a suspension with no fine—for his insubordinate attempt to bunt July 17th. As popular disapproval of the disproportionality of the sentence became apparent, Yankee management went into a posture of defensive alertness; Yankee employees were not allowed to answer reporters' questions, and banners bearing obscene references to Steinbrenner were confiscated by Yankee Stadium security guards. In what Herbert Marcuse would have considered an instance of repressive tolerance, however, signs bearing pro-Billy/anti-Reggie sentiments such as "Billy's the One Who's Sane, Reggie's the One to Blame" were permitted. Ronald Reagan might have cited as an example of capitalism in the service of the spirit of individualism the fact that the Billy Martin photo button previously on sale for $1 at Yankee Stadium jumped in price to $1.50 and then to $2 before further commercial sales of the symbol of vicarious rebellion against Yankee management were banned.

Steinbrenner, despite his authoritarian personality, was also a showman who had backed Broadway plays (most notably, the Tony Award-winning *Applause*), and he realized that the role left to him after Martin's bathetic departure was bad box office. The Yankee owner began to monitor telephone calls coming in to Yankee Stadium following Martin's press conference; over two hundred calls backing Martin were received the day he resigned, and the volume and intensity of his support grew daily. Steinbrenner finally shut down the switchboard and instructed the Yankees' public relations department to tell the press the calls were running 50-50 for and against Martin; in truth, the fans' loyalty to Martin was never greater, a fact whose broad acceptance caused Yankee press releases to be met with more than the usual measure of reportorial skepticism during this period. At the same time the New York papers began to speculate that the New York Mets would hire Martin if Steinbrenner would let the manager out of his contract. Steinbrenner would be damned if he did, since Martin could be expected to draw fans to Shea Stadium and away from the Yankees, and damned if he didn't, since a refusal to release Martin from his contract would result in negative popular reaction too awful to contemplate. Americans may not know much about history, but they remember that Lincoln freed the slaves.

And thus it came to pass that, two days after the Yankees negotiated Martin's departure, they began negotiations with Doug Newton, his agent, to secure his return. Martin emerged from his Hasbrouck Heights, New Jersey, apartment to meet with Steinbrenner at the Carlisle Hotel in Manhattan. Steinbrenner agreed to honor his obligations to Martin for 1979 and to pay him $100,000 during 1980. The clause in Martin's existing contract that gave the club the right to terminate him for conduct detrimental to the Yankees—a standard that Martin found frustratingly vague and inconsistently applied (see Jackson, Reggie)—was dropped. Details as small as Martin's expense account and company car were finalized. Steinbrenner insisted only on two moral victories: Martin would admit publicly that he had made the offending remarks for which he had been fired, and he would apologize for them.

On July 29th the Yankees were scheduled to play the Twins, with the game to be preceded by an Old-Timers' Day game. July would be the Red Sox' first sub-.500 month of the season, while the Yankees, who were 4-9 for the month at one point, had won eight of their last ten games. Still, New York was in third place, eight games behind the Red Sox, and the Yankees needed a revival, both as a baseball team and as an entertainment commodity. Steinbrenner accordingly decided to spring his surprise on the players and the fans during the Old-Timers' game. Martin was brought to Yankee Stadium in a limousine and taken to a small room that contained only a chair. The room was sufficiently secluded that Yankee workmen who had keys to it were known to use it as a hideout from their bosses. Martin sat there for four hours with his agent; his uniform and his old roommate and drinking buddy Mickey Mantle were brought to him by Mickey Morabito, who had played Dr. Kevorkian at Martin's assisted suicide in Kansas City. "Ain't this somethin'," was about all Mantle could find to say.

After the retired Yankees had left the clubhouse, Martin was moved to a boiler room above the home team's dugout. Once all of the other players had been introduced, the tenor of the program shifted for an announcement. Current manager Bob Lemon was to assume the position of general manager in 1980, public address announcer Bob Sheppard said. Managing the Yankees that year, he continued, "and hopefully for many seasons after that will be, Number 1"—but at this point his voice was drowned out by a roar. Martin had emerged from the dugout and joined his teammates from the past, and the ovation that followed his reunion with them was estimated to have lasted ten minutes, nearly as long as any such outburst in Yankee history.

The Boss

With Bucky Dent's return to the lineup on July 30th, the Yankees were at full strength for the first time since June 10th, a stretch of 49 games. And Reggie Jackson was hitting again, going 16 for 28 with seven runs batted in since returning from his suspension, even though he seemed disturbed by something, although it wasn't clear what. He took his nameplate down from his locker and replaced it with a piece of athletic tape with the words "Badland Territory 44 Blame." While Jackson's behavior would have seemed perfectly natural in the clubhouse atmosphere that prevailed when Martin was in charge, under the peaceful regime that Bob Lemon had installed it seemed out of place, in much the same way that a pedestrian muttering to himself goes unnoticed on the streets of Manhattan but would be institutionalized for doing the same thing in, say, Poughkeepsie.

Although he wasn't talking, Jackson's distemper stemmed from the fact that Martin had been reinstated, disrupting a rare period of calm in his tenure with the Yankees. "You can't imagine what that was like," he said in a state of wonderment. "You come to the park and there are no reporters around your locker, waiting to get your reaction to the latest story in the papers. You can dress in peace. You can pick your game bat out, think of the opposing pitcher, clear your mind. . . .The art of hitting is combining physical skill with mental discipline, concentration, seeing that baseball in the pitcher's hand, studying it, watching it. . . your mind totally on that mission. I could breathe free again." As a reader can judge from this reverie, Jackson was a fabulist whose capacity for fiction and figurative speech made Martin's accusation true—he was a born liar, if by liar one means a mind capable of fiction, trope, metaphor, irony, sarcasm, synecdoche, simile and numerous other forms of deviant discourse.

Martin's assessment of Steinbrenner was accurate as well. George M. Steinbrenner, III, born on the fourth of July, 1930, would be indicted forty-four years later by a federal grand jury in Cleveland for falsifying records and obstructing a federal investigation relating to illegal corporate campaign contributions by his business, American Ship Building, to the Committee to Re-Elect the President (namely, Richard Nixon), an organization known by the ominous acronym "CREEP". In Steinbrenner's version of the events that led to the charges, his payments were baksheesh intended to solve various problems with government agencies that American Ship was experiencing, including antitrust scrutiny, a $5.4 million dispute over a contract with the Coast Guard, and a $10,000 fine as a result of a fatal fire aboard a ship under construction. In truth, Steinbrenner's scheme pre-dated these problems and included payments to Democratic officials as well. Steinbrenner's plan called for the payment of apparent bonuses to himself and certain trusted employees. The monies would be turned over by the individuals to various political organizations, thereby avoiding the ban on corporate campaign contributions. Steinbrenner claimed, among other things, that despite the tangled web he wove he was unaware that corporate contributions were illegal. This was implausible; he had previously been an active participant in fund-raising activities on the national level for the Democratic party.

Martin had been fired because he had attacked Steinbrenner's reputation as an honest man. Steinbrenner was punctilious in his repayment of debts, going so far as to repay corporate debts of the bankrupt Cleveland Pipers basketball team for which he wasn't personally liable because he was embarassed that he had induced investors to part with their money. He cultivated political connections for reasons having to do both with ego gratification and bottom-line business considerations; he was a friend of congressmen from both houses (to the extent that the relationship between a politician and an individual who can raise ample campaign funds is properly characterized as friendship), and his efforts to obtain federal subsidies for Great Lakes shipping companies had resulted in the passage of the Maritime Act of 1970, a law that allowed the Kinsman Marine Transit Co., the business that had been in his family for more than a century, to survive. His good name and access to politicians were thus matters of some importance to him.

Martin had been rehired, however, and this despite the widespread disbelief in both the sincerity of his apology and his initial denial that he had called his boss a liar. Steinbrenner was thus reluctantly forced to admit that, at least by implication, he had been less than honest in the CREEP episode. In his mock-contrite revision of this period of his life Steinbrenner was disingenuously critical of himself, saying that while he was convicted of an isolated "election violation," "that's part of life, that's what you live with, and I live with the plaques and few honors that I managed to get (he offhandedly reminded a sports writer) the same way I live with that; and it's going to come up again and again, and I should live with it." In other words, Steinbrenner would have to bear the burden of his failings in the realm of political ethics just as he lived daily with the ineffable suffering endured by someone who has been named Outstanding Young Man of the Year by the Ohio Jaycees.

As to whether Steinbrenner was guilty of something more than an election violation, let facts be submitted to a candid world. On April 7, 1972, a new campaign finance law was to go into effect that would require disclosure of the names of donors of large gifts. In March of that year Steinbrenner had met with Herbert Kalmbach, a representative of CREEP who was also President Nixon's personal attorney. He emerged from that meeting with the impression that a contribution of $100,000 more or less would facilitate AmShip's proposed acquisition of a competing shipyard, a transaction that would be subject to review by the Justice Department and the Federal Trade Commission for antitrust considerations. At Steinbrenner's direction, Robert E.

Bartlome, AmShip's corporate secretary, informed one Matthew E. Clark, Jr., among several other employees, that he was going to get a $5,000 bonus and to make out two checks totaling $3,100 to organizations whose names had been supplied to Steinbrenner by CREEP. The company deducted $1,300 from the bonus to pay Clark's income tax liability, and the remaining $600 went into a slush fund. Steinbrenner worked a similar calculation on a $75,000 bonus he arranged for himself, and a courier flew the combined contributions to Kalmbach on the day the checks were cut, just meeting the deadline established by the new law.

Common Cause, the good-government group, filed a suit to obtain the names of individuals whose contributions were received on the day before the law went into effect. CREEP succeeded in destroying its records of the contributions, but Rose Mary Woods, the secretary to President Nixon who would later become better known for an erasure of an Oval Office tape recording, did not. After the names of the AmShip contributors became public, Steinbrenner had Bartlome prepare a memo dated April 5, 1972, the day before checks were issued to employees, but actually prepared on a later date, to make it appear that the payments were part of a bonus plan approved in the fall of 1971. Steinbrenner then obtained the company's records of the bonuses and destroyed them. The participating employees were then asked to sign statements certifying that their bonuses were in "no manner, directly or indirectly, conditioned upon or subject to the making by me of any contribution, whether charitable, political or otherwise," and that at no time had "any director, officer or supervisory employee of the company, directly or indirectly, directed, requested or suggested that I make contributions to any charitable or religious group or organization or to any political organization or candidate and that any contributions to any charitable or religious group or organization or to any political organization or candidate and that any contributions so made by me during the year 1972 were entirely voluntary and of my own choosing." Like any too-earnest effort to cover one's tracks, the statements, backdated to 1971, did more to alert the FBI to an attempt at concealment than they did to throw the legal bloodhounds off the scent.

At Steinbrenner's direction, AmShip's corporate secretary was first directed to characterize the bogus bonuses to its employees as rewards for meritorious work on the company's claim against the Coast Guard, but this clearly wasn't true. AmShip didn't get a cent back from the government out of that dispute and had to pay an additional $200,000 penalty after the individuals selected by Steinbrenner had passed on their illegal contributions. In April of 1973, with the Watergate investigation under way, Steinbrenner called in the company's corporate secretary and told him to change the minutes of the board of directors' meetings to indicate that the bonuses were compensation for "effective operation of the company during the year just ended." In testimony before the Senate Watergate committee, Bartlome, the company's record-keeper, was asked: "Mr. Steinbrenner directed you to change the minutes?" His answer: "Yes." Prosecutors went after Steinbrenner alone among more than twenty other corporate contributors because he, unlike the others, had tried to cover up what he'd done and then tried to cover up the cover-up.

The FBI began to interview various officers of AmShip,

who somewhat sheepishly followed a script prepared by Steinbrenner to the effect that the contributing employees had been simultaneously struck by a desire to contribute to President Nixon's reelection campaign in gratitude for his role in the passage of the Maritime Act of 1970. This cultlike declaration of mass faith in a distant leader gave rise to suspicion on the part of the inquisitors, and a federal grand jury was impaneled. Faced with the terrible majesty of the criminal courts and the images of long servitude they are capable of inspiring, the human spokes of Steinbrenner's wheel within a wheel began to break. Three of the officers closest to the hub of the conspiracy—Bartlome, Clark, and company treasurer Stanley Lepkowski—decided they weren't going to perjure themselves, and they so informed Steinbrenner. Efforts to quash the subpoenas were unsuccessful, and the recusants were tortured with Steinbrenner's entreaties to accept the doctrine of the immaculate conception of their bonuses even as they were being driven to the grand jury hearing.

Steinbrenner hired Edward Bennett Williams, a highly-regarded Washington lawyer who would hold interests in various professional sports teams in his lifetime, to represent him before the grand jury. Employees of AmShip were told that their interests were in conflict with Steinbrenner's and that the company would hire a separate attorney to represent each of them. To this generous offer was added the proviso that the employees would be required to reimburse the company for the cost of counsel if their testimony should result in "improbity or illegality." To a lawyerly mind this may seem like a fair and ethical condition; after all, who could fault a business that valued truth and justice more highly than a gratuitous fringe benefit it extended to its workers? A deponent made self-conscious by the baleful glare of the bald eagle on a summons could give these words a slightly different reading, however: If I tell the truth, I'll have to pay, but if I tell it George's way, I won't.

Steinbrenner persisted in his program of shopping for political support even as the grand jury was hearing the testimony that would lead to his indictment. He began a fake expense account program under which employees signed blank reimbursement forms that were filled in by the company in order to justify cash deposits to a slush fund. Contributions from this pot were made to, among others, Senator Danuel Inouye (D-Hawaii), a member of the Senate Watergate committee, in July and August of 1973, as the committee was meeting before a national television audience. His money, his pleadings and his browbeatings of employees were, for one of the few times in Steinbrenner's life, unavailing. On April 5, 1974, he was indicted on fourteen separate counts that alleged violations of federal laws including obstructing an FBI investigation and suborning perjury. Thus, contrary to Steinbrenner's later claim, violating election laws wasn't the half of his problems.

Despite the testimony of two high-ranking corporate officers and another employee involved in the scheme, Steinbrenner maintained that he was innocent. "I feel it very important that I state publicly why I have chosen to fight. . . .There is no way I could plead guilty to a charge involving willful conspiracy. . .or any other charge that may be part of an indictment, because I am not guilty of any such violation." A short time later he did just that, as he pleaded guilty in

August of 1974 to the crimes of making illegal campaign contributions, a felony, and to two misdemeanors, devising a
false and misleading explanation for his employees to tell the
FBI and attempting to influence and intimidate employees to
lie to the grand jury. He could have been sentenced to six
years in jail, but instead he was fined only $15,000 and his
company was fined another $20,000.

The path from the trade of journalism to the profession of
law has been described by one who traveled it as the route of
the intellectual hobo, which may explain why a reporter facing Steinbrenner and Williams on the steps of the federal
courthouse viewed the Yankee executive's guilty plea as a fit
subject for further effort on the part of his counsel. "Will you
appeal?" he asked Williams. To that newsman, at that time,
$15,000 must have seemed a sum beyond the dreams of
avarice, while the mention of the same figure to a young asso-
ciate in Williams's law firm would have been met with a
slightly lower level of interest. "Appeal what?" Williams
replied. In the lawyer's view, there was nothing not to like in
the result he had obtained for his client.

August

O n August 2nd the Red Sox came to New York for a two-game series, leading the Yankees by six and a half games but having lost 12 of their last 15 games. Boston was hitting only .199 over its last 14 games, and Jim Rice, at one point so feared by opposing pitchers, had sunk into a .240 hitting slump. Rick Burleson had played on July 28th after missing 17 games, but he had not yet had an appreciable impact on the Red Sox' play. Since Burleson's return to the lineup the Sox were 2-3, and they were vulnerable to a comeback in the same way that a boxer who has absorbed a series of body blows while complacently holding onto a lead is liable to suffer more from a shot to the head than he would have in the opening rounds. Kill the body, goes the old fighter's maxim, and the head dies. The Yankees gave the Sox a staggering blow to open the series, pushing five runs across the plate before the Sox scored, but Boston recovered, scoring two runs in the fourth inning on a wild pitch by Dick Tidrow and an infield out. In the sixth inning Goose Gossage came in from the bull pen after throwing only fifteen warm-up pitches and walked Yastrzemski for one run and then walked Jack Brohamer for another.

In the eighth inning after Jim Rice doubled, Gossage had an 0-1 count on Yastrzemski when the New York skies opened up and a cold rain delayed the game for half an hour. When play resumed, Gossage threw a wild pitch that allowed Rice to go to third base, and Yaz tied the game with a sacrifice fly to center. After fourteen innings of play the time was one o'clock a.m. American League rules prohibit clubs from beginning an inning after that hour, and play was postponed. When the game resumed the next day the Sox got four hits and two runs to win, 7-5. The way in which those runs scored was particularly annoying to members of the Yankees who were hoping that Martin's departure would cause Reggie Jackson to come out of his funk and display some degree of hustle. In the seventeenth inning Dwight Evans hit a foul ball off Ken Clay into right that Jackson pursued lackadaisically and then watched as it fell into the stands. He then began his return to right field with the same nonchalance that marked his pursuit of Evans's foul. Clay, meanwhile, had turned to face the batter on the incorrect assumption that Jackson would return to fair territory with some degree of alacrity, and he delivered a pitch to Evans while Jackson was still jogging back to his position. Evans connected, hitting a pop-up to shallow right field that fell for a single because Jackson was out of position. Butch Hobson then advanced Evans to third on a hit-and-run, Burleson singled to right to score Evans, and a single by Jim

Rice gave the Sox their two-run margin of victory. Jackson tried to shift responsibility to Cliff Johnson, who was catching at the time, for failing to call time until Jackson was ready. "Ain't that a bitch," said Johnson. "They blaming me for losing that game." Mike Torrez beat the Yankees in the second game, 8-1, and the Sox' lead was back up to eight and one-half games.

On August 4th the Sox fell to Milwaukee, 6-2, as Bill Lee lost his sixth game, while New York lost to Baltimore, 2-1, with Guidry losing only his second decision of the year. The Sox recovered to beat the Brewers 8-1 August 5th, but the Yankees countered with a 3-2 win over Baltimore. The Sox lead was still eight and a half games. That week a story on Bill Lee appeared in *Sports Illustrated* that repeated his characterization of Don Zimmer as a gerbil. Like lightning and thunder, Lee's words may have crackled when first uttered, but by the time they were repeated in print in a national magazine they gave off a duller noise. Amid the pressure of the now-hotter summer of the American League Eastern division race, and with Lee having lost six straight games, the left-hander's metaphor for his beleaguered manager seemed not quite so poetic. Dick Williams, Red Sox manager from 1967 through 1969 who went on to win two World Series with the Oakland A's, was the first to identify the cause of the highly variable quality of the left-hander's humor; "Bill Lee," he said, "is a lot funnier when he's winning."

Meanwhile Tiant, whose cojones continued to serve as a counterweight to Lee's affected gravitas, provided the ballast necessary to right the Sox with a 4-0 win over Milwaukee August 6th, his third shutout of the year and the 46th of his career, striking out nine. Catfish Hunter responded with a 3-0 victory over Baltimore and fellow Hall of Fame shoo-in Jim Palmer, throwing a five-hit shutout, the 42nd of his career. It was Hunter's first shutout since July 21, 1977, his first complete game since August 25, 1977, and it meant that Hunter had now pitched 17 consecutive scoreless innings. The Cat, the New York media agreed, had regained his old form, and they concocted a facile rhyme that was picked up by his Yankee teammates, who murmured in stage whispers as they passed his locker, "The Cat is back."

For the Yankees, Hunter's redemption had come at an opportune time. The veteran pitcher's right shoulder had required manipulation in late June, a procedure that mandated that he be given general anaesthesia. As he slept, the discussion in the visitors' clubhouse at Yankee Stadium, then occupied by the Red Sox as they celebrated a 4-1 victory over New York, turned to Hunter's fate. The Sox wished him well—Yaz said he hoped he'd come back to pitch, and George Scott felt moved to offer him a tribute on the occasion of what could have been a proud competitor's pitching obsequies. "I'll tell you one thing," the man they called "Boomer" shouted to no one in particular.

> The man don't have nothing to be ashamed of, no matter how he goes out. He went out and challenged peoples. He went out and beat peoples. He battle your tail. The man coulda alibied a lot of times, 'cause he was pitching hurt, but I never heard him alibi once, cause he ain't that type. I'd give him the ball in a big game before I'd give it

to anyone, not no Tom Seaver, not nobody. He
pitched his 300 innings and won his 20 games for
years. He's a Hall of Famer, Jack. (All dialect as
rendered by the New York *Times*.)

Hunter's comeback over the course of the year had been
like a long, drawn-out faith healing, given the exigencies of
pitching to major league hitters and actually getting them out.
In the month of June he had pitched only one inning after a
spell on the 21-day disabled list. That inning came on June
21st against Boston, in the rubber game of the first Yankees-
Red Sox series of the season, and Hunter's performance had
been awful, as he gave up four hits, including two home runs,
before striking out Yastrzemski with the bases loaded. Some
writers had suggested at the time that Yaz had gone down
intentionally, but given Yaz's competitive nature this is
unlikely. The next day Hunter again went on disability leave,
this time at his own suggestion, to see if something could be
done to restore his arm to the strength of his early years in the
majors. At the time, he had already secured his place in baseball history as one of only four pitchers to have won 200
games before turning 31; the others were Cy Young, Christy
Mathewson and Walter Johnson. He had been pitching in pain
since 1976, however, when he nonetheless won 17 games; the
next year he would win 9 games, and in 1978 he had won only
2 games when he began the program of arm manipulation
that enabled him once again to cock his arm, however
unsteadily, in imitation of the effortless motion that had characterized his early years with the Athletics.

On August 8th the Sox beat the Indians 9-7, and New York

beat Milwaukee 3-0 with Dick Tidrow holding the Brewers to three hits in eight innings and Gossage getting two strikeouts in the ninth inning and the save. The Sox' lead stood at eight and a half games. On August 9th Billy Martin called a press conference to explain what his duties with the Yankees would be until he returned to manage the team in 1980. A reporter diverted his stream of consciousness from its intended course, however, and a torrent poured forth over the rocks of his relationship with Reggie Jackson. Jackson, said Martin, was the main reason he had resigned, but he had no malice in his heart towards the man; it was just that it was "sickening" playing in New York, he told the members of the working press. "I didn't treat him like a superstar because he doesn't play like a superstar," Martin added. "Sometimes I even rate Fred Stanley above Jackson."

The concealed weapon of Martin's hatred for Jackson was visible through the cloak of his pretended candor, and the race of the tattling reporters to the newsroom was on. When George Steinbrenner heard that Mickey Morabito had set up the news conference for Martin, he lashed out at the Yankees' public relations man. "If this hits the papers tomorrow, you're fired," he threatened. But like a deus ex machina improbably appearing in the last act of a Greek drama, a pressmen's strike suddenly halted publication of New York's three daily newspapers, the *Times*, the *Daily News*, and the *Post*. Martin's quotes never made it off the pages of the reporters' notebooks, and Morabito's job was saved. New York beat Milwaukee 8-7 that day when, down by four runs in the bottom of the ninth, the Yankees scored five runs to win, two on a home run by Mickey Rivers and the winning run on a squeeze play that featured a misfired bunt by Lou Piniella that was mishandled by the Brewers' catcher, allowing Chris Chambliss to score.

In an ideal world, coverage of baseball by the news media would have no more effect on the game itself than a road map has on soil erosion; the game would exist as a series of human actions and decisions and the writing and reporting about it would occupy the paper on which it was recorded or the signals by which it was transmitted, and never the twain would meet. The world of that imagining does not exist; professional athletes are different from the rest of us in many ways, but one of the most important is that they have to answer questions about the quality and quantity of their work at the end of every day, usually before they've changed their clothes, and their answers are made public before they next take the field. The normal process of seepage and percolation by which workplace problems are submerged and come to the surface over time is correspondingly compressed, with the result that the possibility of explosive outbursts between players and between player and manager is enormously increased.

As a result, the local press plays a role in the progress of a team's fortunes that is rarely examined and never for long, since it would require the sort of self-regarding analysis on the part of the news media that is difficult for all of us and painful for most. It hardly needs to be mentioned that such self-examination would be unlikely to increase a newspaper's circulation or a television or radio station's ratings. Double-blind testing of the relationship between the mood of local journalists and the success of the sports teams that they cover is impossible in an open society where free speech is protected by law. We can only look to those situations where a team has

operated under both intense press scrutiny and its absence as
a result of external forces, such as newspaper strikes and the
presence or absence of particularly newsworthy individuals.
While the sample is small, what evidence there is indicates
that the cynicism of a press corps, which in small amounts is
essential to its proper functioning, can be harmful if present in
excessive amounts, in much the same way that the human
body cannot function without bile but becomes jaundiced if
that humor becomes part of its lifeblood. In 1968, the Detroit
Tigers won the World Series while the local newspapers went
unpublished during a strike. In 1971 the Pittsburgh newspapers were on strike from May to September and the Pirates
won the pennant. The Yankees would similarly win 35 games
while losing 14 during the strike that started August 10th. As
Bucky Dent would later point out, during the strike "everybody started thinking about playing baseball instead of all the
nitpicky, chaotic stuff that you read about in the papers."

Thus, on the day the Yankees would begin a period of
play in which they would go unwatched by disapproving
eyes like children playing in the twilight of late summer, the
presses in Boston rolled on, with the *Globe* advertising a com-
plimentary team picture to be included in the next Sunday's
edition by the claim that the "'78 Red Sox is (sic) a great ball
club—one of the best ever in Boston and in baseball history."
The Yankees won their fifth game in a row that day, beating
Milwaukee 6-0 on a three-hitter by Ron Guidry, while the Sox
were losing to Rick Wise and the Cleveland Indians 5-1, the
third time in the 1978 season that Wise had beaten his former
teammates, each time allowing them only one run. Bill Lee
had pitched a one-hitter for five innings but had to leave the

game with a blister on his thumb. Did Wise find beating the Red Sox to be a pleasurable experience, a reporter asked. "Sure I do. Damn right I do," replied the erstwhile Buffalo Head.

The next night in Baltimore the Yankees won when, with Catfish Hunter holding the Orioles to four hits through five innings, the rains came causing the game to be called and giving Hunter his sixth win of the season. The Sox, meanwhile, lost to Milwaukee, 10-5. The Yankees' six-game winning streak came to an end the next day as the Orioles beat them, 6-4, and the Sox regained their composure, taking a double-header from Milwaukee. Jim Rice hit his twenty-eighth home run, and Jim Wright, after 36 relief appearances, started and lasted seven innings to give the Sox the promise of a rainy-day reserve for a rotation that might need it down the stretch. Both Rick Burleson and Jerry Remy had 17-game hitting streaks going and Mike Torrez won his fourteenth game the next day against Milwaukee; Torrez's record was 14-6, and he led the team in wins.

The forces of nature again intervened in the course of the Yankees' comeback August 13th, this time causing time to be called in the middle of a New York rally in the top of the seventh inning that had given the Yankees a 5-3 lead in Baltimore. The Yankees protested that the Baltimore grounds crew didn't act quickly enough to protect the field after play was suspended, leaving the field in an unplayable condition and causing the game to be called with the score settled as of the last complete inning—Orioles 3, Yankees 0. Communal frustration among the Yankees nearly caused a spontaneous work stoppage as the players considered a clubhouse vote to refuse to play the next day in protest over the iniquitous interruption. Reggie Jackson positioned himself as a leader of the insurgents, and Sparky Lyle was cast against type in the role of labor peacemaker. "Let's hold a meeting and put not playing to a vote," Jackson suggested. If they did, Lyle demurred, it would set off a dispute between the American League and the players' union that wouldn't resolve anything and would jeapordize negotiations for players whose contracts expired at the end of the season. Lyle recommended that the issue be referred to Bob Lemon, whose cooler head could be relied upon to consider the matter in a more tranquil fashion. Lemon called a meeting the next day and told the players, "I know it's been tough and we got screwed last night, but the same thing happened to them two nights ago when they called the game. I want you guys to try and forget about it and go out and win this game." The players recognized the wisdom of that advice, and went out and beat the Orioles and Jim Palmer, 4-1.

While the Yankees were winning the Sox were losing to Milwaukee, 4-3, getting 13 hits but leaving 11 men on base as Bill Lee lost his ninth game in twelve decisions since May 26th. They lost to California the next day, 5-2, as the Yankees beat Oakland 6-0, closing the Sox' lead to seven games from their greatest margin of 14 games a month before. Dennis Eckersley was the loser as Frank Tanana beat the Sox for the fifth time without a loss at the Angels' home field in Anaheim.

Tiant stopped the Sox' slide the next day with a 4-2 win over Nolan Ryan, giving him a 6-1 career record against the Hall of Fame fastballer. Tiant gave up more hits than Ryan (6 to Ryan's 4) and struck out only four while Ryan fanned thirteen, but Tiant found a way to win, as two of his strikeouts came with two runners on. For his part, Ryan was the author of his own obituary for the game, walking George Scott, overrunning a bunt by Butch Hobson and then throwing wildly after catching a popped-up bunt by Rick Burleson. A writer made the mistake of pestering Don Zimmer for a glowing comment on Ryan's pitching performance in the clubhouse the next day. "Ryan sure had a great one, didn't he," prompted the writer. "Tiant pitched a great game," Zimmer said in the oblique way by which he suffered fools. "Ryan really had the strikeout pitch going, didn't he," the writer unwisely persisted. "Let Ryan have his ____ing strike-outs, and Luis Tiant will take the wins, thank you." Quoth the Gerbil, nevermore.

Yastrzemski's wrist was injured, his fourth debilitation since late July, the first a lower back injury suffered while swinging at a pitch, the second a knot in his shoulder, the third a hurting in his back caused by a strenuous throw. Age was catching up on the Sox' captain, and he sat out the victory over Nolan Ryan and the Angels. The Yankees kept pace with the Sox by beating Oakland, 5-3, on a home run by Bucky Dent in the seventh; it was their ninth win in eleven games, and Catfish Hunter was now 7-4. The Sox beat the Angels and Ken Brett 8-6 the next day as Bob Stanley's record ran to 10-1 and Jim Rice got his 99th run batted in of the season; he led the majors in home runs and runs batted in and was only marginally behind the batting average leader. Boston then traveled north to beat the Oakland A's, 6-3, as Rice stroked his thirtieth home run along with three other hits and passed the 100 RBI mark for the third time in four years. The Yankees were playing slightly further north in Seattle, and bested the

Mariners 6-1 on the strength of Ed Figueroa's twelfth win, a four-hitter that represented his ninth complete game. Reggie Jackson broke a tie in the seventh with a single and a stolen base, advancing to third on a wild pitch and scoring on a single by Bucky Dent.

The beginning of the end of Bill Lee's season began August 19th as he lost to Oakland 8-4 on a night when, with Fred Lynn out, Boston had so loaded its lineup with right-handers against A's left-hander John Henry Johnson that Carlton Fisk started in left field, the first time in his major league career he had played the outfield. (With Fisk so positioned, Jim Rice, who would never be mistaken for Willie Mays, was dispatched to patrol center.) Lee was now 3-9 since May 26th, having gone from 10-3 to 10-10. His earned run average over his last 41 innings was 5.27. He had given up 54 hits and 25 earned runs in losing his last seven starts. Asked by a reporter how long he'd be willing to stick with Lee, Don Zimmer said simply, "I don't know." As the fourth leg of the Sox' pitching stool began to crack, a skeptical observer of their prospects might have noted that the Yankees' staff included the pitchers with the lowest and second lowest earned run averages in baseball: Ron Guidry (1.79), and Goose Gossage (1.89).

Lee responded to his decline with a bit of dramatization one day for the assembled media representatives. "This is a test," Lee intoned in an imitation of the portentous voice heard at the opening of the 1960s science fiction series *The Outer Limits*. "Your dials are locked. You are no longer in control. This is a test for Don Zimmer. It wasn't when I was pitching well. But now this is a test of his patience. The rotation being traded. That's his problem." And indeed, former Buffalo Head Ferguson Jenkins retired 27 of 28 batters two days later to win his twelfth game, a 4-1 win over the Minnesota Twins. But the past was past, and it was impolitic of Lee to have brought it up. The Sox were getting ready for the last game of a three-game series with Oakland when Lee, who was scheduled to pitch next against the Seattle Mariners, asked Zimmer whether he should take an early flight to Seattle to rest up for his start, as is customary among major league teams on the road. "No," Zimmer snapped at him. "Get out in the outfield and run." The next day Lee was removed from the Sox' starting rotation in favor of Jim Wright; he was banished to the bull pen, with Dick Drago to occupy the role of spot starter for the time being.

"I'll go out there and work hard," Lee told reporters. "They've needed me before to bail out this club and maybe they'll need me again. I'll do it. I'll do it for my teammates and for baseball," he went on, in a self-aggrandizing style that Reggie Jackson might have admired. "But I won't do it for those two guys. Zimmer didn't make the decision by himself. Sullivan helped him." Sullivan responded to the charge by saying that the decision as to who started and who relieved was "strictly up to the manager." But, he added, "I don't disagree with him. The bottom line is that when you get to this time of the season you want to win. You go with your best. That's the number one priority." Lee was quick to turn Zimmer's sympathy against him. "A week ago he said with any luck I'd be 13-6. Now this. I'd say that's rather contradictory."

Despite Lee's dissension, and the sense that things were

beginning to fall apart, the Sox achieved a respectable record of 19-10 in August after a sluggish July, while the Yankees went 19-8. Zimmer tried to explain to reporters that there was no immediate cause for concern after the Sox had beaten the A's, 6-0, on August 25th. "The Yankees have 38 games to go. If they go 28-10," he began, scribbling on a piece of paper, "they'll have 93 wins and we'll have to go. . .uh." He paused. "Aw the hell with it. I'll leave the figures to someone else. The only thing to do is to go out and play the games." Ron Guidry won his eighteenth game against two defeats in Oakland that day, 7-1, as Reggie Jackson hit a grand-slam home run in the sixth inning to break open the game. On the odometer of Jackson's career records, the grand slam was his seventh such blast and it produced his 1,001st run batted in.

On August 26th Jim Wright won his first start since replacing Lee in the Sox' rotation, a 7-1 decision over California. Graig Nettles kept the Yankees from falling behind by hitting his 21st home run, giving New York a 5-4 win over Oakland. The Sox produced a dramatic, extra-inning win the following day over the Angels, who had tied the game at 2-2 in the eighth inning and gone ahead, 3-2, in the twelfth. Yaz, who was three for three up to that point as designated hitter, led off for the Sox with a single to right, and Jerry Remy replaced him as a pinch runner. Remy went to second when Lynn walked. On a 3-2 pitch George Scott hit a ground ball to Carney Lansford at third and Lansford's throw pulled Joe Rudi off the bag at first. Remy kept running and slid under the tag to tie the game. Butch Hobson then singled to center, scoring Lynn with the game-winning run. The Yankees matched that win with a 6-2 victory over Oakland, however, as Catfish Hunter won his sixth game in a row.

On August 27th Dwight Evans was hit in the back of the head by Seattle's Mike Parrott and knocked unconscious. The Sox won the game, 10-9, but Evans was admitted to a hospital and would suffer the effects of the beaning through the rest of the season. Ron Guidry would be hurt the next day by a flying bat from the hands of the Orioles' Ken Singleton, but it didn't stop him from winning his nineteenth game and it would not prevent him from pitching down the stretch drive. At the end of August the Yankees were six and a half games behind the Sox, an improvement of only one game over the course of the month.

September

The death rattle of the Sox' asphyxiation by choking in the fall of 1978 began with a four game series against the Yankees at Fenway Park beginning September 7th. On that day, the Sox led the Yankees by four games as they took the field, with the two teams' heavyweights, Mike Torrez and Catfish Hunter, scheduled to pitch the first game. The Yankees had lost three straight games to the Sox and six out of the eight games the teams had played to that point in the season, but they had won thirteen of their last fifteen and were 36-14 since they had started their run to catch the Sox from the depths of their depression in July.

The Yankee onslaught in the opening game of the series came so quickly that there was barely enough time for Boston fans to buy a hot dog before the Sox were hopelessly behind. When Catfish Hunter had to leave the game in the fourth inning with a groin pull, more than a few Boston fans were already trying to get their cars out of the cramped parking lots surrounding Fenway Park before they were blocked in by latecomers. By the middle of the fourth inning the first four batters in the Yankees' lineup had come to bat four times and the score was 12-0. Before the game, the Yankees had asked for extra batting practice at 3:30 the next afternoon; in the fifth inning they called to cancel. Thirteen Yankee players ultimately combined to produce 21 hits, five for extra bases, none of which reached the outfield wall, in a 15-3 victory. It was the horsehide equivalent of the death by a thousand cuts.

Torrez, who had failed for the fourth time in four consecutive starts to give his team a win, was now 1-2 against New York for the season. Yankee first baseman Chris Chambliss downplayed the suggestion that his team's destruction of Torrez in the series opener was motivated by a special animus towards their former teammate. "I don't think there was any grudge at all. We would have gone out the same way no matter who was pitching, Bill Lee or anybody." Lee was in fact the fans' choice to staunch the Sox' bleeding. Groups of bored, waggish or desperate Fenway spectators began to chant "We want Lee" as the Yankees revolved around the bases, but Lee, despite his long-standing hatred of the Yankees, couldn't (or wouldn't) answer the call. "The people wanted Bill Lee," Zimmer said when asked, "but he told (pitching coach) Alvin Jackson he didn't want to hurt his arm by pitching because he had a bad foot." One of Lee's feet was inflamed because, in Zimmer's words, "he hasn't gotten the shoes he wants and says he needs." To Zimmer, Lee's podiatric disability had the odor of hypochondria about it; the manager had called out to the bull pen for Lee earlier in the week when Eckersley got into a jam against Baltimore, but Lee was in the clubhouse. "He screams about not pitching," Zimmer pointed out, "then when I try to pitch him he's in the clubhouse." The Yankees were three games out. After the game Zimmer sat in his office talking to reporters. "Close the door, will you," he said to an interviewer at the edge of the crowd. "There's a breeze coming in—a chill."

The next day, Friday, the two teams sent their subalterns— Jim Wright for the Sox and Jim Beattie for the Yankees—out to do battle. Wright gave up 17 hits and lasted only four innings while Beattie retired 18 batters in a row at one stretch as the Yankees won 13-2. Dwight Evans had to leave the game due to continuing side effects from his beaning on August 28th; Evans could see only when he was looking straight ahead, not up or down, a serious handicap for an outfielder. Evans, the gold standard among the Sox in the field, was consigned to the bench, and the team's gloves seemed to obey a sort of Gresham's law of baseball defense, with bad fielders driving out good. The team had now committed 23 errors for 19 unearned runs in 9 games; Butch Hobson alone had four throwing errors and a ball go through his legs in five chances. Zimmer felt he couldn't bench Hobson because of Hobson's power, even though the Alabaman would finish the season with the worst fielding average of any Sox starting third baseman since James Edward "Red" Morgan in 1906. The Yankees were two games out.

On Saturday the two teams had their best pitchers available, Ron Guidry and Dennis Eckersley. Eckersley didn't allow the Yankees to score in the visitors' half of the first inning, the first time in the series that a Red Sox pitcher had thrown a shutout in the opening frame. Guidry allowed two singles in his turn on the mound, but the Sox didn't score. In the Yankees' fourth Thurman Munson led off with a single but overestimated the power of a Reggie Jackson fly ball to left field that was held up by the wind, and thus ran himself into a 7-4-3 double play. Chris Chambliss followed with a double, and Graig Nettles was walked intentionally. The Sox' poor fielding then took the form of nonfeasance rather than their more recent misfeasance. Lou Pinella hit a pop-up to right field that fell to earth despite the close proximity of Burleson, Lynn, Scott, Duffy and Rice, a play that a healthy Dwight Evans probably would have made. Roy White was walked intentionally, bringing up Bucky Dent. Dent singled to left where Yaz muffed the ball as two runs scored. Mickey Rivers singled and Eckersley's day on the mound came to an end, the first time he had failed to reach the fifth inning all season. The Yankees won, 7-0, as Guidry allowed no hits after the first inning. The Sox' lead was down to one game.

On Sunday the Sox' cupboard of rested pitchers was bare—according to Zimmer—except for Bobby Sprowl, who would oppose Ed Figueroa. Tiant had offered to pitch—nay, pleaded with pitching coach Al Jackson to let him pitch—on three days' rest, but Zimmer wanted to save Tiant for the game the next night against Jim Palmer and the Orioles. Other members of the team argued the case for Bill Lee, but Zimmer was still angry over Lee's absence without leave against Baltimore and his sick-out when asked to mop up in the first game of the series with the Yankees. Sprowl, who had been consistent the first half of the season against Double-A hitters, was coming off two unimpressive months with the Sox'

Triple-A farm team, the Pawtucket Red Sox. "The kid's got icewater in his veins," Zimmer told members of the media before the game, more than a little defensively, since the rookie had faltered in his first start, a 4-1 loss to Jim Palmer on September 5th. Sprowl walked four and Bob Stanley gave up 10 hits as the Sox lost 7-4; Figueroa got his 16th win and Gossage his 23rd save.

New York's totals for the series: 42 runs, 67 hits, 5 errors. Boston's numbers—9 runs, 21 hits, 12 errors, including 7 in one game. No Sox starting pitcher finished the fourth inning, and only one got five outs. George Scott was 0 for 25, while the Yankees as a team came close to hitting .400—they were .396 for the series. Bucky Dent drove in seven runs for the Yankees during the series to lead the team. Two Yankee batters—Willie Randolph and Thurman Munson—went three for three in a game before the Red Sox' ninth batter made it to the plate. By a historical allusion that occurred to many Sox fans at approximately the same time, the series was immediately dubbed, and will forever be known, as the Boston Massacre.

The Sox had stumbled the final four steps of their descent into a tie with the Yankees by losing four straight games to their pursuers, a feat of fearful symmetry. The degree of civic agony that the Sox' fall precipitated in Boston could be measured by the next day's headline in the Boston *Globe*—not on the sports page, but the *front* page, where the news of the Sox' collapse was placed above the fold in the area normally reserved for news of national or international consequence. In a post office in Brookline, Massachusetts, a man in summer whites, apparently making a belated return from a summer vacation beyond the reach of the American news media and baseball box scores, muttered under his breath as he waited in line to collect his mail: "I knew they'd blow it. I knew it." A coin flip held the morning of September 11th to decide where a one-game playoff would be held if the two teams ended the season in a tie would be the Sox' only victory over the Yankees in the series; the Sox won, and they elected to play the game at Fenway Park.

The Yankees' sweep of the series that ended September 10th turned the rest of the season into a twenty-game sprint to the finish. The Sox hoped to hold on until Remy, Evans and Yastrzemski were healthy enough to come back, but the team had much to be discouraged about. The pitching staff's performance during the second half of the season was a mirror image—that is, reversed—of their success before the All-Star Game. Lee, who had won his first six games, had lost seven in a row. Tiant was 2-7 in his last twelve starts. Jim Wright, who had once been 5-1, went through a stretch of three starts in which he retired only 16 batters. Torrez was 4-4 since the All-Star break. His last win had been August 19th and in his last ten and one-third innings he had given up 18 hits and 13 runs, 11 of them earned. Nonetheless, the Sox kept their heads above water, winning their next game, 5-4, as they beat the Orioles on Jim Rice's 40th home run in the 8th inning off Jim Palmer. The Sox were back in first if only by a percentage point or two over the idle Yankees.

Both New York and Boston lost the next day, the Sox 3-2 to the Orioles, the Yankees 7-4 to the Tigers. On September 13th the Sox lost 2-1 to Cleveland, while the Yankees won 7-3 over Detroit, and for the first time since May 23rd the Sox had no claim to first place in the American League's eastern division.

Bill Lee, a man who in his sullen moments communicated by silk-screened T-shirt, wore one that day showing the standings of the division at the All-Star break. It had taken New York 158 days to reach first place but, as folk poet Reggie Jackson put it on the occasion of the Yankees' arrival at that summit, "What counts is where you are when the leaves turn brown, not when they're green."

The following day the Sox lost to Cleveland as discarded Sox pitcher Mike Paxton pitched a perfect game for four and two-thirds innings on the way to his eleventh win, a 4-3 decision that the Sox could have won had they advanced Carlton Fisk, who opened the ninth inning with a double, to third base. Fred Lynn, batting next, hit away to shortstop Tom Veryzer rather than bunting; Veryzer held Fisk, forced Lynn at first, and two fly balls by Butch Hobson and Jack Brohamer were wasted. Meanwhile, Graig Nettles's two home runs gave the Yankees the offense they needed to lead the Tigers 4-2 going into the eighth. Sparky Lyle returned from his exile as stopper to quiet a Tiger rally by forcing Jason Thompson to hit into a double play. The Yankees now held a game and a half lead over the Sox. They were 41-15 since falling 14 games behind on July 19th.

Boston and New York then met for their last regular season series, a three-game encounter in Yankee Stadium. The Sox' bus was met each night by a crowd of Yankee partisans estimated by a sportswriter who was there to have been approximately 1,000 strong, wearing hastily made-up T-shirts bearing slogans such as "Boston is Dead," "Boston Chokes" and, in defiance or ignorance of orthographic convention, "Red Socks Suck." Ron Guidry opened for the Yankees against Luis Tiant. Guidry struggled in the early innings by comparison to the form that had produced a record of 22-2 going into the game, running up 3-2 counts on seven batters in the first four innings. He righted himself to finish with a two-hitter, his second in a week against the Sox, as the Yankees won 4-0. The Sox were two and a half games out of first place.

In the second game of the series Catfish Hunter again opposed Mike Torrez. Jim Rice staked Torrez to a lead in the first with a two-run homer following a single by Jerry Remy, who was playing with a broken wrist. In the Yankees' half of the fifth inning Reggie Jackson suffered a broken nail while waiting in the on-deck circle after being hit by a foul ball off the bat of Thurman Munson. He came to bat anyway and homered on an 0-2 pitch when Torrez failed to get his slider to move inside. "I got a hitter's pitch and a pitcher's mistake," Jackson said. In the ninth inning, with the score tied 2-2, Torrez made another mistake on an 0-2 pitch. Yaz was playing leadoff hitter Mickey Rivers in close, as Torrez was pitching him low. Yankee third base coach Yogi Berra alerted Rivers to the outfield alignment: "Look how they're playing you—you got the gap." The next pitch from Torrez was up, and Rivers hit it over Yaz's head for a triple, putting the winning run 90 feet away from home plate. Willie Randolph tapped a grounder to Burleson, who held Rivers and retired Randolph at first. With one out and first base open, Zimmer elected to pitch to Thurman Munson, a tough out in a clutch situation. Munson hit a line drive to Rice in left that was deep enough to score Rivers for the Yankees' sixth consecutive win over the Sox. The Yankees were now three and a half games ahead of the Sox, their biggest lead of the season.

The next day Boston had Dennis Eckersley pitching, but more importantly their bats regained their springtime vigor as Boston produced 11 hits. In the third Burleson singled and stole second as Munson bobbled a pitch; he scored when Yaz hit a blooper to left. In the seventh Evans led off with a walk, advanced to third on a ground-rule double by Burleson and scored on a sacrifice fly by Remy. In the eighth Fisk walked and Duffy failed to sacrifice him to second but then, with two strikes, redeemed himself with a single past third baseman Graig Nettles. George Scott then failed to lay down a bunt as well, but followed Duffy's lead and doubled. Hobson doubled Scott home—6-3, Red Sox. In the home half of the eighth Jackson hit a ground ball to Jerry Remy who misplayed it for an error that went into right field. Jackson challenged the arm of Dwight Evans and tried to reach second; he lost as the rightfielder threw him out, leaving the bases empty with two out and killing a potential rally. Yaz hit a solo homer in the ninth, and the Sox won 7-3. The Yankees were 90-58 and the Sox were 88-61, two and a half games back. "We have to win 12 out of our next 13 games," Yaz said after the Sox had broken the Yankees' six-game hoodoo.

The Comeback

With two weeks left in September and their chances to gain ground on the Yankees by direct attack now over, the Sox began a test that would determine whether they would look back on the 1978 season with happiness or regret, and if the latter, whether or not mitigated by a strong finish that would prove they weren't quitters. The Sox started the homestretch against the Detroit Tigers on September 18th in a game that went into extra innings. Andy Hassler worked out of a jam in the tenth inning and Jerry Remy singled in the eleventh to drive in the winning run in a 5-4 Sox victory. It was only the 39th game (out of 150 thus far in the season) in which the Sox' eight regular starters had taken the field together. It was also the first time the Sox had won consecutive games since August 30th, after which they had lost fourteen of seventeen.

In New York the Yankees matched the Sox as Mickey

Rivers singled in the winning run in the bottom of the eighth against Milwaukee, giving Ed Figueroa a 4-3 win, his sixth straight win and his eighteenth of the year against 9 losses. Figueroa was on a personal crusade to become the first native-born Puerto Rican pitcher to win twenty games, a milestone he had almost reached in 1976 when, with 19 wins to his credit, he had lost his last two starts. The next year John Candelaria had won 20 for the Pittsburgh Pirates, but in the mind of Figueroa and many of his fellow Puerto Ricans, Candelaria's accomplishment was not the genuine article since he was born in New York to Puerto Rican parents. Figueroa had something else to prove as well. He had chafed under Billy Martin's rule because Martin wouldn't let him pitch on a cycle of three days' rest, and the manager insisted on calling pitches in the late innings of close games when Figueroa was on the mound, a practice that the pitcher felt had caused him to lose two games in Martin's portion of the season. Figueroa thrived under Bob Lemon's looser managerial style, however, and his revival paralleled the Yankees' comeback. It was Figueroa who had thrown a six-hitter on July 19th to reverse the tide of the Yankees' fortunes at their lowest ebb of the season.

The next day the Sox beat the Tigers again, 8-6. Four batters into the game Yaz hit a three-run homer that normally would have been enough of a lead for Luis Tiant pitching in a pressure game, but Tiant left after facing only four batters, the last of whom, Jason Thompson, hit a grand-slam home run. The Sox generated 12 hits and their four-run fourth inning was their biggest in a month. Jim Rice got his 200th hit and as a result became the first American League hitter since Al

Rosen of the Indians in 1953 to have 200 hits, 40 home runs and 100 runs batted in over the course of a season. Bill Campbell relieved in the fourth inning and pitched the Sox into the ninth. He got only his fourth save of the year when, with two on and one out, George Scott snagged a softly hit ball by Rusty Staub, stepped on first and threw to Fisk to beat Aurelio Rodriguez to home plate for a 3-2 double play.

That same day Milwaukee beat the Yankees 2-0 as Mike Caldwell became the only 20-game winner in the majors besides Ron Guidry. It was Caldwell's third shutout victory over the Yankees for the '78 season, the first time any pitcher had accomplished that feat since Dean Chance of the (then) Los Angeles Angels in 1964. Caldwell had a 3-1 record and a .99 earned run average against New York for the season, and his victory enabled the Sox to narrow the Yankees lead to a game and a half with less than two weeks to go.

On September 20th the Yankees split a doubleheader with Toronto, but the Sox couldn't gain ground on New York as the Detroit Tigers beat Mike Torrez, 12-2. Torrez had historically finished the season with a second half that was stronger than his performance in the springtime and early summer; he had been 38-11 after the All-Star Game in the four preceding seasons, but his loss that day was his seventh straight start without a win. A cruel assessment of Torrez's performance began to circulate—he had won it for the Yankees in 1977 and was doing it again in 1978. The Sox began their game against Detroit with the Blue Jays' first-game victory over the Yankees already on the board; the Tigers got 5 runs in one and two-thirds innings off Ron Guidry, breaking Guidry's string of 22 straight scoreless innings coming into the game. The loss meant that the Sox had failed to capitalize on one of Guidry's rare failures and that their pitching remained inadequate or, viewed from another angle, poorly used. When Torrez gave up a walk and a single in the fifth, Bill Lee, who had declined to warm up against the Yankees, began to throw *sua sponte*. Zimmer ignored him and brought in John La Rose, who pitched out of a no-out, bases-loaded situation. Whatever help Lee was capable of providing, Zimmer was at this point unwilling to accept. The Sox were two games out.

Eckersley pitched the next day, his third consecutive start on three days' rest, and threw a six-hitter for his eighteenth win as the Sox beat the Tigers 5-1. The only flaw in his performance was a homerun ball he threw to Detroit's Jason Thompson. As the pitcher put it in his peculiar pidgin tongue of Eckspeak, "Yeah, he went ta-ta in front of 15 grand." (Translation: He hit a home run in front of 15,000 fans.) Known throughout his career for his tendency to give up home runs, Eckersley will one day enter baseball's Hall of Fame but he will always be remembered most vividly for the pitch he threw in the bottom of the ninth inning of the first game of the 1988 World Series to the Los Angeles Dodgers' Kirk Gibson; Gibson, with a two-strike count and ailing legs that would prevent him from appearing in the remainder of the series, hit a two-run home run that won the game, 5-4. He threw another memorable gopher ball in postseason play to Toronto's Roberto Alomar in the fourth game of the 1992 American League Championship Series. In fact, when Eckersley retires, he will do so as the leading pitcher of all time in at least one category—most home runs allowed. As this is written, he already holds the major league record of 341.

Catfish Hunter matched Eckersley with a 7-1 victory over Toronto, his 11th win of the season. The win gave Hunter 8 wins and 1 loss since the beginning of August, a better record than either Guidry or Figueroa, but he left after six innings with a groin pull. The Sox were still two games out.

On the 22nd, Bill Campbell failed to save a game against Toronto that Bob Stanley and Andy Hassler had held for the Sox through eight innings. Stanley had been effective, at one point retiring 12 batters in a row. After pitching out of trouble in the eighth, Hassler gave up a single to Bob Bailor to open the ninth, retired Alan Ashby on a popped-up bunt, and then allowed a second single by Dave McKay. After a walk loaded the bases, Campbell came in and gave up a third single that scored two runs, giving the Jays a 5-4 win. As a result, the Sox would not win twelve of their last thirteen, the number of victories Yaz had predicted would be required to win the pennant, but perhaps they wouldn't need to. The Yankees also lost that day, to the Cleveland Indians, on a series of miscues in the tenth inning. With two out, Goose Gossage had walked Duane Kuiper, who advanced to second on a passed ball and then to third on a wild pitch. Gossage gave Bernie Carbo an intentional walk after running up an unintentional 3-0 count. Rick Manning then hit a ball to second base that Fred Stanley was able to knock down but unable to turn into an out, allowing Kuiper to score for an 8-7 Yankee loss. Ed Figueroa was denied his nineteenth win on his march towards twenty, and the Sox remained two games out.

The next day Luis Tiant allowed thirteen Toronto runners to reach base, nine of whom made it to second base or further. Only one of them scored, however, while the Sox pushed across three of their own to win their 92nd game. In the first Rick Burleson singled, stole second and scored on a two-out single by Yaz. In the fourth Hobson doubled and came home on a two-out single by Brohamer. The game marked Butch Hobson's last appearance at third base in 1978, however. "I'm no quitter but I just can't get it over there (to first). I had to get out of there before I got someone killed," he told reporters, an improbability, perhaps, but not by much. Hobson was still hitting hard so he would become the designated hitter for the remainder of the season, while Jack Brohamer would play third. Dwight Evans, who was 9 for 54 since his beaning, would be benched, and Jim Rice would play right field.

The Yankees, meanwhile, fell early to Cleveland as Jim Beattie gave up four runs in the second and Dick Tidrow gave up four more in the next two innings. The eventual 10-1 loss left the Sox one game out with seven to play. In the 20-game season that had begun on the day the Yankees finally caught the Red Sox, Boston was now 7-6 while New York was 6-7.

On the 24th Torrez started against the Jays and left the game behind 4-3. He was now 0-6 in his last eight starts with a 5.37 earned run average. Bill Campbell gave up three in the top of the ninth to give the Jays a 6-4 lead. In the ninth Jay pitcher Victor Cruz, who had struck out the side in the eighth, walked two of the first three batters up and left the game in favor of Balor Moore. Moore balked the runners over to second and third and walked Bob Bailey to load the bases. Rick Burleson then hit a ball that Willie Upshaw couldn't handle, scoring two runs to tie the game.

The Jays put runners on base in every inning that day, and the extra innings were not recommended viewing for the frail elderly. Dick Drago took over from Bob Stanley in the tenth inning and stopped a rally, and then repeated the feat in the eleventh when the Jays put two men on. Don Zimmer called for an intentional walk to Roy Howell to get to Otto Velez, loading the bases, but the Jays failed to score when Velez grounded out to shortstop. In the twelfth Willie Upshaw led off with a single but Fisk caught a popped-up bunt by Doug Ault and threw to Jerry Remy covering first for an unusual 2-4 double play. In the thirteenth Zimmer repeated his strategy of the eleventh and Otto Velez again accommodated him by grounding out to Frank Duffy. In the fourteenth Jim Rice, who was 0 for 5 to that point, singled—his 388th total base. He moved to second on an infield out and then on to third on a high-hop single by Fisk. Then a ball hit by Butch Hobson struck a seam in the artificial turf and rose up to hit third base-man Roy Howell in the throat. Howell recovered but threw wildly to first, giving the Sox a 7-6 win.

The Yankees had Guidry that day, however, and he threw another two-hitter, his third two-hit shutout in his last four starts, as New York beat Cleveland 4-0. Guidry was now 23-3 with a 1.74 earned run average. Fourteen of his twenty-three wins had come after a New York loss. He had won 13 straight games, and opponents had a .194 average against him; the batting average of hitters against all American League pitchers that year was .263. The Sox remained one game out with six to play, but they would need to use Eckersley twice more before the season ended, while Guidry would have only one more turn in the rotation. He would be available for the one-game playoff, if it came to pass, but Eckersley, the Sox' best pitcher at 18-8 with a 3.16 earned run average, would not.

On the 26th Eck earned his nineteenth win, a 6-0 shutout of the Tigers and his fourth straight start on three days' rest. That same day Ed Figueroa got his nineteenth win, however, a 4-1 decision against Toronto, and the Yankees began accepting orders for World Series tickets. The Sox were still one game out, but now with only five games to play. The most momentous event of the day in the history of baseball was not the result of a ball thrown, caught or batted, however. On the 26th of September, 1978, for the first time in the history of baseball, female reporters were permitted to enter the New York Yankees' locker room under the authority of an order by Judge Constance Baker Motley, who had ruled that women were legally entitled to interrogate undressed sportsmen on the same basis as that offered by the ball club to male reporters.

The ruling caught the older generation of Yankees in varying states of dishabille. Clyde King left the showers with only a towel around his waist and, upon learning of the revolution in equality that had occurred, retreated to an area where Sparky Lyle had stockpiled extra towels and there covered himself. Pitching coach Art Fowler had his boxer shorts pulled down by a clubhouse jester. The younger generation of Yankees generally accepted the development in a more equable manner. "I'm not the type of guy who's going to change," said Willie Randolph. "I'm not going to walk around with clothes everywhere I go. If she wants to talk to me while I'm getting dressed that's cool. Anyway, they're grown women." Jay Johnstone, on the other hand, ran up a flag of protest like a racing yacht claiming a foul, hanging a sign above his locker that expressed his dissenting opinion, to wit: "U.S. JUDGE CONSTANCE MOTLEY SUCKS RATSHIT."

The Comeback

On September 27th Tiant, working on three days' rest, pitched the Sox into the sixth inning when he was forced to leave with a hamstring pull. George Scott sailed out of his personal batting doldrums with three hits in four at bats, including a two-run home run in the second. Andy Hassler held the Sox' lead into the ninth, when Bob Stanley came in with two men on—following a walk and a single—and none out. Stanley's appearance in relief was an indication of the Sox' depleted pitching stock, since he was also scheduled to start the next day. He threw only three pitches, one that Milt May, a left-handed hitter, sliced to left field on a sinking line drive that Yastrzemski barely caught sliding on one knee. The other two pitches produced outs as well as the Sox beat the Tigers 5-2 for their eighth win in ten games.

The Yankees next called on Catfish Hunter, who continued his revival, giving up only 6 hits to the Toronto Blue Jays. Graig Nettles hit his 27th home run and Reggie Jackson hit his 25th as the Yankees beat the Jays, 5-1. Hunter's record since his embarassment on July 27th, when he had failed to retire a single batter against Cleveland, was now 9-1 with a 1.71 earned run average. New York's starters had allowed only 2 runs and 14 hits in the last three games. The Sox remained one game out with four games to play.

Guidry would pitch the next day on three days' rest, although it wasn't clear he needed more than that since he used fewer pitches in winning than most pitchers—he had thrown only 149 in his last two outings, the first of which was his abbreviated appearance against Toronto on September 20th. The Sox accordingly needed a win from their starter, Mike Torrez, since Guidry was unlikely to lose. Torrez redeemed himself with his first victory after eight unsuccessful starts, a 1-0 win over the Tigers. The score disguised the labor-intensive nature of Torrez's accomplishment. He had walked seven men and still pitched a shutout, mainly by keeping his pitches down; only two outs were fly balls. The parade of Tigers who took to the base paths failed to reach home due to two timely double plays and a throw by Fred Lynn that beat Jason Thompson, running on a sprained ankle, trying to score from second. Jim Rice's 45th home run of the season produced the only run of the game. In later years Rice's ability to hit under pressure would become a subject of fans' derision, with one Boston writer suggesting that his number should be changed to 6-4-3 due to his tendency to hit into double plays. In 1978, 31 of his 46 home runs either tied the game or put the Red Sox ahead. Unfortunately for the Sox, however, Ron Guidry would win his last start of the regular season that day, keeping the Sox one game back with three games to play. Guidry's record was now 24-3, the best winning percentage (.889) for a pitcher with a least twenty wins in baseball history, passing Lefty Grove's 31-4 mark (.886).

On the 29th the Sox routed Toronto 11-0 behind Bob Stanley, who threw a perfect game until a two-out walk in the fifth inning, and a no-hitter into the sixth inning. There were several notable milestones passed that day. Stanley's victory meant that two twenty-three-year-olds on the Sox staff, Stanley and Eckersley, were a collective 34 and 10 for the season. Jim Rice got his 400th total base, a feat which, with his other statistics, marked a baseball milestone, namely, only the eleventh time in baseball history that a hitter had produced at least 400 total bases, 100 runs batted in, 100 runs, 40 home runs, 200 hits, 20 doubles and 10 triples in a season. Finally,

Don Zimmer became a grandfather in the third inning.

New York's Jim Beattie and Cleveland's David Clyde were meanwhile pitching dual shutouts before the Indians scored on a Tom Veryzer double and a Rick Manning single with two out in the top of the eighth inning. The Yankees rallied on singles by Willie Randolph (who pulled a hamstring running out an infield hit), Reggie Jackson, Lou Piniella and Thurman Munson (who had stitches in one hand after putting it through a glass window in a clubhouse sauna) and won 3-1 to keep their one-game lead with two games left.

On Sunday, September 30th, both Eckersley and Figueroa got their 20th wins as the Sox beat Toronto 5-1 and New York beat Cleveland 7-0. Eckersley struck out the first two batters on six pitches, gave up a home run (his 30th gopher ball) to the next batter, Roy Howell, but settled down after that. Figueroa had reached his goal of becoming the first native-born Puerto Rican to win twenty games by winning thirteen of his last fifteen decisions and eight straight without a loss to end the season. The Yankees' pitching since Figueroa won the July 19th game that started the team's comeback had been uniformly exceptional, but Figueroa, with a 13-2 record in 18 starts, had produced more wins than any starter during that stretch, including Guidry. His wife and five brothers had flown in from Puerto Rico to watch the game, which was transmitted by both radio and television to the island. The Yankees still led by one game with one game to play, and so the season would be decided by one game, or possibly two. The starting pitcher for the Sox against Toronto would be Luis Tiant, two months shy of thirty-eight years old as he took the mound.

Loo-ie

While Luis Clemente Tiant was correctly viewed by fans and his teammates as an idiosyncratic master of the pitching arts, a sort of Thelonious Monk of the mound, and while he got along well with Bill Lee, the self-conscious nonconformist, the contrasts between the two were deep. Lee had grown up in Southern California, the model for America's affluent postwar style of living, and he had gone to college at the University of Southern California, which had one of the nation's premier college baseball programs under coach Rod Dedeaux. Lee signed with the Red Sox when they drafted him after his Southern Cal team won the College World Series in the spring of 1968; he was in the majors by June of the next year after Jim Lonborg, the pitching stalwart of the Sox' Impossible Dream team of 1967, injured his toe attempting to bunt. Within two years Lee had won nine games while losing two for the Sox as a long reliever, the pitcher who would hold a lead or keep a game close for the Sox' short reliever, Sparky Lyle, and he stayed with the team for ten years.

Thus, despite his reputation as a rebel and an iconoclast, Lee had advanced to the majors and developed his skills there by a straight and steady progression. He had even, during the early years of his career, served in the army reserves. Perhaps Lee's desire to make a spectacle of himself on occasion grew out of the relatively humdrum course his life and his baseball career had traversed. By contrast, Tiant's childhood in Cuba had been happy but lacking in material comforts, and his years in baseball had been marked by some long detours and genuine setbacks. Further, during his years in the majors he lived under circumstances that would have burdened the strongest heart.

Tiant's father, Luis Eleuterio Tiant, pitched for the New York Cubans in New York's major league stadiums when white teams weren't playing, and he retired in 1948 with a tired arm when Luis the younger was eight years old. After his pitching career came to an end, Luis the elder bought a truck and became a furniture mover in Cuba. Tiant's parents were strict; his father sent him to private school because it had a longer school day and because in private school Luis could learn English, which his father thought he would need some-day. Tiant's father was a highly-regarded hurler in his time, but he discouraged his son from pursuing a career in baseball because he believed a good education was more likely than pitching skills to equip him for a life in which he would end up somewhere besides the driver's seat of a furniture truck.

Tiant's first professional job was with the Mexico City

Tigers in the winter of 1959; following an outstanding career as a Juvenile League pitcher he had first tried and failed to make the Cuban League, a winter league in which talented Cuban players mixed with American major leaguers. Bobby Avila, a second baseman for Cleveland in the early '50s and then an Indians' scout, had inside knowledge of Tiant's pedigree and talent because he had been a batboy on the elder Tiant's team, and he recommended him to the Tigers' general manager. Tiant accepted an offer of $150 a month from Mexico City after he failed to attract the interest of the Cuban League's Havana Sugar Kings. He was sixteen years old.

His first season with Mexico City was an uneven one; his record was 5-19 but his five wins included three complete-game shutouts. That winter he again tried out for the Havana Sugar Kings and this time made the roster, but he was cut after the team opened the season with a losing streak. Fermin Guerra, the team's manager, promised to call when things got better; he never did, and Tiant spent the winter of 1959-1960 pitching in Nicaragua. The next season with Mexico City his record improved to 17-7 and he pitched well in the postseason series as the Tigers were the champions of the Mexican League.

After the 1960 regular season with Mexico City, Tiant was met at the Havana airport by his parents and the man who never called back, Fermin Guerra. Tiant signed with the Sugar Kings even though he was still miffed about his treatment the previous winter. He returned to Mexico City for the 1961 regular season when his winter with the Sugar Kings ended, but due to an injury he appeared in only 24 games in his third and final season there. That summer Tiant pitched in the Pan

American Association All-Star Game, however, a game he won in relief. A Cleveland Indians scout saw him pitch that day and on the basis of his performance persuaded the Indians to purchase his contract from Mexico City for $35,000.

Luis Tiant's coming of age as a pitcher coincided with Cuba's transition from life under Fulgencio Batista, who twice came to power as the result of military coups, to rule by Fidel Castro, leader of a group that overthrew Batista in 1959. Castro promised free elections as had Batista before him, but he instead delivered a reign of terror marked by military trials and executions. In 1960 Castro began an affiliation with the former Soviet Union and instituted a socialist form of government that expropriated property and anaesthetized the spirit of the Cuban people. In the first two years of Castro's regime, 10 percent of Cuba's population left the island and as a result emigration was curtailed in 1961. Dissenting voices were stifled—one of Tiant's boyhood friends was executed by a firing squad.

Luis was married in the middle of the 1961 season, and he and his wife, Maria del Refugio Navarro, decided to postpone their honeymoon until the fall. They planned to go to Nicanor del Campo, Luis's hometown, to meet his parents, and then to an island off the southern coast of Cuba. When the newlyweds called Tiant's home, however, his parents told them to stay in Mexico. They went to Puerto Rico where Luis would spend the winter preparing for the 1962 season in the Cleveland Indians' farm system. He would not see his father again for 15 years. Tiant would also be separated from his wife and children for long stretches of the first thirteen years of his marriage. He spent his summers in Cleveland, Minnesota and Boston and his winters in Nicaragua, Venezuela and Puerto Rico while his wife and children lived in Mexico City. It was not until 1974, when his wife was pregnant with their third child, that he bought a home in the Boston area and spent the majority of his time with his family.

Tiant's first year in the minor leagues—1962—included stops in Charleston, South Carolina (Class A, Eastern League) Jacksonville, Florida (Triple A, International League), and back to Charleston after developing a sore arm, while his wife was pregnant and living in Mexico. He then played winter ball in Mexico, where his first son was born September 5th. He pitched well that season and was invited to try out for the Indians in the spring of 1963. He didn't make the final cut in his first try at the majors at the age of 23, and was assigned to the Indians' Burlington, North Carolina, club in the Class A Carolina League. He had a good year, leading the league in strikeouts with a 2.56 earned run average and a 14-9 record, which included a no-hitter over the Boston Red Sox' Winston-Salem affiliate.

In 1964 Tiant was a member of a troika of young, strong arms in the Cleveland system along with "Sudden" Sam McDowell, a fastball pitcher with a collection of oddities and narcissistic pretensions (he claimed, for example, to be the world's greatest drag bunter) and Sonny Siebert, who like Tiant would one day end up with the Red Sox. Siebert made the team, McDowell was sent to Portland, the franchise's AAA farm team, and Tiant was sent back to Burlington. Tiant was subsequently brought to Portland after another pitcher was injured, but he felt slighted by his belated promotion to AAA and by the reception he received when he arrived. He noted that his uniform had holes in it, unlike those of the other players, and that his locker was off in a corner with another Hispanic player. While these embarrassing items may merely have been all that a minor league team had left to give him at that late point in the season, to a prideful Tiant they were further evidence that he was not considered the top prospect in the franchise. Luis wasn't a starter at first, but he became one after striking out eight in a four-inning appearance in relief of a faltering McDowell. He won his first 8 games as a starter, lost a 2-0 decision, and then won seven consecutive games. With a show of pitching momentum like that to recommend him, he was called up to the parent club. When his minor league manager gave him the news, however, he said he didn't want to go.

Tiant was irritated that McDowell had been called up a month earlier with an 8-0 record while the Indians had waited for Luis to post a 15-1 mark before deciding to promote him. Not surprisingly, Tiant's pique subsided as his competitive spirit overcame his wounded pride. A day after arriving in New York on a plane from the west coast, Luis won his first major league start, defeating the Yankees, then the American League champions, and their premier starter, Whitey Ford, 3-0. Tiant struck out 11, allowed only a bunt single through the first five innings and only four singles in all. In the next ten and a half weeks he went 10-4, with nine complete games and 3 shutouts, including a 5-0 decision over the Red Sox. By a difficult and tortuous path, he had finally arrived.

Tiant labored with the Indians when they were a mediocre team, and his record of 75 wins and 64 losses during his six-year tenure there seems to suggest that he was no better than his teammates. A closer look at his statistics indicates that he was a stronger pitcher than his weak-hitting club permitted him to be, however. During those years his earned run average—the most common measure of a pitcher's ability considered apart from the runs properly attributable to his teammates' errors—was never higher than 3.71, and for four of his six years there he allowed fewer than three earned runs per nine innings. During 1968, his best season, he led the league with a 1.60 earned run average, the lowest in the American League since Walter Johnson's figure of 1.49 in 1919, as he won 21 games and lost only 9. Tiant took himself out of a game late in the season because of stiffness in his elbow, however, and manager Alvin Dark used the occasion to speculate to the press that Tiant's disability was the result of the gyrations the pitcher put himself through every time he threw to the plate.

Tiant was known for a pitching motion that made him look like a man trying to screw in a lightbulb while climbing out of a cement mixer, a collection of elaborate flourishes that angered many batters. The essence of Tiant's wind-up was concealment and confusion. He began by turning his back to the batter and facing, on his more limber days, a point close to straightaway center field. "If Tiant's not right," observed Carlton Fisk, his principal catcher over the course of his career, "he can't swivel." As he turned towards the plate Tiant's head would cock, his left arm would flail out as he began his forward motion and then (and only then) would he deliver the ball from one of three different latitudes; overhand, three-quarters or sidearm. To most batters, the effect was to take the normal image of a pitcher's delivery and refract it through a kaleidoscope. An ancillary component of his delivery was constant motion. "I'll try doing anything that I think will help my career. . . .All through life you should be prepared for something new," he said in 1975. "This is my 12th year up here, and I'm still trying to find something new to throw at hitters." Carl Yastrzemski, no one's fool at the plate, once struck out three consecutive times against Tiant when the Cuban was pitching for the Cleveland Indians. "Luis comes at you from all angles and throws your timing off," Yaz explained by way of justification. "There's no zone you can look for and know that's where the ball is coming from."

In 1965 both the Washington Senators and the Red Sox sought to have Tiant's motion declared illegal, and those complaints led to an investigation by the American League. The league's inquiry, led by umpire-in-chief Cal Hubbard, found probable cause to indict, but Tiant got off with only a warning. "He's walking the fine line of a delayed delivery," Hubbard told an assemblage of reporters.

He can come down with his lead foot and delay his arm motion as long as he wants, just so long as he continues in motion without stopping. It's a very tough pitch, and it's amazing how he can do it just inside the rules and still control it. He's the trickiest pitcher in the league. I can't believe how many pitches and deliveries he's got. He's the only guy I know of who can throw sidearm, crossfire from the stretch, while stepping in the opposite direction.

Hubbard laid down a rule that, if Tiant were ever found to

have thrown an illegal hesitation pitch, runners would be allowed to advance and the pitch would be called a ball if no men were on base. The penalty was never imposed, as Tiant proved to be as adept at evading detection as he was at deceiving hitters.

Tiant disagreed openly and vehemently with Dark's diagnosis that his delivery was the cause of his stiffness late in the 1968 season, and he seemed to have the better side of the argument since his claim that the Indians' lack of support caused him to work harder to win was borne out by the facts; his teammates rarely gave him more than three runs to work with, and he compensated for their anemic production by treating every batter as a crucial out. And he was the winningest pitcher on the Indians' staff, no matter how unorthodox his delivery.

Unfortunately (but characteristically for Tiant, a streak pitcher all his career), the next year he lost his first seven games, the result (he thought) of the Indians' decision to prohibit him from pitching in the winter, as was his custom. The lack of work over the winter caused Tiant to suffer from adhesions in his pitching shoulder, a formation of scar tissue that results from a return to activity after a period of rest and which reduces mobility in the joint. Winter ball had helped Luis keep his shoulder functioning fluidly in the past, and the forced layoff resulted in the slow start from which he never recovered. After leading the league in a positive respect the year before, he led his circuit in two negative categories a year later, as his 20 losses and 129 walks topped (or bottomed) all others.

Alvin Dark again attributed Tiant's decline to a pitching motion he believed caused a lack of concentration on the pitcher's part. "You've got to keep your eye on the target," Dark told a reporter. "You can't throw your head up into the air, then look over at the scoreboard and then pitch a baseball," Dark claimed, ignoring the fact that Tiant had done just that for the previous five years, winning 66 games in the process. While continuing as field manager, Dark took over as de facto general manager from Gabe Paul during the 1969 season, thereby acquiring the power to sell and trade players. In December of 1969 Tiant would learn that he had been traded to the Minnesota Twins.

Tiant's lineup in Minnesota featured a great many more potent hitters than he had been able to count on in Cleveland. The Twins had finished first in the American League Western division the year before, powered by Rod Carew, the league's best hitter for average, Harmon Killebrew, who led the league in home runs and runs batted in, and Tony Oliva, who had more hits and more doubles than any other batter in the league. Tiant won his first six games with the Twins before fracturing a bone in his shoulder, the result of the effort that he put into his pitches in order to disarm major league hitters. He was ordered to rest, and he finished the season at 7-3, winning one and losing three decisions after returning from his injury without his best fastball. He agreed to take a $10,000 pay cut following his unexceptional showing in 1970, but in the spring of 1971, after a frustrating winter of inactivity intended to aid his recuperation, he pulled a muscle in his rib cage and pitched poorly. On the last day of spring training in 1971, he was given his unconditional release by the Twins—not sent to the minors, not put on the disabled list, and not traded. The conventional wisdom among baseball professionals was that his career was over.

Tiant didn't give up. He signed a 30-day contract with the Atlanta Braves and reported to their Richmond, Virginia, farm team. There he made two appearances against the Louisville Cardinals, a Red Sox affiliate, and piqued the interest of future Boston manager Darrell Johnson. Lee Stange, a pitching coach in the Sox system, went to see Tiant, although Stange couldn't formally approach Tiant about joining the Red Sox until his 30-day contract with Atlanta expired. Atlanta declined to bring him up to the parent club, and so he signed with Louisville. He was then 2-2 with a 2.61 era, but in 31 innings he had fanned 29 and walked only 11. The control and speed that he had demonstrated in his days of domination were still there.

Tiant joined the Red Sox on June 3, 1971, and was placed in the starting rotation on June 11th. The results were not encouraging; he lasted only one inning against the Kansas City Royals, giving up three hits, three walks and five runs. By July he was 0-4, and was sent to the bull pen. He was 0-6 before getting his first win on August 31st. Manager Eddie Kasko explained to Joe Fitzgerald of the Boston *Herald* why he stood behind Tiant:

> You know what made me like that guy so much? His professionalism. I know that sounds corny, but it's true. With all of the things that were on his mind that summer, he never showed any signs of discontent, even when I finally had to send him to the bull pen. He never bitched or moaned. The man was a professional in every sense of the word.

The Year of the Gerbil

When the season ended Tiant's record stood at 1-7, and the question whether his career was or should have been over was a legitimate one. Could he hold off the young pitchers who might show promise in spring training? To this question, Tiant answered with a proverb that may have been devised specifically for the occasion: *"Deja a los otros caballos correr primero y levantar polvo yo los alcanzare."* Loosely translated, "Let the young horses run first and make a lot of noise and dust. I will catch them."

In 1972 a strike delayed the start of the season for ten days, an unexpected gratuity for a hot-weather pitcher such as Tiant. The Sox continued a pattern that had begun for Tiant in Cleveland, however, giving him fewer runs to work with (2.45 per game) than any other Sox pitcher. He was 0-1 at the end of May, but in June he made 10 appearances, 9 in relief, gaining 2 wins with a 1.80 earned run average and averaging a strikeout every inning. He went 5-0 in August, including four consecutive shutouts. He went 15-5 for the year, no slight achievement in view of the fact that he didn't get his first start until the third week of June. During the period from August 19th through September 29th, he was 9-1, with six shutouts and an 0.96 earned run average, and all of his wins were complete games. It was the beginning of Tiant's reputation in Boston as the pitcher to turn to for a win in important situations, since the Sox had been seven games under .500 in June and came from eight and a half games out of first place to a half-game lead over Detroit with three games to play, primarily on the strength of Tiant's pitching. The Sox came to Detroit for the last three games of the season; whoever won two would win the pennant.

Loo-ie

The story of that season's end has been properly personified in the image of Luis Aparicio slipping and falling—twice—as he rounded third base with the lead run on a hit by Carl Yastrzemski in the third inning of the first game of the series. When Aparicio finally made it back to third he found Yaz, who was retired when he was forced to retreat to second. Mickey Lolich didn't give the Sox another chance and the Tigers won 4-1, reversing the standings and putting Detroit in first place by a half game. But the pennant was lost the next night when Tiant faced Woody Fryman, whom the Tigers had acquired on waivers from Philadelphia. The teams were tied 1-1 in the seventh when, with one out, a man on second and first base open, manager Eddie Kasko elected to have Tiant pitch to Al Kaline. Kaline singled to left, scoring Dick McAuliffe with the winning run.

The Sox were eliminated but Tiant had acquitted himself admirably, allowing only one earned run in the deciding game of the season. For the year he ended up with the lowest earned run average in the American League, 1.91, the second time in his career he had done so, becoming the first Red Sox pitcher to lead the league in earned run average since Mel Parnell in 1949, and the first Sox pitcher with an earned run average under two runs per game since Carl Mays in 1917.

Tiant would win twenty games or more the next two seasons, in each case leading the team in wins. He had transformed himself in a year from a has-been to one of the best pitchers in baseball at a point in his life (his early thirties) when most pitchers begin the slow decline towards coaching or some other form of sedentary employment. He had also, in a display of protracted eccentricity that a Carbo or a Lee would never have emulated, much less duplicated, worn white throughout 1974 after deciding at the end of the 1973 season, his first twenty-win season with the Sox, to devote one year of thanksgiving to God and Saint Barbara for his good fortune. Thus does simple piety sometimes give rise to novelties more striking than those produced by adolescent rebellion.

Tiant would again win twenty games in 1976, but he slipped to 12-8 in 1977 following a three-week contract dispute in the spring. He quarreled that year with Zimmer over the preference of the manager (and the rest of the pitching staff) for a five-man rotation; Tiant's need to avoid adhesions required that he pitch frequently. He took himself out of games twice that year, complaining that his lack of work caused his control to suffer. He was playing out the final year of his contract in 1978, and holding a 7-0 record when, on June 24th, he suffered a groin pull and a leg injury. His performance declined sharply thereafter as he won 2 games and lost 7 in his next 12 starts, a reversal that mirrored Bill Lee's decline from 10-3 to 10-10. Still, Tiant was pitching in September, not Lee; was it anything more than Zimmer's feelings of spite towards Lee that caused it to be so? In view of Tiant's history, the answer is probably yes.

Over his career with the Red Sox, Luis Tiant won nearly three-quarters of the games he pitched during the month of September, when pennants are won or lost. In 1975, the year of the storied World Series between the Sox and the Reds, Tiant would end up with 18 wins and 14 losses, but his contribution to the team's pennant drive was not susceptible of measurement by normal statistical categories. On September 11th he returned from a three-week layoff caused by a bad back and beat Detroit, 3-1, after pitching a no-hitter into the eighth inning. He would beat Cy Young Award winner Jim Palmer and the Baltimore Orioles four nights later by a score of 2-0, giving birth to the "LOO—IE, LOO—IE" chant by which Sox fans would exhort him to strike outs and victories down the stretch for the rest of his career in Boston. Then, in his final start of the regular season, he would shut out Cleveland, 2-0, spiritually, if not mathematically, clinching the pennant for the Red Sox. Lee, by contrast, won his last game of the season August 24th, shutting out the White Sox.

Tiant was the winning pitcher in two of Boston's World Series victories against the Reds, and he pitched seven innings in the fabled sixth game, thereby taking part in all three of the team's wins, while Lee won none. When manager Darrell Johnson took advantage of a rain delay to pass over Lee in favor of Tiant to start the sixth game, Lee did not go gently into that Sox bull pen, calling the decision "stupid." "Darrell's been falling out of trees and landing on his feet all season," he observed to the wayward press. Then, in a lapse of pitching judgment in a pressure situation, Lee threw his Leephus ball to Tony Perez in the sixth inning of the seventh game and watched it sail out of the park much faster than he had thrown it in, cutting the Sox lead to 3-2. The Reds went on to win 4-3.

Tiant's performance during September of 1978 was consistent with his past. On September 6th he shut out the Orioles, 2-0, in a pitching standoff in which both he and Dennis Martinez took one-hit performances into the seventh inning. On September 15th he lost 4-0 to the Yankees and Ron Guidry, whose record upon throwing the final pitch was 22-2. By September 20th only two Sox starters had won a game all month—Tiant and Eckersley, who had beaten the Yankees. On September 23rd Tiant won again, putting his record at 11-8, as he beat Toronto 3-1. The victory was not the casual affair the final score might imply; Tiant threw 142 pitches, thereby depleting himself before his final two starts of the year. The win gave Tiant a 26-12 record in September over his career with the Red Sox, a figure that proved by cold statistics, lest it be doubted, the proposition that the Cuban was a formidable opponent in games that counted for more than a simple win.

Tiant was a pitcher whose commitment to winning, not just throwing good pitches, caused him to prevail in games that counted the most. Even Lee himself recognized the difference in Tiant's character. "Here's where Luis and I are different," Lee was quoted as saying.

> I get upset when I make a terrible pitch because I strive for perfection. But if I make a good pitch and the guy still gets a hit, it doesn't bother me. I figure there was nothing I could do about it. See, I can attain perfection and still lose the ball game. But Luis—he's just win, win, win. It's his whole life. It's an inbred thing. I don't want to fail out there. I'm afraid of failing. I'm not afraid to lose; I'm afraid to fail. You see, losing and failing are not the same things to me. But Luis thinks he's failed if he loses. I've trained my mind to take the animal fears that he and I both feel and convert them to mental feelings. That's the only difference between Luis and me as far as our competitive natures are concerned.

But it was enough of a difference to persuade a manager and a pitching coach who needed a win October 1st to salvage a season that had begun with such promise and subsided for the former Boston Pilgrims into their own slough of despond. On the Friday before Tiant's third win during the month of September, the Sox had dropped a disheartening decision to the Blue Jays in the bottom of the ninth inning after leading in the top of the eighth. The loss left the Sox two games out with eight games to play. "Let's face it," a competitor as fierce as Rick Burleson had to admit. "Tonight finished us." Tiant considered this autopsy to be defeatist and premature. "Boolcheat," Tiant (phonetically) said. "Win today, win tommorow, win the next day. The easy thing in life is to give up. Too many players on this team don't know what it's like to be treated like cheat most of their lives." Tiant did, which is why he rather than Lee was pitching down the stretch and on October 1st, when the Sox needed another win to play another day.

Burleson, apparently in a manic-depressive mood swing that reflected the erratic turns of his team's fortunes, took the view that the game against the Toronto Blue Jays that afternoon would be "the biggest day of our lives." The Sox and the Jays played scoreless ball for four innings, but in the bottom of the fifth inning Butch Hobson singled and George Scott hit a hopping ground ball to second that bounced off Dave McKay's ankle for an error, putting men on first and third. Jack Brohamer then hit a soft ground ball that scored Hobson and Jerry Remy followed with a ground rule double that scored Scott, giving the Sox a two-run lead. It was all Tiant needed on a day when he put the final coat on the high sheen of his reputation as a clutch pitcher; he gave up no hits until the fourth inning and only two singles in all as the Sox won, 5-0. The Sox had won their last eight games, four of them by shutouts, and had played errorless ball in doing so. Afterwards, Tiant would agree with Burleson's assessment about the significance of the game, with one caveat: "It may have been the most important game of my career, but I've been there before."

During the Sox game a girl in the right-field bleachers handed Bob Stanley a transistor radio to follow the action in New York, where Catfish Hunter would be pitching on three days' rest for the first time since September of 1976 against Cleveland's Rick Waits. Hunter failed to finish the second inning, giving up home runs to Andre Thornton in the first and Gary Alexander in the second, the first time Hunter had given up two home runs in a game since he allowed Fred Lynn and George Scott to do so on June 21st. Rick Waits, who had three losses and a 5.40 earned run average in his five starts against New York up to the last day of the season, gave up two runs in the first but none thereafter as the Indians beat the Yankees, 9-2, forcing the second one-game playoff in American League history. The Fenway Park scoreboard flashed a routine announcement to describe this unusual event: "NEXT GAME—TOMORROW, 1:30, GUIDRY (24-3) VS. TORREZ (16-12)." And a more heartfelt message as well: "THANK YOU RICK WAITS."

The Game

The 1978 American League Eastern division playoff game marked the third time that Boston and New York teams had met on the last day of the season to determine a championship. In 1904, the then-Boston Pilgrims faced the then-New York Highlanders at New York's Hilltop Park for a doubleheader, with the New Yorkers needing to win both games to win the American League Championship. Jack Chesbro, a 41-game winner with a 1.82 earned run average and 48 complete games in 51 starts, was the starting pitcher for New York in the first game. In the ninth, with the score tied 2-2, Boston's Lou Criger singled to open the inning and advanced to third on a sacrifice and a groundout. In those days the application of foreign substances to the ball was legal, and Chesbro's best pitch was his spitball. Chesbro moistened his fingers and, following the prescribed procedure for obtaining the maximum effect from his lubrication, threw the ball hard at the batter. He threw it too hard, however, as the ball sailed over his catcher's head, allowing Criger to score the pennant-winning run for Boston.

In 1949 the Sox held a one-game lead over the Yankees with two games left to play against New York. The Sox lost the first game 5-4 after leading 4-0, leaving the two teams tied with one game to go on a Sunday afternoon. In the bottom of the first the Yankees gave their starter Vic Raschi a 1-0 lead. Raschi and Sox starter Ellis Kinder battled into the eighth, when Boston manager Joe McCarthy, seeking an advantage in the days before the invention of the designated hitter, sent in a pinch hitter for Kinder. The Sox didn't score, and Mel Parnell, Boston's other starter of quality, was sent in to relieve him. Parnell gave up a solo home run to Tommy Henrich, and McCarthy sent in reliever Tex Hughson. In his final major league appearance, Hughson loaded the bases and then gave up a weakly-hit double to Yankee infielder Jerry Coleman that cleared the bases, making the score 5-0. Raschi gave up three runs in the top of the ninth, but Casey Stengel let him stay in. The Yankee starter finished and won the game, and with it the pennant.

There had been only five previous regular seasons that had ended in ties, four in the National League and one in the American. The National League settled such matters by best-of-three series in which one team was the Dodgers, either Brooklyn or Los Angeles; the Cardinals had beaten the Brooklyn Dodgers in 1946, the New York Giants had beaten the Brooklyn Dodgers in 1951, the Los Angeles Dodgers had beaten the Milwaukee Braves in 1959, and the San Francisco Giants had beaten the Los Angeles Dodgers in 1962. The sole

American League playoff had been the 1948 playoff between the Red Sox and the Cleveland Indians. The Indians won that one, 8-3, as Sox manager Joe McCarthy, the winningest manager in both Red Sox and major league history, started Denny Galehouse, a journeyman right-hander who usually ended up on the wrong side of the .500 mark at the end of a season, instead of Mel Parnell, the best pitcher on the staff with a 15-8 mark for the season, or Ellis Kinder, with a slightly better record for the year. Galehouse gave up home runs to Lou Boudreau in the first inning and to Ken Keltner in the fourth, and will forever be remembered by Red Sox fans as the man who shouldn't have started.

From the retrospective point of view of a Red Sox fan looking back over the summer, the 1978 playoff game should never have happened. While there were many games during the season that were remembered with regret, the recollection of one game that wasn't played was especially painful. The Sox-Yankees game scheduled for July 4th that was rained out would have pitted a Red Sox pitching staff at its peak against a Yankee staff with as many pitchers on the disabled list as starters. The game was rescheduled to September 7th, and on that date Mike Torrez didn't last two innings as the Yankees crushed the Sox 15-3, beginning the four-game sweep of the Sox that brought the Yankees from four games back to a tie for first place.

October 2, 1978, was a bright fall day in New England, and a crowd of 32,925 filled Fenway Park for the playoff game. Both teams would be missing a starter; rightfielder Dwight Evans for the Red Sox was still suffering from his August beaning, and second baseman Willie Randolph was out for the Yankees with the hamstring pull he had suffered September 29th against the Indians. Mike Torrez would start for Boston against Ron Guidry for the Yankees. The thought of this matchup was unnerving to Boston fans and players alike. Torrez was 1-3 against New York for the season, and he had only recently redeemed himself from his late-season losing streak. He also had a habit of falling behind in the early innings, then settling down as the Sox hitters produced their daily quota of hits and runs. On this day, however, an early deficit would involve a higher degree of risk for two reasons; first, the playoff was a one-game affair, and the loser's season would be over when the last out was made. And second, the pitcher for the Yankees that day was Guidry, the best pitcher in baseball over the course of the year, with a 2-0 record against the Sox for the season.

Torrez's first inning began inauspiciously, as leadoff man Mickey Rivers walked on four pitches and then stole second on the first pitch to Thurman Munson. Torrez retired the next two men, however, bringing up Reggie Jackson—Mr. October, now in his month. Torrez had Jackson down in the count 0-2 when he made a mistake and threw a fastball in the strike zone that Jackson hit towards the left-field light towers, a drive that confirmed the hard-earned pessimism of every Boston fan watching or listening to the game—until it dropped short of the left-field wall and fell into Carl Yastrzemski's glove, held back by an autumn wind from the north. Torrez had been saved by natural forces from an early Yankee lead. Guidry retired the Sox in order in the bottom of the first, striking out Burleson, caught looking, and Rice, swinging.

The Game

Torrez retired the Yankees in order in the top of the second, striking out Roy White to end the inning. The pitcher was forced to pause momentarily in his progress while signs put up by fans in the center-field bleachers were removed so as not to cloud batters' eyes from incoming pitches; he threw warm-up pitches while this renovation took place, as spectators began to bundle themselves against a growing chill. In the home half of the second inning, the leadoff hitter against Guidry was Yastrzemski. Guidry had dominated Yastrzemski throughout the regular season, but the Red Sox' captain, a fastball hitter at the end of his career facing one of the best young fastball pitchers in baseball, hit Guidry's second pitch, a fastball up and in, over the wall that circumscribes Fenway's short rightfield on a line drive that curled like a slicing tee shot around the park's extended foul pole. Sox 1, Yankees 0. Yankee announcer Phil Rizzuto noted that the wind that had held up Jackson's drive had now shifted, and this turn of the weather had helped keep Yastrzemski's drive from going foul. Two improbable outcomes in two innings, and the state of mind of many Sox fans must have been like that of a bum who finds two dollar bills in a stretch of two city blocks. Carlton Fisk and Fred Lynn followed with two well-hit balls off Guidry, Fisk sending Roy White back to catch a long fly to left and Lynn causing Rivers to retreat to the warning track in the deepest part of Fenway Park. Guidry's fastball was not at its best, since he was working on three rather than four days' rest, and the Red Sox were driving his customary "out" pitch hard and far. Guidry thus had to rely more heavily than usual on his slider, his second-best pitch and a slower-moving target for the Red Sox hitters.

The Year of the Gerbil

In the top of the third the Yankees got their first hit of the game, a double by Mickey Rivers with two out, but he was followed by Munson, whom Torrez would strike out for the second time. The Sox missed a chance to get more in the third inning when George Scott doubled to lead off and went to third on a sacrifice bunt by Jack Brohamer, but he was stranded there when Rick Burleson grounded to third for the second out of the inning and Jerry Remy flied to Roy White. It was the twenty-fifth time since September 1st that the Sox had failed to score a runner from third with fewer than two men out.

Sox fans had cause to be provisionally pleased with Torrez's performance in the early goings. It took the Yankees four innings to get their second hit, a single by Lou Piniella off Rick Burleson's glove, and Torrez killed that potential rally by retiring the next three batters. Torrez would give up only two hits, strike out four and walk only three batters through the visitors' half of the sixth inning. Jim Rice's play in right field in substitution for Dwight Evans was similar cause for furtive rejoicing among Bostonians; he had made two tough catches through four innings, the first of a softly-hit ball by Bucky Dent that threatened to fall between Fred Lynn and Jerry Remy in the third inning, the second of a line drive into the sun by Reggie Jackson in the top of the fourth inning, which Rice followed with a strong throw to first, nearly catching Lou Piniella, an indifferent base runner, off guard. In the home half of the fourth the Sox went down in order as Rice grounded out, shortstop to first, on an off-target throw by Bucky Dent that required Chris Chambliss to make a sweeping tag of Rice as he ran by. Yaz then struck out on a 2-2 count and Fisk hit a deep fly ball that Mickey Rivers caught up to in center field.

Torrez walked Roy White on a 3-0 count to start the fifth inning; it was the third lead-off batter he had allowed to reach base, a sign that he was perhaps overachieving despite his otherwise steady performance. White advanced to second on a fielder's choice, but Bucky Dent popped up to his counterpart Burleson for the second out of the inning. Rivers then gave the Sox' shortstop another chance, this time a grounder; Burleson threw to Brohamer at third to catch White, although his throw nearly hit the runner. The Sox put a man on in the bottom of the inning as Graig Nettles was unable to handle a shot by Butch Hobson, but George Scott struck out and Jack Brohamer flied out to Roy White to retire the side.

Thurman Munson opened the Yankees' sixth inning by striking out for the third time; Torrez then retired Piniella on a long fly to Fred Lynn in center field and Reggie Jackson on a groundout. The score thus remained unchanged until the home half of the sixth inning. Burleson opened the inning with a double down the third-base line, moved to third on a sacrifice by Remy and scored on a single to center by Jim Rice. It was Rice's 213th hit, 406th total base, and 139th run batted in of the year. Sox 2, Yankees 0. After an infield out and an intentional walk to Fisk, Fred Lynn, a left-hander, came to bat with two men on. Lynn worked the count to 3-and-2, then hit the next pitch, a slider by some accounts, a fast ball by others, into the right-field corner. There, Lou Piniella fought off the sun and correctly judged the force of the wind on the ball to make the catch running to his left. Piniella was playing Lynn further toward the line than a normal defensive alignment would have called for, and what would ordinarily have been an extra-base hit was thus merely a tough out. The Yankee outfielder claimed that the adjustment was the result of precise calibration based on his observation, confirmed by Thurman Munson, that the Sox' hitters were pulling Guidry's slower-than-usual stuff that day, and in part on his deduction that Guidry wouldn't throw a curve with a full count. Others are of the opinion that Piniella—an inveterate gambler known to receive Belmont Park racing results via hand signals from the Yankee bench—had played a hunch and won. Whatever the reason, it was the first happenstance that day to go the Yankees' way.

So while the Yankees could have entered the top of the seventh inning down by at least 4-0, they instead left the field trailing the Red Sox by a score of only 2-0. Torrez retired the first batter, Graig Nettles, on a fly to Jim Rice, but then gave up consecutive singles, the first to left field by Chris Chambliss, the second to center field by Roy White. Andy Hassler, a left-hander, and Bob Stanley, a right-hander, got up to throw in the Sox bull pen. Don Zimmer walked to the mound, ostensibly to caucus with his battery and infielders but in fact to give his relievers time to warm up; one lonely fan had the audacity to boo him as he came out of the dugout, an effrontery that was not seconded by his fellow spectators, who understood the tactical nature of the manager's move and the solemnity of the occasion. Bob Lemon sent in Jim Spencer to pinch-hit for Brian Doyle, who was in turn subbing for the injured Willie Randolph. Spencer had won four games pinch-hitting for the Yankees over the course of the season, but Torrez got him out on a sharply-hit ball to Yastrzemski. Two outs, two on, with Bucky Dent—0 for 2 on the day— scheduled to come to bat. Short of infield help with Randolph injured and Doyle now out of the game, Lemon was forced to let Dent hit.

Torrez's first pitch was a ball, and Dent fouled the second pitch off his left shin, falling to the ground. Dent, who had a tendency to foul pitches off his left leg, had at various times during the season worn a shin guard on his left ankle to protect himself from just such an occurrence, but he wasn't wearing his protective gear that day. The Yankees' trainer, Gene Monahan, came out to spray Dent with painkiller. Mickey Rivers, the next batter, noticed, or claimed to notice, that Dent was using a cracked bat. He sent the batboy to the plate to give Dent another bat, allegedly the same model as Dent was holding but one that was uncracked. Dent would later explain away this odd exchange by noting that he and Rivers were using the same model bat at the time—a "Max 44" originally purchased for Roy White—and that Dent had cracked one of their joint stock during batting practice. Dent and Rivers had continued to use the damaged bat during batting practice, according to Dent, because the Yankees were waiting for a new shipment to arrive and were down to the last of the bats that White had ordered. By this account, Rivers had prior reason to know of the defective bat, and the acute powers of observation he displayed that day, which might otherwise have seemed unusual, were thus at least plausible. Rivers's version of this incident, as recounted to the Boston *Globe*'s Dan Shaughnessy, is consistent with Dent's in most significant respects, with the addition of the Butterfly McQueen-like exclamation, "Homey, Homey, that bat is cracked, you got the wrong one!"

As adjustments were made to Dent's body and armament,

the Red Sox threw the ball around the infield while Torrez stood idle for a period that he would later estimate to be four or five minutes, but which a tape of the game reveals to be much shorter, just shy of a minute and a half. Fisk did not call for warm-up pitches during the interruption, and Torrez, who had kept himself loose by throwing during a similar pause in the second inning, didn't either, trying to conserve his energy as he concentrated on the task ahead of him, seven outs to victory. Two outs, two on, two strikes. Dent stepped back into the batter's box and choked up a good four inches or more on his bat, an indication of his humble hitting ambitions and limited long-ball capacity. Torrez went into his stretch position and threw—a fastball, down and in. Dent swung and hit a fly ball that, six innings earlier, might have fallen harmlessly into Yastrzemski's glove in left field, as Jackson's drive had in the first inning. Torrez claims he started to walk off the field and Fisk reported that he felt a sense of relief over a poorly-thrown pitch. Their recollections have a quality of wishfulness about them, however; Bill White, the former all-star first baseman for the St. Louis Cardinals who was doing play-by-play for the Yankees, immediately called Dent's fly a well-hit ball with a note of rising expectation in his voice. Yastrzemski circled under the wall in left field and looked up, but the shifting wind was still blowing from right field to left. The ball was gone. Yankees 3, Red Sox 2.*

Baseball is, in the broadcaster's cliche, a game of inches, but Dent's blow could be gauged in various units of measure.

---

* Red Sox players are not the only ones who have suffered lapses of memory regarding this supposedly unforgettable moment. In the book *Sweet Lou* by Lou Piniella and Maury Allen, Piniella asserts that Jim Rice was playing left field for the Sox at the time, and Allen does not correct him.

The Game

Had Torrez thrown the fateful pitch a few inches closer to
Dent, he might have broken the shortstop's bat. Had the
Yankees won the coin toss to decide where the playoff game
would be held, or had the Red Sox chosen (as Torrez would
have preferred) not to play the game in Fenway Park, Dent's
hit would have been an out in the spacious veld that is left
field in Yankee Stadium. Had the wind not shifted by half the
park's compass between the first and seventh innings,
Yastrzemski probably would have edged his way along
Fenway's outfield wall and picked off the dropping fly ball
with no more difficulty than one might experience changing a
ceiling lightbulb.

A subsequent comment by Rivers to Torrez gave credibility to the suspicion of some Red Sox fans that Rivers had
passed a corked bat to Dent as they engaged in their batting
circle byplay. Both Dent and Rivers would deny that charge,
again with slightly different responses, Dent claiming that the
comment was a joke and Rivers asserting obliquely that Dent
didn't need to use a corked bat to hit a home run. On the contrary, if anyone could have used a prosthesis in that situation
it was Dent; his hitting powers, never considerable, had slowly declined over the years from a .274 average in 1974 to a .243
figure in 1978. For the season, he had driven in only thirty-
seven runs and had hit only four home runs. The enormity of
his feat was attested to by Phil Rizzuto, a Yankee shortstop
from an earlier day and one of the team's announcers present
at the site: "I let out three 'Holy Cows' in the press box with
all those Red Sox fans there," he said. "I thought Frank
Malzone," the former Red Sox third baseman, "was going to
bite me on the ankle."

257

Mickey Rivers then worked Torrez to a 3-2 count and walked. Thurman Munson was up next, and although Torrez had already struck him out three times, Zimmer called in reliever Bob Stanley to pitch to him. The improbability of Dent's homer and its fortuity may have disrupted Torrez's concentration, and Zimmer needed to keep the game within reach. Rivers stole second on a one-hop throw to second by Fisk, and Munson hit a double to left-center field, scoring Rivers. Piniella flied out to right, ending the inning. As the Sox left the field, the score stood Yankees 4, Red Sox 2.

In the bottom of the seventh, Guidry struck out Hobson leading off, but George Scott followed with a single. Zimmer decided to send right-handed hitting Bob Bailey up to pinch hit for left-handed hitting third baseman Jack Brohamer against the left-handed Guidry, playing for the minuscule advantage that a batter standing on the opposite side of the plate normally has over one who must take a pitch from the pitcher's throwing side. As soon as Bailey was waved in by the home plate umpire, Yankee manager Bob Lemon responded to the change by bringing in the right-handed pitching Rich Gossage. Even before Lemon chose to neutralize Zimmer's strategic move, however, the match was uneven. Bob Bailey hit .257 during his major league career and .188 during his season and a half with the Red Sox. He was 1 for 12 in pinch-hitting appearances in 1978, and the Yankee television announcers joked that, from the looks of his overhanging gut, he was out of shape. Nonetheless, Bailey was a favorite of Zimmer's, the first player that the manager named to the team in spring training. He was also all Zimmer had; the pinch-hitting hero of the 1975 World Series, Bernie Carbo, was gone,

and as Bill Lee had predicted, he was now, in the most important game of the year, sorely needed. Gossage, on the other
hand, had struck out 122 batters in relief appearances in 1978,
a Yankee record, on the strength of a fastball that traveled the
sixty feet, six inches from pitching rubber to home plate at
nearly 100 miles an hour. After one outside pitch, he struck
out Bailey on a foul ball and two called strikes. The power of
Gossage's fastball may be deduced from Bailey's postgame
comment that one pitch "sounded low," as if to admit that
Bailey's hitting radar couldn't pick up the relief pitcher's
superior weaponry. Burleson grounded out, shortstop to first,
to end the inning. Bailey, Zimmer's pinch-hitting hole card,
would never come to bat in the major leagues again.

In the top of the eighth Reggie Jackson led off with a home
run to center field, making the score 5-2. On his way back to
the dugout Jackson gave a "high five" greeting to Yankee
owner George Steinbrenner, who was sitting in the front row
of Fenway Park on the visitors' side of the field, as if to confirm Billy Martin's suspicion that Jackson's primary allegiance
as a player in the age of free agency was to the man who
signed his paychecks, not to his manager or his teammates.
Jackson's home run produced a calm in the crowd not unlike
that which prevails in a well-run funeral home; the shock of
Dent's home run had been absorbed and Jackson's long ball
seemed like the ceremonial conclusion to a fate that now was
accepted as inevitable.

Jerry Remy doubled over first base in the bottom of the
eighth, however, and scored when Yastrzemski singled to center field, his right arm wheeling as he rounded third base as if
to balance himself and avoid the fate of Luis Aparicio in 1972.

Carlton Fisk faced Gossage next and worked him strenuously, fouling off one fastball after another until, on the tenth pitch, he singled. Lynn followed with another single, sending Yastrzemski home and making the score 5-4. Runners on first and second, one out, Butch Hobson up, with George Scott to follow. Gossage forced Hobson to fly out to Piniella, who caught the ball on the heel of his glove, and Scott struck out to end the inning.

The Yankees didn't score in their half of the ninth inning, and the game came down to three final outs for the Red Sox, and one run. Dwight Evans pinchhit for Frank Duffy and popped out to left field on the second pitch. Rick Burleson drew a one-out walk, bringing up Jerry Remy. Gossage got two strikes on him, then challenged him again with a fastball rather than waste a pitch. Remy connected, sending the ball to right field, where Lou Piniella was unfortunately standing directly in its path. Burleson hesitated between first and second, assuming that Piniella had the ball in his sights and could make the play. Piniella, however, was blinded by the sun and couldn't see the ball coming towards him. "I had told Bob Lemon about the seventh inning when that big orange ball of fire was going over the roof of the third-base grandstand that I hoped they didn't hit the ball to me on a line because it was impossible to see," Piniella recalled to a Boston *Herald* writer some years later. "He said 'Do the best you can.'" When Remy's ball leapt off his bat, it rose into the sun that blinded Piniella. "I saw it leave the bat, then for the longest time I lost total sight of it," he remembers. The veteran outfielder had the presence of mind to play possum, however; he made a show of preparing for the catch, striking a pose with his arms out to his sides as if to call off the center-fielder and steady himself for the catch while he backed up to keep the ball in front of him. The decoy worked, as Burleson froze between first and second to make sure he could get back to first if the ball were caught on the fly. Instead, the ball land-ed in front of Piniella, and he caught it on the first bounce with a lunge to his left. "I knew sooner or later the ball had to come out of that sun, and then just as it got to me I saw it, stuck out my glove and there it was." Burleson was thus at second instead of third, where he would have ended up if Piniella had panicked.

Some have criticized Burleson's baserunning, finding in it a trace of Bostonian conservatism that fits neatly within the template by which distinctions between New York and Boston are inevitably tested. In this case, at least, the prejudice against prudence in favor of reckless daring is unfounded. Burleson would have been out by a city block (or a country mile, depending on your preference) had he tried for third, as Piniella's decoy had stalled him in his tracks and the throw from right field reached third base on one hop. In any event, instead of runners at first and third with one out, Jim Rice came to the plate with runners on first and second, one out. Among other might-have-beens noted by those who dwell on this game, the fact that Piniella was playing right field that day meant that Reggie Jackson, a left-hander, was not. If Jackson had been in Piniella's position, he would not have had his glove hand in a position to stop the ball and most like-ly would not have made the play. To paraphrase Mark Twain, speculation is a marvelous thing; one gets a wholesale return of regret from a trifling investment of facts.

The Year of the Gerbil

Rice flied out to right field, deep enough to advance Burleson to third and to have brought him home had he made it to third on Remy's hit. The Red Sox were down to their final out and Yastrzemski, who had homered, singled and driven in two runs thus far, was at the plate. The tying run was ninety feet away, the winning run on first. Some great hitters, like Hank Aaron, are a picture of relaxation at the plate. Others, like Stan Musial with his coiled crouch, are models of concentration. In Yastrzemski's case, his stance was more a matter of physick than physics, a triumph of will over the depreciation caused by age and regular play. He was then a little more than a month past his 39th birthday and five seasons away from retirement, and at that point in his career had adopted a stance that was a piece of patchwork improvisation not unlike the home-built stall showers one sees attached to cottages on Cape Cod for use by swimmers returning from the beach—a construct of pieces that varied in strength held together at joints weakened by constant exposure to the elements. Both hands were taped and one was gloved, his bat held gently but directly in front of him and upright, not slanted backwards in anticipation of the swing to come. He seemed to slope downwards towards the mound, his bat held high, his front shoulder dropped, as if to maximize the gravitational force behind his swing and thereby minimize the effort required to get around on the pitches of younger men like Gossage. Then he cocked his eye at Gossage like a skeptical shopper, ready to ask if his fastballs were really fresh.

Gossage, by comparison, was at the start of a five-year stretch during which he would set Yankee relief-pitching records for earned run average (2.03) and strikeouts (506). He was younger, stronger, and at or near the peak of his powers. Yaz had been there before, but the prior outcomes, if a fan had the presence of mind to remember them, were not auspicious; in 1967 he had been the last man out for the Sox in their World Series loss to the Cardinals, and in 1975 he was the last out in their World Series loss to the Reds. Gossage reared back, his windup so fierce it seemed like an amateurish parody of a rube pitcher trying to blow one by a batter, and let go—ball one. Working quickly, he snagged the toss back from the catcher, squared himself, and waited for Yaz to get back in the batter's box. When Yaz was ready, Gossage rocked into his pitching motion and threw again. Yastrzemski swung and popped the ball up towards third base, causing Graig Nettles to back up into foul territory behind third base, where he caught the ball with little effort beyond that required to restrain himself from prematurely jumping for joy.

There is perhaps nothing so forlorn in all of sports as the mounted guard of police assembled for the joyful riot of fans that never comes because the home team loses. A troop of blue-coated mounties of the Boston police force, their horses impassive, ringed the infield at Fenway Park as the Yankees retired to the visitors' clubhouse. The 1978 Red Sox-Yankees playoff has been compared to the 1951 playoff in which Bobby Thompson's home run won the National League pennant for the New York Giants over the Brooklyn Dodgers, but the last hitter in that game caused his team to win, while Yaz's pop-up meant that the team with the last at bat had to lose. Moreover, Thompson hit his home run at the Polo Grounds and as such was greeted with wild cheers, while Yaz's pop-up came down on Boston sod, which meant that you could hear the plop of the ball into

Nettles's glove and anything else you cared to listen for immediately thereafter until the organ at Fenway Park began to
resound with Sousa's "Stars and Stripes Forever". If, as Karl
Marx archly put it, history repeats itself, the first time tragedy,
the second time farce, the history of the Red Sox should by now
have exhausted the various dramatic forms available for the
depiction of human misfortune, comic and tragic.

The Sox had finished the season with 99 wins, more than
forty-five previous winners of the American League pennant
had been able to accumulate. The Yankees subsequently won
the American League Championship Series (over the Kansas
City Royals, 3 games to 1), the third time in three years that
the Yankees kept the Royals from the World Series. The
Yankees also won the World Series over the Los Angeles
Dodgers, 4 games to 2, the eighth time in ten World Series
meetings between the two teams that the Yankees had prevailed over a Dodger team, six times while they were in
Brooklyn, twice since they moved to Los Angeles. Today more
people remember how the Yankees got to the 1978 World
Series than how they did there, however. They got there by
beating the Boston Red Sox in a one-game playoff with a double by Thurman Munson, a solo home run by Reggie Jackson,
and a home run with two men on in the bottom of seventh
inning by Russell Earl Dent, better known as "Bucky".

Epilogue

O
n November 10, 1978, Sparky Lyle got his wish as the Yankees traded him to the Texas Rangers. He signed a three-year contract with them the next day worth about a million dollars, plus a television broadcasting contract that would bring him another half million dollars, thereby putting an end to his tramp through the vineyards where his sour grapes over George Steinbrenner's gulling of him in the early days of free agency were stored. He would play for Texas, Philadelphia and the Chicago Cubs before retiring at the end of the 1982 season. He recently (and counter-intuitively, in light of the fact that he rarely made a curfew during his playing days) became the manager of the Somerset, New Jersey Patriots, a minor league team that will play its first games during the summer of 1998.

On December 7, 1978, a day which will live in infamy, Don Zimmer called Bill Lee to tell him that he had been traded to the Montreal Expos for Stan Papi, an infielder. When Lee heard the news, he waited to hear who else the Expos were giving up for him; when he realized that Papi was the sole item of compensation, he placed him mentally in the category to which fellow Buffalo Head Ferguson Jenkins had once consigned Zimmer—lifetime .230 hitter. In fact, Papi would hit only .188 in fifty-one games over two seasons and would end up a career .218 hitter. Lee would win 16 games while losing 10 for Montreal in 1979, but just nine games in three years thereafter before walking out on the club over the release of Rodney "Cool Breeze" Scott, the team's second baseman, much as he had walked out over the sale of Bernie Carbo in 1978. (At one point in the 1979 season Lee had worn one of his didactic T-shirts to summarize his view of the 1978 playoff game: "Here comes Gossage, here comes Bailey. . . where's Bernie?") At this point in his career Lee was 36 years old and no one was interested in his services. He suspected a conspiracy, but he needn't have; the truth was not so convoluted.

Since retiring Lee has held a variety of jobs. He has worked for The Sox Exchange, a Montpelier, Vermont, business that organizes trips to Florida on which vacationers can play baseball and socialize with former Sox players. He won the presidential nomination of the Rhinoceros Party in 1988 in the first New Hampshire primary to be held in the state of Vermont. He has played and coached for the barnstorming New England Grey Sox and pitched in senior league baseball games. He currently works with a group called Planet Baseball, which sponsors father-and-son clinics, and has a daily radio show, *Answers from Space*, on station CIQC, the

Epilogue

Montreal Expos' principal broadcasting outlet. He also owns a farm in Vermont. His 1975 World Series ring was recently auctioned off by a New York sports memorabilia dealer on behalf of one of Lee's former girlfriends.

As this is written, Jim Rice is not in baseball's Hall of Fame, even though his 1978 season represented the midpoint of a span in which he, alone among all major league baseball players, had two hundred hits and thirty-five home runs in three consecutive seasons. He played with the Sox for 16 years, retiring after the 1989 season. He finished his career with a .298 average; but for his dismal last year, when he managed only 45 hits, he would have ended up a .300 hitter. He led the American League in home runs five times, and in RBIs twice. Critics point to the fact that he is also near the top of the list in another, unfavorable statistic—namely, double plays hit into. It is worth noting that the all-time leader in this regard is Hank Aaron. Rice now coaches for the Red Sox.

Don Zimmer would last two more years as the Red Sox manager. His 1979 team won 91 games and lost 69, finishing third. The next year the Sox were 82-74, 36-45 at Fenway Park, when Zimmer was fired with seven games to go. He subsequently managed the Texas Rangers and the Chicago Cubs and has since coached for the Yankees, the Giants, the Cubs, the Red Sox (in 1992 under Butch Hobson, his third baseman during 1978), the Colorado Rockies and then the Yankees again. He is still with New York and recently began his 50th year in professional baseball; by his own recollection, he has never cashed a paycheck that wasn't drawn on a baseball team's account.

On October 27, 1978, Jerry Lemon, the son of Yankee

manager Bob Lemon, was killed in a car accident near Phoenix, Arizona. When the father arrived in spring training in early 1979, he seemed understandably weakened by the tragedy and incapable of the conviviality that others had experienced with him before. As the Yankees staggered through May and June, Yankee owner George Steinbrenner began to blame the team's lack of success on Lemon's apparent loss of appetite for baseball's cycle of competition and tedium and decided to bring back Billy Martin a season ahead of schedule.

On August 2, 1979, at 3:02 p.m., Yankee catcher Thurman Munson was killed when his plane sliced into a bank of trees 1,000 feet short of runway 19 at the Canton-Akron, Ohio airport as he was practicing landings.

Luis Tiant was eligible to become a free agent after the 1978 season ended. "Before you think about becoming a free agent," Tiant claims Sox' owner Buddy Leroux said to him in August, "think about your age. I hope you have a lot of money in the bank." Insulted, Tiant shopped his wares around and received an $840,000, two-year contract with the Yankees, while Boston offered him only a one-year contract. "I was wise to their bool cheat," Tiant would tell George Kimball, then a reporter for the Boston *Phoenix*. Tiant would win 25 games and lose 24 in four more years in the big leagues, two with the Yankees, one with Pittsburgh and one with the California Angels. He recently became baseball coach for the Savannah College of Art and Design.

Ron Guidry played with the Yankees for ten more years, winning twenty games two more times, in 1983 and 1985. He retired after the 1988 season.

Epilogue

On Christmas Day, 1989, Billy Martin, returning to his farm in Binghamton, New York, after a day of drinking, was killed when his pickup truck slid into a drainage ditch. Before he died, he had been rehired and fired by Yankee owner George Steinbrenner four more times.

Bernie Carbo left the Cleveland Indians after the 1978 season, and then lasted two more years with the St. Louis Cardinals and the Pittsburgh Pirates. He recently filed suit against major league baseball claiming that an image of his home run in the sixth game of the 1975 World Series had been used in a commercial without his permission.

Dennis Eckersley stayed with the Red Sox until 1984, when he signed with the Chicago Cubs. He stayed with that club for three years, converted himself into a relief pitcher, and then went on to the Oakland A's in 1988, where he spent the next decade. On December 9, 1997, he signed a contract that brought him back to the Red Sox for the 1998 season.

Reggie Jackson played his last season with the New York Yankees in 1981, hitting .237 with 15 home runs after one of his best years in 1980, hitting .300 (the only season in his career in which he did so) with 41 home runs (only the second time he had hit 40 home runs in a season). He spent the next five years with the California Angels, and ended his career with the team that had first signed him out of college, the Oakland Athletics. He is now a special consultant to the Yankees, among other part-time occupations.

Mike Torrez stayed with the Red Sox for four more years, compiling a career record of 60-54 with the team, before ending his career with the New York Mets in 1984. He is out of baseball and lives and works in New York.

The Year of the Gerbil

Bucky Dent played with the Yankees until 1982, when he joined the Texas Rangers. After two seasons, he left to join the Kansas City Royals and retired after the 1984 season. He is now a coach for the Texas Rangers.

ON FIRST LOOKING INTO CHAPMAN'S GERBIL

Much have I read in the books of sport,
And many goodly plates and base paths seen;
Round many eastern stadia have I been
In houses as Ruth built, and similar sort.
Oft of Fenway's green expanse had I been told
That great-gutted Zimmer ruled as his demesne;
Yet did I never breathe its pure serene
Till I heard Chapman speak out loud and bold:
Then felt I like some watcher of the skies
Who some much-heralded comet spies
And says with a skeptical distaste
That's it? For this my time's a waste?

Acknowledgments

To supplement my memories of the 1978 season and of games I watched that year in Boston, New York and Baltimore, I reviewed a number of sources, primarily newspaper accounts from the Boston *Globe*, the Boston *Herald* and the New York *Times*, articles in *Sports Illustrated* and *Sport Magazine*, and two videos, "It Don't Come Easy" (New York Yankees Video Library) and "Baseball's Greatest Games, 1978 American League East Playoff" (Major League Baseball Home Video). Much of the statistical data was derived from John Thorn and Pete Palmer's "Total Baseball", a CD-ROM published by Creative Multimedia. In addition, I consulted the following works, among others:

Allen, Maury, *Damn Yankee: The Billy Martin Story*, New York, Times Books, 1980.

Allen, Maury, *Mr. October: The Reggie Jackson Story*, New York, Times Books, 1981.

Berry, Henry, and Berry, Harold, *The Complete Record of Red Sox Baseball*, New York, Macmillan Publishing Company, 1984.

Gammons, Peter, *Beyond the Sixth Game*, Lexington, Massachusetts, The Stephen Greene Press, 1986.

Golenbock, Peter, *Wild, High and Tight: The Life and Death of Billy Martin*, New York, St. Martin's Press, 1994.

Halberstam, David, *Summer of '49*, New York, Avon Books, 1989.

Higgins, George V., *The Progress of the Seasons: Forty Years of Baseball in Our Town*, New York, Prentice Hall Press, 1989.

Honig, Donald, *The New York Yankees: An Illustrated History*, New York, Crown Publishers, Inc., 1981.

Lee, Bill "Spaceman", and Lally, Dick, *The Wrong Stuff*, New York, Penguin Books, 1984.

Lyle, Sparky, and Golenbock, Peter, *The Bronx Zoo*, New York, Crown Publishers, Inc., 1979.

Mercurio, John A., *New York Yankee Records*, New York, S.P.I. Books/Shapolsky Publishers, Inc., 1993.

Piniella, Lou, and Allen, Maury, *Sweet Lou*, New York, G.P. Putnam's Sons, 1986.

Riley, Dan, ed., *The Red Sox Reader*, Boston, Houghton, Mifflin, 1991.

Schaap, Dick, *Steinbrenner!*, New York, G.P. Putnam's Sons, 1982.

Acknowledgments

Shaughnessy, Dan, *The Curse of the Bambino*, New York, Penguin Books, 1991.

Thorn, John, *Baseball: Our Game*, New York, Penguin Books, 1995.

Tiant, Luis, and Fitzgerald, Joe, *El Tiante: The Luis Tiant Story*, Garden City, New York, Doubleday & Company, Inc., 1976.

Weinberger, Miro, and Riley, Dan, eds., *The Yankees Reader*, Boston, Houghton, Mifflin, 1991.